Thomas Michell

Russian Pictures

Drawn with pen and pencil

Thomas Michell

Russian Pictures
Drawn with pen and pencil

ISBN/EAN: 9783337165109

Printed in Europe, USA, Canada, Australia, Japan

Cover: Foto ©Thomas Meinert / pixelio.de

More available books at **www.hansebooks.com**

Russian Pictures

Drawn with Pen and Pencil

BY

THOMAS MICHELL, C.B.

AUTHOR OF "MURRAY'S HANDBOOK FOR RUSSIA, POLAND, AND FINLAND," "THE SCOTTISH EXPEDITION
TO NORWAY IN 1612," ETC

WITH THREE MAPS AND ONE HUNDRED AND TWENTY-FOUR ILLUSTRATIONS

NEW YORK
SCRIBNER AND WELFORD

LONDON
THE RELIGIOUS TRACT SOCIETY
56 PATERNOSTER ROW AND 164 PICCADILLY
1889

LONDON:
PRINTED BY WILLIAM CLOWES AND SONS, Limited,
STAMFORD STREET AND CHARING CROSS.

AN ILLUMINATION FROM A MS. OF THE FOURTEENTH CENTURY, IN THE IMPERIAL
PUBLIC LIBRARY, ST. PETERSBURG.

PREFACE.

THE object of this volume is to represent graphically the salient features
of the Russian Empire and its inhabitants. Readers of the previous
volumes of the 'Pen and Pencil Series' will remember that their contents
are uniformly limited, and, be the country dealt with large or small, the
number of pages is the same. Indulgence must, therefore, be claimed for
the unavoidably incomplete character of a work that attempts to sketch by
the aid of both pen and pencil the lands and peoples embraced in so vast
an area as that which stretches from Poland to Kamchatka, and from the
Arctic Ocean to the 'frosty Caucasus.'

The execution of this task has been facilitated by the generous permission of Mr. John Murray to draw upon the information contained in the
Handbook for Travellers in Russia, Poland, and Finland. The thanks of
the author are also due in a special degree to Captain J. Buchan Telfer,
R.N., for his friendly contribution of a chapter on the Crimea and Caucasus,
on which he is a high and well-known authority.

The ancient illuminations that head the chapters of this volume have
been copied from M. Boutoffsky's *Ornement Russe.* It will be seen that
their purely Byzantine character was preserved through the tenth century

and for a good part of the next, while at the end of the eleventh century the Byzantine style began to be mingled in Russia with elements of native genius, which was gradually much influenced by the art of India and Persia.

Russia received its first strong impulse from Peter the Great, at a time when the printing press was already an active force, when the wall that had surrounded 'Muscovia' had been considerably breached, and when inter-communication with the rest of Europe, by sea and by land, had become comparatively easy and free from danger. It is therefore as in a glass hive that the Russian bees have ever since been toiling under the guidance of gifted and ambitious rulers to build up the colossal fabric we view to-day with an amazement which is not unmingled with disquietude, when only the area of the modern Russian Empire presents itself for consideration.

The foreign criticism and animadversion to which Russia has been liable since the days, more especially of its great Reformer, have not been produced by racial or religious prejudice. They have been the natural consequence of the great position which Russia acquired so late in her political life, in the eyes and under the keen observation of states that had long been more or less solidified and advanced in the spirit and the form of their civilization and government.

Hence, so far from being a *terra incognita*, Russia, especially that part situated in Europe, has been the subject of such numerous literary productions that it is well nigh impossible to say, or to depict, anything by pen and pencil that will not appear to a large class of readers to be more or less a *réchauffé* of other travellers' notes and artistic labours. Nevertheless, the hope is not forbidden that the book produced in these circumstances may not only please the eye of the reader into whose hands it falls, but also, by giving him accurate, if somewhat scanty, information about the history peoples, lands, and cities of Russia in both Europe and Asia, add something to the interest he may already take in the subject.

In short, the work may be introduced to its readers somewhat ap-propriately in the words of an English writer at the end of the seventeenth century:' 'Tis true, this relation will not afford the same variety of beautiful structures, gardens, statues, and other niceties as that of Italy; nevertheless, the more remote the manners, religion, and policy of the Muscovites are from other nations of Europe, the more abstruse their history and surprising in the event, among a nation guided for the most part merely by instinct, and consequently hurried on from one extreme to another, the more, I say, they may deserve our particular observation at this juncture of time.'

---

[1] Dedication to *The Antient and Present State of Muscovy*. By Dr. J. Crull. London, 1698.

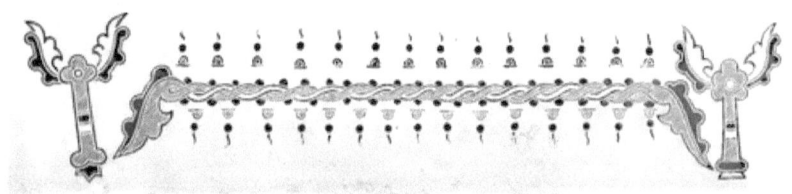

CONTENTS AND LIST OF ILLUSTRATIONS.

CHAPTER I.

EXTENT AND ORIGIN OF THE RUSSIAN EMPIRE.

CHAPTER II.

WESTERN RUSSIA.

CHAPTER III.

THE MODERN CAPITAL: ST. PETERSBURG.

CHAPTER IV.

THE NORTHERNMOST PROVINCES OF EUROPEAN RUSSIA.

CHAPTER V.

MOSCOW: THE ANCIENT CAPITAL.

CHAPTER VI.

A VOYAGE DOWN THE VOLGA.

CHAPTER VII.

SOUTH RUSSIA.

CHAPTER VIII.

THE CRIMEA AND CAUCASUS.

CHAPTER IX.

SIBERIA.

CHAPTER X.

CENTRAL ASIA.

CHAPTER XI.

POLAND.

CHAPTER XII.

FINLAND.

MAP OF RUSSIA IN EUROPE.

AN ILLUMINATION FROM A MANUSCRIPT OF THE THIRTEENTH
OR FOURTEENTH CENTURY, IN THE IMPERIAL PUBLIC
LIBRARY, ST. PETERSBURG.

CHAPTER I.

EXTENT AND ORIGIN OF THE RUSSIAN EMPIRE.

OCCUPYING one seventh part of the land surface of the globe, and about one quarter of its entire superficies, the Russian empire had, in 1886, an estimated population of one hundred and nine millions, of which eighty-four per cent. was spread over an area of over two million square miles in Europe, the remainder being more or less permanently settled in Asia, on territories measuring about six and a half million square miles. The vastness of these combined possessions, already covered with 17,000 miles of railway, is exceeded only by the magnitude of the British empire (9.314.000 square miles), with a population almost three times as large as that which is now under the sway of the Russian sceptre.

On the north the Russian empire has an arctic coast-line that embraces more than one hundred and forty degrees of longitude, and which fails to reach the Atlantic only by the interposition of the kingdom of Norway. Its eastern limits are on the Pacific Ocean, from Behring Straits down to the frontier of the Chinese empire, which forms also its southernmost boundary, before the latter is carried westward across Central Asia to the confines of

Persia and Turkey, countries with which the empire also comes into close contact, severally, on the Caspian (practically a Russian lake), and on the Black Sea, of which it holds the northern and eastern shores from the Danube to Batoum. On the west, the Grand Duchy of Finland is conterminous with Norway and Sweden, after which the Baltic and Polish Provinces establish contiguity to the empires of Germany and Austria, while the modern kingdom of Roumania has become a neighbour on the lower course of the Danube.

The dominant population of Russia Proper is Slavonic; the Slavs or Slavonians having been a branch of the Aryan or Indo-European race, by which the greater part of Europe has been occupied from time immemorial. Settled in a country so remote from the centres of Greek and Roman culture, the Slavs made a late appearance on the stage of history. They are referred to by Pliny the elder (A.D. 79) as the *Veudi*, inhabiting 'the country beyond the Vistula.' Tacitus mentions them as the *Veneti*; and the Teutonic tribes designated their early eastern neighbours as the *Winedi*, or the Wends, who survive in Lusatia. In King Alfred's *Orosius* the Anglo-Saxon designation of the Slavs south of the Baltic is *Winedas* or *Weonodas*, while in the eleventh and twelfth centuries the Scandinavian name for the same people was *Vender*. To this day the Finlanders know Russia only as *Venäjä*, and their racial brethren, the Esthonians, on the opposite side of the Baltic, call it *Vene*.'

From the Vistula, where the earliest historical records locate them, the Slavs extended eastward to the Dnieper, and northward into the territory that later became the dominion of Novgorod the Great. During the first centuries after Christ they were cut off, in their woods and marshes, from the events which at that period disturbed the greater part of Europe. Whether from external pressure, or from an inherent nomadic tendency, they began soon after their short-lived subjection to the Goths (in the third or fourth century) to spread themselves to the west in two distinct streams.

One mass crossed the Vistula, and populated the tracts between the Carpathian Mountains and the Baltic, down to the Elbe, in succession to a previous German element exhausted by internecine conflict, or by deadly struggle with the Roman empire. Except in Poland, Bohemia, and Moravia, few of their descendants survive. The other mass followed the course of the Danube, and became known as the South Slavonians, composed of Bulgarians, Servians, Croatians, and Slovéns. These have played an important part with regard to the entire race, inasmuch as they were the link between early Christianized civilisation and their own kindred heathen tribes. It was to the Danubian Slavs that, in the early part of the ninth century, Cyril and Methodius preached the gospel in their mother tongue.

the 'old Slavonic,' which by the spread of Christianity was, until a few centuries ago, the vernacular, in a slightly varied form, of all the Slav nations.[1] The same language, written in the alphabet composed by Cyril and Methodius, is still used in the services of the Russo-Greek Church.

We first hear in Nestor's[2] *Chronicle* of the Slavs who remained in their ancient home, now the western part of the country we are engaged in sketching. He records that even in the ninth century of the Christian era they were not yet a nation, but divided into a number of rude and independent tribes around Lake Ilmen, with Novgorod as a capital, and near the sources of the Volga, the Dvina, and the Dnieper, with Smolensk as their chief settlement. One of the most important of those tribes was that of the *Poliàné*, whose capital, Kief, later played so great a part in Russian history; while the easternmost Slavs were the *Viatichi*, in the basin of the Oka, which joins the Volga at Nijni Novgorod. It is only the latter tribe that had reached, at the period in question, the centre of modern Russia Proper.

Beyond these principal limits of the primitive Slav world, the greater part of 'Russia' (a designation that long remained unknown) was peopled by Finnish tribes, and by hordes of Tartar or Turkish origin more or less nomadic in their habits. The most redoubtable of the latter—the Khazars—had in the latter half of the seventh century formed on the Volga a State ruled from a city near the site of modern Astrakhan. Gradually, the greater part of Southern 'Russia' fell into their hands, and the Slavonic tribes nearest their boundaries became tributaries to them. Their power was, however, crushed, A.D. 969, by the Rurik princes.

Between the Volga and the Slav territories, as well as throughout the northern part of what is now Russia, dwelt the Finnish tribes. We shall find some of them extant on our voyage down the Volga. Those who occupied lands nearest to the Slavs on their eastern side have long been absorbed by the Slavonic race, and survive only in name as the *Muroma*, the *Meria*, and the *Ves*. North of the Slavs of Novgorod were the *Chud* or Finnish tribes that spread around the Gulf of Finland and the Lake of Ladoga, and who, together with the Lett and Lithuanian races to the south of them, completely excluded the Slavs from the Baltic and the waters appertaining to it.

We thus find that in the ninth century the extensive country we are dealing with was peopled by a number of ethnologically unrelated heathen tribes, warring more and more among themselves as their numbers multiplied or as they approached each other's territorial confines, and having each a primitive, patriarchal form of government, without any common political tie.

In these circumstances Nestor asserts that the Slavonian and Finnish

---

[1] To this day anyone acquainted with the modern Russian language has no difficulty in understanding Bulgarian, Servian, or Czech.

[2] The earliest monkish historian of Russia.

groups of the north combined to send the following message to the Scandinavians, from whose depredations they had already begun to suffer: 'Our land is great and bountiful, but there is no order in it; come ye and rule over us.' Dr. V. Thomsen points out, however, that another monkish legend places almost the same words in the mouths of the Britons by whom the Saxons were 'invited' to come over the sea.

Clearly it could have been only as a conqueror that Röric, sailing over in his viking ships to the south coast of the Gulf of Finland, penetrated inland, and establishing himself, A.D. 864, at Novgorod, founded what could

THE EMPEROR OF RUSSIA.

then for the first time be called a *Russian* monarchy, from *Rhos* or *Russ* the clan to which he belonged.

The Scandinavian character of the ruling race at Kief was probably not preserved for more than a few generations. Röric's grandson already bore a Slavonic name, and by the year 1000 the reigning princes who succeeded to the throne of Kief in priority of descent, in accordance with the law of *Oddsret*, had become essentially Slavonicized. Their adoption of the Greek religion must have had some effect in estranging them from their Roman Catholic brethren at home

After the period to which we have brought down our observations, the
stream of settlers ceased to pour in from Scandinavia, but it had by that
time deposited so strong a contingent that a contemporary writer describes
the population of Kief in 1018 as consisting 'chiefly of Danes,' or men
from the north. Novgorod long continued to keep up its character of a
'Varangian'[1] city, and its Scandinavian element gave way only in the
thirteenth or fourteenth century to the Germans of the Hanse Towns, by

THE EMPRESS OF RUSSIA.

whom its lucrative trade was absorbed. That intimate personal relations
were maintained, even at the close of the eleventh century, between the
Princes of Kief and the country of their ancestors, is proved by the fact
that in about 1070 Vladimir (Monomachus) married Gyda, the daughter of
King Harold, after she had fled with her brothers to the Danish Court.
Their son espoused a daughter of Ingo Strenkelson, King of Sweden.

[1] Varangar (Old Norse: *Vaeringjar*) signified only the Scandinavian body-guard of the Emperor of Byzantium,
not Scandinavians in general. The term was later adopted by the Slavs in the form of *Variag*, to denote Northmen.

Dr. Thomsen gives a long list of proper names of Scandinavian root which long survived the Slavonicization of the 'Russ.' He has also discovered in the Russian language a host of words (principally for household objects in incipient civilized life) that are unmistakably Scandanavian in their origin. Even the word *knút*, or whip, with which criminals were punished or executed within recent times in Russia, is derived from the old Norse or Swedish *knut-r*—a knot. We have indeed found in Norway many more such words than the learned professor has cited. For instance, *peich* or *petchka*, the Russian for stove, is still as *peis*, the Norse for hearth or oven.

The first Russian code of laws, compiled in the reign of Vladimir (tenth century), was essentially Scandinavian or Teutonic in its principles. Thus it introduced, in lieu of the primitive law of vengeance and retaliation, penalties or compensation for manslaughter, under the name of *Weregeld*, converted into *Vira* in Slavonian.

We have already alluded to the law of *Odel*, still prevalent in Norway. This was the origin of the Russian *Udél* system, under which the successors of Röric fought amongst themselves for the paramount throne and facilitated by their dissensions the occupation of Russia by the Tartars during two centuries. Until that catastrophe occurred, Russia had followed the general European path of civilization and development in its social life, its laws, and its internal government. Even the Saxon Witenagemotes had been reproduced under the Slavonic name of *Véché*, and survived more especially at Novgorod and Pskof (in the form of Republics), until the Russian sovereign power was concentrated at Moscow.

It was Ivan III. (1462–1505) who assumed the title of Grand Duke (or Prince) of Novgorod, Vladimir, Moscow, and 'all Russia,' and added to his arms the double-headed black eagle, after his marriage with Sophia Paleologus, of the imperial Byzantine blood. His successor, Vasili III. (1505–1534) absorbed the principalities that had remained independent of Moscow; and his son Ivan IV. the Terrible (1534–1584) found himself in the position of being able to take at his coronation, the first in Russia, the title of 'Tsar,'[1] and 'Autocrat of all the Russias.' He was well read in Byzantine lore, and desired to be recognised by the Patriarch of Constantinople, to whom he sent a costly present of sable skins, as the representative of the extinct imperial line, through Anne, sister of the Emperor Basil and wife of Vladimir, the first Christian Prince of Kief. Russian historians are now agreed that the legend of Vladimir Monomachus having received investiture at the hands of the Emperor Constantine is a mere legend fabricated in the reign of Ivan IV.

Having thus sketched the development and consolidation of Russia down to the age of Peter the Great, we bring this chapter to a close, and begin our rapid but extensive travels through the empire.

[1] Czar is a corrupt German spelling of the title.

RUSSIAN SLEIGHING AND COURSING.

AN ILLUMINATION FROM A RUSSIAN MS. OF THE TWELFTH OR THIRTEENTH CENTURY, IN THE PUBLIC MUSEUM, MOSCOW.

CHAPTER II.

WESTERN RUSSIA.

LIKE the great majority of British and American travellers bound for St. Petersburg, our first objective point is Berlin, which we reach from London in about twenty-four hours. We can proceed the same night and in about fifteen hours more enter the Russian Empire at the frontier station of Wierzbolow or Wirballen. Dreary as we may have found the plains of East Prussia, we miss suddenly their neat homesteads, their well-kept roads, and their trim avenues of poplars, when we cross the brook which separates the two great empires. Instead of these we catch a glimpse of the blue and gold dome of a Russo-Greek church, and scarcely require to be reminded, by a demand for our passports, that we are in 'Holy Russia.' But geographically we are only in a province of the Kingdom of Poland, inhabited chiefly by Poles and Jews. Even at Kovno, sixty miles beyond, we are not on ancient Muscovite ground, but in the venerable Duchy of Lithuania, dynastically joined to the Crown of Poland in 1386, united with that kingdom in 1401, and finally incorporated with it in 1569. At the third partition of Poland (1795), Lithuania fell to the share of Russia.

Prettily situated at the confluence of the Vilia with the great Niemen River, in a fertile and pleasantly accidented district, Kovno, notwithstanding its present squalor, is of interest as the last stronghold of paganism in

Europe, and one which held out until the end of the fourteenth century, or three hundred years after its foundation. Ten miles beyond it, on the Niemen, now stands a Roman Catholic church, on the site of a sacred grove within which the pagan worshippers maintained a perpetual fire until they were driven from their last and holiest shrine. Their chief priest, whose iron sceptre, when produced by his messengers, secured the implicit obedience of pagan kings and princes, resided at a more ancient place of the same name—Romnové—in East Prussia, on the River Alle, which was burnt when Boleslas of Poland invaded Prussia in 1015, and forced its inhabitants to accept the religion of Christ. Dusburg, a chronicler of the thirteenth and fourteenth centuries, relates that niches in the sacred oak of ancient Romnové contained effigies of Perkun, the sun-god, with a red face surrounded by rays; of Petrimpa, the god of springs, sources and fertility, in the form of a beardless youth; and of Pikol, the moon-god having power over death and misfortune, and therefore represented as a grey-headed old man of deathly pallor, with a white band round his head.

Only eighty years ago, in the neighbouring province of Courland, could be seen erect some of the sacred oaks of ancient days, the last mementos of the extinct but once paramount authority which had been wielded by pagan high priests over the greater part of the country between the Baltic and the Carpathians. Strife and warfare, originally in the name of the true faith, later for political objects, in which the Teutonic knights, the Lithuanian grand dukes, the Poles, and the Russians, are mixed up to a degree that will not admit of any clear account within the limits of these pages, have not permitted the survival of any very ancient remnants of architecture. The church of St. Peter and St. Paul at Kovno, the largest Roman Catholic edifice in Lithuania, was dedicated in the fifteenth century, like the church of St. George; while the chapel of St. Gertrude is known to have existed since 1503. In 1812 the town was devastated and pillaged by the French, whose ultimate disastrous retreat is commemorated in the following inscription on a monument which stands in the market-place: 'In 1812, Russia was invaded by an army numbering 700,000 men. The army recrossed the frontier numbering 70,000.' We may add that out of eight hundred guns, only nine were carried back by the French, and we shall later find a good display of them within the Kremlin at Moscow.

Passing junctions of lines that lead severally to the port of Libau, in the Baltic, and to Warsaw, the capital of the Kingdom of Poland, we halt for refreshment at Vilna, the 'Little Paris' of the Lithuanians in happier days, and now the chief town of a Russian province of the same name. The beauty of its situation on the Vilia River, amongst hills that rise to the east, south and west, is not very apparent from the large and handsome railway station, and its attractions not being in other respects sufficient to encourage a break in the journey, we must be content to read in 'Murray'

that this also was a centre of heathen fire worship in days of remote
antiquity. The Jagellon Castle (1323), of which an octagonal red brick
tower still remains, crowns the hill at the foot of which a fire was kept
uninterruptedly burning until the triumph of Christianity. Roman Catholic
as the province of Vilna now is, Count D. Tolstoy[1] points with pride to the
fact that the Gospel was brought to Lithuania by Russians at a period
when Latinism was completely unknown, notwithstanding that the inhabitants
of the provinces of Vilna, Grodno, Samogitia, and part of Courland were
not kindred in race to the Slavs. The remains of the first martyrs of
the faith, Anthony, John, and Eustace, killed by the Lithuanian idolaters,
under Olgord, their prince in the fourteenth century,
repose in the church of St. Nicholas, 'the Miracle Worker,'
at Vilna.

In further corroboration of such
a wide and early establishment

VILNA.

of Greek orthodoxy in the present
north-west provinces of Russia, the
testimony is adduced of Baron
Herberstein, ambassador from the
Emperor Maximilian, of Germany (1517-1526), and of Alessandro Guagnino,
an Italian officer in the military service of Poland (1560), to the effect that
in their time there were more Russian than Roman Catholic churches in
Vilna. They assert that even in the reign of King Stephen Bathory (1575-
1586) there were already thirty Russo-Greek places of worship in that city,
and that the most illustrious houses in Lithuania belonged to that confession,
after seceding from the Church of Rome. Sustained as it was by the advice
and the personal visits of the Patriarch of Constantinople, and partly by the
influence of Muscovy, whose Grand Duke, Ivan III., had married the

---

[1] *History of Romanism in Russia*, by the late Count D. Tolstoy, 1874.

daughter of the Grand Duke of Lithuania, the Greek Church held its own, notwithstanding the proclamation of the union of the Latin and Greek Churches by the Council of Florence in 1438.

The famed Teutonic knights had in the fourteenth and fifteenth centuries done their best by violence to introduce Romanism into Lithuania; but it was only when Jerome of Prague visited the country (in the fifteenth century) that Rome began to achieve some success. The pope then assumed the right of nominating and confirming bishops without the preliminary consent of the Kings of Poland, who, however, at the dawn of the sixteenth century, vindicated and exercised the right of filling the episcopal sees. This led to the disorganisation of the Latin clergy and religious orders, the authority of the bishops appointed by the king being frequently disputed. The Reformation movement found Lithuania in this condition, towards the middle of the sixteenth century. The upper classes were ready for it, both as a result of the preaching of John Huss, and by the liberty of the press, established since 1539 in Poland. It was accepted with such enthusiasm that the Lithuanian Senate soon became composed almost exclusively of Calvinists and Lutherans.

The Roman Catholic clergy being unable from venality and disunion to struggle against the Reformation, Lithuania was flooded with Jesuits, who established, in 1570, a college at Vilna, which was a few years later raised to the dignity of a university. Vast estates were gradually conferred upon them by the King of Poland, and by the great nobles, who re-entered the pale of the Church. Even Prince Nicholas Radzivill the Black, the powerful protector of the Calvinists, at whose expense the Bible had, in 1563, been printed in the Polish language, passed over to Romanism, drove the ministers of the Reformed Church from the estates which they held, and gave their churches, printing presses, and libraries to the Jesuits. By the year 1632 there was not a single ' Dissenter' in the Polish Senate.

Having suppressed the Reformation, the Jesuits attacked with increased activity the Russo-Greek Church established in the outlying Polish provinces. Constantinople was distant, and Moscow was absorbed by her own disastrous affairs. The Greek priesthood was, at the same time, in a very degraded position. A Russian noble of the period states that the clergy of that faith often ' passed their time in drinking-houses,' pillaged their own churches, and that it was impossible to find one among them who could translate the works of St. John Chrysostom into Slavonic. Some of their bishops were gained over, and submitted their Church to the pope, who thereupon proclaimed the union of the two Churches, under which, as a measure of conciliation, the rites and doctrines of the Greek Church could be preserved, ' in so far as they were not contrary to the Roman Church.' Thirty years later, the inhabitants of Lithuania were professed *en masse*, the great noble families having already left the Greek Church and embraced Romanism.

After this digression on the ecclesiastical history of Lithuania, explanatory of the present predominance of Roman Catholicism, we notice some other stirring events in the history of Vilna. After much suffering in wars with Teutonic knights, Tartars, and Russian princes, the city was plundered and destroyed in the seventeenth century by Swedes, Russians, and Cossacks. In 1708 it was occupied by Charles XII., and in 1794 it fell to the Russians, after a gallant defence. It was the centre of the French operations in 1812. The memory of Napoleon's triumphal entry into Vilna, when he occupied the Episcopal Palace, now the residence of the Governor-General, is dimmed by the recollection of his ignominious flight in disguise from the Grand Army, which had been reduced, in little more than five months, to the condition of a rabble train, leaving in one hospital alone 7,500 corpses 'piled like pigs of lead one above the other,' the total number of sick and wounded abandoned by the King of Naples having been 20,000. More recently disasters overtook the Lithuanians, when they joined the Polish insurrection of 1831, and in 1863 and 1864, when General Mouravieff sternly carried out from Vilna the measures which averted a threatened dismemberment of the empire.

An imposing iron-lattice bridge next takes the train at a solemn pace over the Western Dvina, which, like the Volga and the Dnieper, rises in the Valdai hills, between St. Petersburg and Moscow, and which falls into the Baltic at Riga, after running a sluggish course, occasionally accelerated by rapids, for about 650 miles. Except towards its mouth, this shallow and tortuous stream dotted with islands that become in spring, together with the sandy banks, mere swamps tenanted by storks, snipe, and every other variety of wild fowl—is navigated only by the barges of light draught which we momentarily see as we move on towards the great railway junction (with Riga on the one hand, and Smolensk and Moscow on the other) at Dünaburg.

We are now in the province of 'White Russia,' as distinguished from 'Great' and 'Little' Russia, or, to use modern terminology, in the province of Vitebsk ; still, however, connected, like the rest of the country through which we have passed, with records of strife and bloodshed, laid to the account of Teutonic knights, Poles, Swedes, and Muscovites. The tide of the battle for Christendom, and, later, the struggle for political dominion in these ancient provinces, have left many traces in the history of Dünaburg, finally ceded by the Poles to Russia in 1772, and now one of her most important fortresses.

Although, politically, the original combatants have disappeared or been rendered powerless, the new interests and combinations that have supervened render the fortress of Dünaburg of high importance. The works form part of the second line of defence protecting the western frontier of Russia, and are intended to render impossible an inimical occupation of the main lines

of railway from Warsaw to St. Petersburg, and from Riga to Vitebsk.
Formidable as a place of arms, the town is also a centre of considerable
trade in flax, hemp, tallow, and timber, sent by barge or rail to Riga.

Detached homesteads are now of less and less frequent occurrence, and
we learn that the broad cuttings through which we are conveyed are the
margins of forests of which bears, wolves, and elk, are still in possession.
Groups of grey and tumble-down-looking log-huts, forming villages of
melancholy aspect, tell the traveller that he is already in Russia Proper,
which is reached at Ostrof, in the province of Pskof. Nevertheless, we are
not yet beyond the reach of ancient Lithuanian and Polish depredation.
The fortress that existed here in the fourteenth century survives only in

LITHUANIAN PEASANT.

three of its towers of grey and red stone.
In 1501 the Lithuanians massacred 4000
of the inhabitants of Ostrof, and in 1581
it was captured by the famous Stephen
Bathory of Poland, who a year later caused
to be built the church of St. Nicholas,
which is still extant. Scarcely twenty-five
miles beyond is one of the most interesting political centres of primitive Russia.

Pskof, supposed to have been founded
by St. Olga, who partially introduced into
Russia the Greek religion, which she had
embraced at Constantinople about A.D. 955,
played an important part in the foundation
of the Russian Empire. It is curious to
observe that the earliest political institutions of the country were of a popular
character, on the model of our Saxon
Witenagemotes. Like Novgorod (the
Great) and Khlynof (now Viatka), Pskof
had its open-air *vechè* (Witenagemote), at which the citizens deliberated (on
one occasion in their shirts) and exercised their right of electing and
deposing their princes. These had good cause for alarm when they heard
the *vechè* bell ring out, and saw the club (mace), emblematical of the majesty
of the law, set up in the great square. The city and its territories formed
part of the Hanseatic League in the earliest period of the great trade with
Germany, of which Pskof was the first Russian outpost. The gradual
absorption of these republics by the Grand Duchy of Moscow will be
described in our account of the Great Novgorod. We need only mention
here that the famed *vechè* bell in the church of the Holy Trinity was taken
down in 1510, amidst the wailings of the citizens over their lost freedom.
Three hundred of the most distinguished Pskovian families were at the

same time removed to the dominions of Muscovy Proper, and replaced by an equal number of families of the trading class drawn from towns on the Volga. The Novgorodians had met with a similar fate thirty-two years earlier.

But the ancient spirit of independence had not been entirely quenched, even by the year 1570, when Ivan the Terrible of Moscow, after ravaging Novgorod, appeared before the walls of Pskof, whose citizens he equally suspected of treasonable designs. However, the city was saved from his fury by a monk, who, according to frequent examples in ancient as well as in modern Russia, pursued mendicancy in the guise, assumed rather than inherent, of an idiot. Capering about on a stick, he addressed the redoubtable monarch as 'Johnny,' offered him raw meat, and exhorted him not to drink the blood of Christians, but to eat of the bread and salt to be presented to him in the cathedral, as a token of submission. On orders being given to seize the idiot, he suddenly and miraculously vanished, but not before he had caused the horse of Ivan to fall, while he was warning him of his death by lightning if he injured a single citizen. Struck with terror, Ivan left the city precipitately, without doing any harm to the inhabitants. In 1581 Pskof was besieged by the Poles, and in 1618 by Gustavus Adolphus, but on both occasions the invaders were ultimately repelled.

Such are the latest vicissitudes to which the ancient city has been subjected. We may well gaze on its stout Kremlin walls, built in 1323. Their base on the east and north is washed by the Pskova River, and on the west by the Velikaya, while 'Dovmont's Wall,' constructed at the close of the thirteenth century, springs from their southern face, and forms a square on which once stood the castle of the reigning prince.

The huge Cathedral of the Trinity almost fills the space enclosed by the Kremlin walls. It was built in 1682 in the so-called 'Russo-Byzantine' style, in succession to an edifice raised in 1368, which again had been preceded by churches built severally in 1266 and 1138. Its site is, however, more especially hallowed by the fact that St. Olga built a church upon it A.D. 957. Among the more conspicuous of the numerous relics in this cathedral is a silver shrine with the remains of a godly prince who died in 1138. Its miraculous properties are assumed to be such that when the Novgorodians, over whom he had previously ruled, claimed his relics, the coffin could not be moved by human force, the sainted prince thereby signifying a desire to abide among his faithful Pskovians. Unfortunately, the original cross which St. Olga raised at Pskof was destroyed by fire in 1509. The tomb of plain oak, in a chapel to the right of the altar screen, is that of St. Dovmont, a Lithuanian chief elected Prince of Pskof, and his sword, suspended near the tomb, was used at the consecration of the old sovereigns of Pskof in this cathedral. Close by is the shrine of 'the

sainted Nicholas Salos, the 'Idiot,' whose service to this city we have already
recorded.

Traditions of miracles performed to the discomfiture of foes attach to
several other churches, and a small chapel opposite the bazaar is in
memory of citizens who fell in an insurrection in 1650. There are also
many ancient and interesting monuments in the neighbourhood, and we may
point out more especially the fortified monastery of Pskof Pechersk, renowned for its catacombs and for the sieges it has sustained.

A railway enables us to reach from Pskof the Baltic Provinces of Russia,
consisting of the Provinces of Livonia, Esthonia and Courland, with a
population of more than two and a quarter millions, and with a sea-board of
the highest importance to Russian commerce. We branch off again into the
ancient activity of Lithuanian Teutonic knights, Poles, Swedes, and Muscovites, but have space to say only that the civilisation and culture of those
provinces is still undeniably German, and must ever remain so. We are
again, since reaching the Russian frontier, in the country of good highways
marked out by tall poplars, in a land of farms and mansions, neat and solid,
and of towns great and small, more or less mediæval-German in aspect.
Every institution is, fortunately for the inhabitants, still Germanic, although
perhaps somewhat too conservative. But this is a question of development
on ancient, rather than on new lines, as advocated by ardent ' Russificators.'

The empire may well be proud of the city of Riga, the capital of
Livonia, which, together with Esthonia, was finally ceded by Sweden to
Russia in 1721 at the Peace of Nystad. The exercise of the Protestant
religion, the official and judicial use of the German language, and all
ancient municipal rights and privileges were guaranteed by the terms of that
capitulation. Commercially, Riga, built by Bishop Albert in A.D. 1200, ranks
as the second port in Russia, although its population is only 170,000. One
half of its trade is with Great Britain.

A couple of thousand ships of all nations discharge or load here
annually, and we have already seen - at Dünaburg—the barges that bring
down the Dvina the grain, linseed, flax, and other native products of the
Russian interior. Although not in the least Russian, the sights at Riga are
interesting.

There is the massive castle, with crenelated towers, dating from the
days when the Teutonic knights were paramount (1494-1515). The effigy
in stone of the Holy Virgin, over one of the archways, will be found
reproduced in miniature in the hall of the Great Guild, and being locally called
the Docke (which is equivalent to the present Danish and Norwegian word
for a doll), suggests that we have here the origin of the 'dock' in which
prisoners stand in our own country. The chairman of the Guild sat under
the Docke, and as ' Dockmann' administered the affairs of the corporation
including, no doubt, the trial of offenders against municipal and other laws.

The Hall of the Blackheads, so called from the device of a Moor's head, which, in honour of Saint Maurice, their patron, they adopted as their heraldic distinction, was built early in the thirteenth century, and contains among treasures of silver, books, and paintings, many ancient relics of the order. Moors' heads distinguish the pews of the 'Blackheads' in the Cathedral of St. Mary, built in the thirteenth, and renovated in the sixteenth century. A letter from Luther to the Senate of Riga and a very ancient Bible are the proudest possessions of the City Library.

South-west of Riga lies Mitau, on the Aa River. This city, the capital of Courland (incorporated with Russia in 1795), was founded in 1271, when also its castle (rebuilt in 1772) was erected by Conrad von Medem, Grand Master of the Livonian Order of Knighthood. In the left wing of this historical edifice is the mausoleum of the ancient Dukes of Courland, beginning with Gothard Kettler, the last Grand Master and first Duke (1517-1587). Most

VIEWS IN RIGA.

of the coffins were closed and secured by iron hoops about forty years ago, with the exception of the coffin of Duke John Ernest Biron, the unworthy favourite of the Empress Anne of Russia, who was originally the grandson of an equerry, or groom, to the fourth Duke of Courland. The German cicerone explains that the remains were ordered by a Prince Dolgorouki to be left exposed, in order that patriotic Russians might have the opportunity of reviling their enemy, and he actually requests visitors not to spit at the mummified body and thereby injure the well-preserved velvet clothing, wig, ruffles, &c. The remains are perfect, all but the eyes and the nose, which, it is asserted, an ardent patriot broke with his clenched fist.

The palace is also interesting from its occupation in 1798 by Louis (later XVIII.) of France, and his Queen, Marie Josephine of Savoy. The daughter of the unfortunate Louis XVI., on being liberated from the Temple, came here to marry her cousin, the Duc d'Angoulême, in a chapel of the palace, at which the Abbé de Firmont, who attended the French monarch on the scaffold, officiated. The hospitality thus offered by the Emperor Paul ceased abruptly in 1792, when the royal exiles were compelled to leave, partly on foot, in mid-winter, for Memel, their eccentric host having suddenly made an alliance with Buonaparte.

Working back by the same railway in the direction of St. Petersburg, we arrive at the picturesque town of Dorpat, the seat of a university, founded in 1632 by Gustavus Adolphus. Its Gothic features were destroyed by a great fire in 1598, and are represented by a few ruins of the cathedral. Several subsequent conflagrations modernised the town, which is supposed to have been founded in 1030 by a Grand Duke of Novgorod.

In old posting days, travellers caught sight on this journey of the navigable Peipus Lake, twenty-three miles long; but the railway now skirts it at some distance on its way to Reval, the capital of Esthonia, one of the prettiest places on the Baltic, and of great commercial importance since its connection by rail with St. Petersburg and the interior of the empire. Its old Danish castle, perched on the top of a rock, and enclosing the 'Ritterhaus,' the cathedral, and many houses of the ancient nobility, is a strikingly picturesque object. One of the oldest churches, dating from the foundation of the town in 1219, is now a chapel attached to the Gothic Rathhaus, or Town Hall. The Guildhall of the 'Blackheads' contains the archives of the Knights of the Sword (a Livonian order), and a large collection of silver plate is interesting from the many English names of donors engraved upon one of the cups.

The environs are as pretty and as interesting as the town itself; but we can only draw attention to the ruins of Padis Cloister, the finest in Esthonia, at a distance of about twenty-seven miles from Reval. It was a famed monastery even in the early part of the fourteenth century.

This chapter must now be brought to a close with a mere mention of Hapsal, the Baltic Brighton, and of Narva, with its splendid waterfall and its prosperous manufacturing industry, while we speed on to St. Petersburg.

THE COLUMN OF ALEXANDER I., ST. PETERSBURG.

ILLUMINATION FROM A RUSSIAN MS. OF THE 14TH CENTURY, IN THE BIBLIOTHÈQUE
IMPÉRIALE, ST. PÉTERSBOURG.

CHAPTER III.

THE MODERN CAPITAL: ST. PETERSBURG.

RISING in Lake Ladoga, the clear and rapid, but treacherous, waters of
the Neva, after flowing a distance of forty-two miles, bear almost on
their surface the modern capital of the Russian empire. The main stream
is confined within solid granite quays, but the city of St. Petersburg rests
on a crust of soil which almost floats on the water-logged marshes selected
by Peter the Great, in 1703, as the site of the 'window' through which he
desired to 'look into Europe.' The crust itself is now secure enough, for it
was well pegged down with the superimposed piles of wood on which the
resolute Tsar laid the foundations of his first buildings. Besides, it is well
weighted with the stones and rubble, with which for many years he compelled all carts and vessels coming to the new city to be laden. The chief
danger to which the city has since been mainly exposed is inundation. In
1824, in succession to many previous floods, the waters of the Neva rose
thirteen feet four inches above their ordinary average level, submerging the
greater part of the capital. Standing on the gallery under the dome of St.
Isaac's, whose huge and heavy mass has visibly sunk into the marshy subsoil,
it is difficult not to accept the possibility, long predicted, of St. Petersburg
being some day overwhelmed by a still greater catastrophe of the same
kind.

However, *après nous le déluge*: we have only to deal with the city as it now is, and to express a fervent hope that the dreaded combination of the elements will never occur. It is certainly a remarkable city, not only from its origin, but also from the colossal character of many of its buildings, and the impression of hugeness and desolation imparted to the traveller by the vast open spaces and wide streets. The best edifices are imposing from their immensity, rather than from the beauty of their architecture. The materials of which they are composed are mostly only brick and stucco. With a population of nearly one million, the city itself in summer looks deserted, and oppresses the visitor with a feeling of insignificance, from being set in so vast a frame. In this respect only is it typical of Russia, which, with its population of more than one hundred millions, is a desert in comparison with every other country in Europe. Nevertheless, it contains objects of such great interest, and artistic treasures of so great and exceptional a value, that scarcely any capital in Europe is more worthy of being described by pen and depicted by pencil.

The best starting-point for a tour of inspection is the great square, partly converted into a neat park, on which stands the Winter Palace, restored in 1839, after a fire which had consumed the interior of the building erected in 1762 and completed in 1769, in the reign of the great Catherine. Unlike the huge spaces of which we have spoken, this immense edifice, 455 feet in length by 350 in breadth, may be considered as emblematical of the magnitude of the empire and of the power by which it is governed and held together. The noble halls and other apartments are replete with works of art, and more especially with pictures of Russian victories by sea and by land since the days of Peter the Great, who is depicted in the hall which bears his name as being attended by the Genius of Russia. Portraits of soldiers and statesmen, renowned in the more modern annals of Russia, cover the walls of a large gallery and those of the Field Marshals Hall. In the Alexander Hall is a portrait of Alexander I. by George Dawe, an English artist of celebrity at St. Petersburg; while equally good full-sized likenesses of succeeding emperors, down to Alexander II., adorn the Round Hall. There is one small, plain room which the visitor should endeavour to see—the study and bed-chamber of Nicholas I., in which he died on the camp bed, still covered with his military cloak. His writing-table remains undisturbed, and on it lies the last military report which the emperor received.

Travellers who succeed in obtaining permission to inspect this palace are sometimes fortunate enough to obtain a view of the crown jewels, securely kept in an upper room. The huge so-called Orlof diamond in the imperial sceptre, purchased from an Armenian by Count Orlof, and presented by him to his imperial mistress Catherine II., is the largest, as the Pitt diamond of France is the most beautiful, of all the known diamonds in Europe. The emperor's crown is adorned with noble jewels, and surmounted by a cross formed of five beautiful diamonds fixed on a very large uncut spinel ruby. Its value is about £100,000.

Connected with the palace, but entered by a noble vestibule from Bolshaya Millionaya Street, is the famed Hermitage, originally the Pavilion, built in 1765, in which Catherine II. spent her leisure moments in conversation with philosophers, men of letters, and artists. The building was reconstructed between 1840 and 1850, in the Greek style. The ground floor is occupied by galleries of antique sculpture, of classical, Scythian, and Siberian antiquities, of original drawings, and by a library of ten thousand volumes on archæology, remnants of the libraries of D'Alembert, Diderot, and Voltaire, now in the Imperial Public Library. The Kertch collection is alone worth a visit to St. Petersburg, for it reveals, in the most perfect specimens, the art of the Greek colonies which were founded on the northern coast of the Black Sea nearly six hundred years B.C. Attracted by commerce and by the wealth of the 'Nomadic' and 'Royal' Scythians, described by Strabo and Herodotus, the Greeks from Miletus engrafted their ancient civilisation on them, and in their artistic productions mingled their mythology, legends and types with those of the barbarians. The process is apparent in this unique and unrivalled collection of objects of antique art, principally in the precious metals.

It may be divided into two classes: objects from the Crimea and adjacent districts, and others from Siberia and Central Russia. They date from the period of the highest civilisation of Greece to the time of the first Mongol invasion of the Russian plains in the thirteenth century. Mr. Alfred Maskell[1] is of opinion that few of the various pieces of goldsmiths' work go back to a period earlier than the third century before Christ, and that most of them are much later. The Crimean (Greco-Scythian) objects are naturally of the highest artistic value. Hidden in a great number of tumuli, essentially Milesian, their existence was first practically revealed by M. Paul Dubrux, who, without pretension to archæological knowledge, pointed out the spots where important discoveries were made, principally in 1831. In that year, the royal Kul-Oba tomb, about four miles west of Kertch, was discovered by soldiers who were quarrying stone for fortifications. It contained the mouldered remains of a Bosporian king, buried in his richest robes and adorned with his most precious ornaments, together with those of his favourite wife or queen (bearing on her head, like the king, a mitre-shaped diadem), and of some of his attendants and horses, with their clothes and trappings. The sarcophagus of carved and painted yew-wood in which the king lay, with his gold-hilted sword and other arms and treasures beside him, now stands in the Hermitage Museum, as brilliant in colour as it was at least two thousand years ago, when the Greek artist

[1] See his *Russian Art and Art Objects in Russia* (South Kensington Museum Art Handbooks), 1884.

D

ornamented it with paintings of victories mounted on chariots, figures of Greek men and women, and warriors with bows and arrows. Unfortunately, after the discovery of its rich contents, the tumulus was not sufficiently guarded, and under cover of night a crowd of people rushed into it and carried away, and subsequently melted down, a large number of the thin gold plates with which the royal dresses were covered as well as much other golden treasure, estimated to have weighed one hundred and twenty pounds, of which only fifteen pounds were recovered by the authorities. But sufficient was rescued to render the Kul-Oba even now, after many other discoveries of a similar character, conspicuous among the treasures of the Kertch collection of the Hermitage—so called from the Museum at Kertch in which Bosporian antiquities were amassed before the Crimean War.

In the Kul-Oba tomb was found a very remarkable vase of electrum. It is lotah-shaped, and on a band surrounding the centre are four groups of Scythians with long hair and beards, and dressed very much like the Russian peasant of the present day, excepting the hood, or *bashlik*, which has been introduced into Russia from the Caucasus within modern times. These groups represent episodes in the life of a chief, who in one scene is having his leg bandaged, in another his tooth drawn. As the skull discovered in the tomb bears evidence of dental affliction, it is presumed that the incidents so skilfully repoussé on the vase refer to incidents in the life of the king in whose tomb it has been preserved. The costumes thus handed down to us, as it were in a photograph, are reproduced in one of the five small statuettes found in the same tomb, and also in electrum—a metal obtained, when not found in a natural state, by the alloying of gold with one-fifth part of silver. We find the same people represented in the nomadic occupation of lassoing and breaking in wild horses on the wondrous silver-gilt Nicopol vase, which stands enshrined in the centre of one of the finest halls of the Hermitage. M. Thiers was so much struck by its beauty and importance that he declared its possession was almost sufficient to form a *casus belli* with the Russian empire. It was found (1863) in a tumulus near the town of Nicopol, on the Dnieper, and is twenty-eight inches high. The work, which is in the most perfect style of Greek art, cannot be of later date than the fourth century B.C.

On the ground floor of the Hermitage are galleries of sculpture and of Etruscan ceramic art. Here also is to be seen the beautiful and matchless king of vases found at Cuma, and purchased by the Russian Government with the Campana Museum; and in a newly-arranged *annexe* of the Hermitage are collections of armour and other objects, which form the Mediæval and Renaissance sections of the Hermitage, adulterated by a large admixture of Oriental trophies and works of art, Polish and Bohemian military standards, and other curios, somewhat incongruous, but of high interest. A whole day might easily be spent in studying this department of the Hermitage alone.

The stately grandeur of the apartments into which we are now ushered makes us feel at once that we are in an imperial palace, although nominally in the picture galleries of the Hermitage. Struck with admiration at the noble tables, vases, tazzas, and candelabra of malachite, lapis-lazuli, porphyry, and jasper that stand on the highly-polished inlaid floors of the principal rooms, we defer for a moment our proposed systematic inspection of the pictures, which cover almost every available inch of the walls, and fill the numerous stands and screens provided for the display of so great an abundance of paintings by the older masters of the principal schools in Europe.

The pictures purchased by Peter the Great were chiefly Dutch and Flemish works, but now the bulk consists mainly of the three celebrated collections of the Marquis de Crozat, Lord Walpole, and the Empress Josephine (Malmaison collection). The gallery contains about 1,800 paintings, of which a little more than one half are of the Flemish, Dutch, and German schools. The art of Italy is represented by about 350 specimens, and that of Spain by 115. The Spanish and Flemish collections are considered to be the most valuable. Indeed, the collection of Spanish pictures is the best and most varied out of Spain, the number of Murillos alone being twenty. The best of the six paintings by Velasquez are the portraits of Philip IV. of Spain, and those of his minister, d'Olivarès.

In the Flemish collection we see much more to interest us, from a national point of view, for it contains portraits by Van Dyck, of Charles I., Queen Henrietta Maria, the Earl of Danby, Sir Thomas Wharton, Philip, Lord Wharton, the Ladies Elizabeth and Philadelphia Wharton, Sir Thomas Chaloner, Archbishop Laud, Inigo Jones, the wife and daughter of Oliver Cromwell, and several other specimens of the great painter. The best of these, and the choicest of the equally numerous paintings by Rubens (in the same room and in Room XIV.), were once the pride of Houghton Hall.[1]

The larger pictures of the Italian school—so largely and worthily represented in the Hermitage—attract attention immediately after passing through the Historical Gallery, in which frescoes represent the progress of Greek art. Here we are in the presence of all the older Italian masters, from the sixteenth to the early part of the eighteenth century. However invidious the task, brevity compels us to name only the St. Sebastian, by Luini, the Descent from the Cross, by Sebastian del Piombo, the many

---

[1] By permitting the dispersion of the Walpole collection, the British nation lost the chance of possessing the finest museum of pictures in the world. In addition to the great number of pictures sold to the Russian Government in 1779 for £35,000, the Louvre acquired from it nineteen of the best pictures now in that gallery, while the Museo at Madrid owes no fewer than 44 of its most valuable paintings to the same opportunity.

pictures by Guido Reni, and the Prodigal Son by Salvator Rosa, formerly one of the treasures of the Walpole collection. A magnificent Canaletto represents the reception at Venice of the ambassador of Louis XV. But there is, in short, scarcely a picture in this room that is not admirable.

The great Dutch and Flemish schools of painting may here be studied to advantage, as the galleries possess many of the finest specimens of all the noted masters. In the far-famed Rembrandt Gallery, for example, are

PETER THE GREAT.

magnificent specimens of every period and subject of the art of that great master. Two portraits, dated respectively 1634 and 1666, show his earliest and his latest style. His Danaë is a chef-d'œuvre of execution ; but the lover of art cannot afford to allow one of his pictures to escape attention. He will especially observe the masterly portraits of old Thomas Parr, of Lieven van Copenal, and the 'Rembrandt's Mother,' a highly-finished cabinet picture on a stand by itself. After glancing at the productions of Franz Hals and Ferdinand Bol, an Englishman cannot fail to recognise the compliment paid to the British school —almost entirely neglected on the rest of the Continent—by the compartment given to it in the Rembrandt Gallery. Sir Joshua Reynolds's Infant Hercules Strangling the Serpent, an allegory of Russia vanquishing the difficulties of its youthful state, was painted for the Empress Catherine II. The Continence of Scipio, from the same brush, is unfortunately unfinished ; but Cupid unloosing the Girdle of Venus (known in two *replicas* in England) here charms the eye.

The French school has enriched the gallery with noble classical landscapes by Poussin, charming pictures by Claude Lorraine, Vernet, Le Moine, Watteau, Greuze, and with a portrait of Mary Queen of Scots, painted, it is supposed, at Fotheringay, by a pupil of Clouet. Numerous other pictures by French artists adorn the Second Hermitage Palace, which is not open to the general public.

Choice specimens of Russian painting and sculpture fill the two rooms through which we make our exit. The earliest Russian painter of any note was Lossenko, who may be said to have founded the Russian school in 1759. Its most important work is considered to be The Last Day of Pompeii, by Brülow. The Brazen Serpent, by Bruni, is a startling academical picture of huge size; but the most interesting examples are the two historical pictures by Ugriumoff—The Capture of Kazan, and the Election of Michael Romanoff—and those by Matveyeff and Shebùef. The former has depicted Peter the Great questioning his son, and the latter Igolkin, a Merchant of Novgorod, who is represented as a captive in chains at Stockholm, on the point of being seized by his gaolers for having killed a Swedish soldier who spoke disrespectfully of Peter the Great. Ivanoff's Christ Appearing to Mary Magdalene, and Bruni's Christ in the Garden of Gethsemane, are typical of the Russian realistic treatment of Scriptural subjects, so different from the conventional Byzantine style of ecclesiastical painting which gives extensive employment to the native iconograph. Aivazofski, who, like Vereschagin, has a world-wide reputation, is seen in two of his most extraordinary efforts, The Creation of the World, and The Deluge.

Peter the Great's Gallery is entered from the Hermitage, although it forms part of the Winter Palace. Here we find objects illustrative of the life and activity of Peter the Great, and presses crowded with valuable nicknacks of every description. The chief interest centres in the relics of the founder of the Russian empire. We see the small gilt chariot in which he sometimes drove; the horse —now stuffed—which he rode at the battle of Poltava; the heavy iron staff which his gigantic strength enabled him to carry with ease; a slender stick, with a notch marking his height at about seven feet; his books, mathematical and other instruments, tools, turning lathes, and a collection of the teeth he had extracted from the jaws of suffering subjects. The stuffed Danish hound in one of the glass cases still wears the collar under which Catherine I. was in the habit of placing petitions in the name of his canine favourite. In the centre of the gallery is a wax effigy of the great Tsar, clad in the dress which he wore at the coronation of Catherine I., who embroidered it for that purpose. The casts on either side were taken from his features after death; but the wax mould of his face, furnished with hair and moustaches, must be the exact image of him, for it was executed at sittings which he gave the artist.

Having exhausted the manifold objects of interest in the Winter Palace and the renowned Hermitage, we cannot do better than mount the dome of

St. Isaac's for a bird's-eye view of the city. This gives us also the
opportunity of visiting one of the most remarkable of the modern cathedrals
in Russia. It was erected between 1819 and 1858, on the site of a wooden
church built in 1710, but replaced in 1801 by an edifice which had been
commenced in the reign of Catherine II. Its foundations (364 feet by 315),

ST. ISAAC'S CATHEDRAL, ST. PETERSBURG.

laid on a forest of piles twenty-one feet long, alone cost £200,000, while
the total cost of construction and decoration (not including the subsequent
cost of propping it up) exceeded three millions sterling. Its form is that of
a Greek cross, and its three chief portals of gigantic bronze work are
approached from the level of the vast square on which it stands by broad
flights of steps composed of entire pieces of polished granite from Finland.

The one hundred and twelve polished granite monoliths that support the four peristyles are sixty feet in height and seven feet in diameter; weighing one hundred and twenty-eight tons each, and crowned with massive Corinthian capitals of bronze, they support on each of the four sides of the edifice a frieze with a text in letters of bronze. Translated, the several texts are: north, 'The king shall rejoice in Thy strength, O Lord;' south, 'Mine House shall be called an House of Prayer;' east, 'In Thee, O Lord, do I put my trust; let me never be ashamed;' and west, 'To the King of Kings.' The cupola, covered with thickly-gilt copper, is sixty-six feet in diameter and two hundred and ninety-six feet high, the entire height of the cathedral to the top of the golden cross that surmounts the elegant lantern being three hundred and thirty-six feet. Four belfries, with cupolas resembling in miniature the central dome, contain bells fifteen to twenty-nine tons in weight. The three principal bronze portals are the largest in the world, and yield to none in costliness of material and beauty of execution.

The interior of St. Isaac's is well calculated to inspire feelings of solemnity and veneration, and to impress the imagination of the visitor. As in all Russian churches, the purposely-subdued light brings into relief the glittering sumptuousness of the *ikonostas*, or screen, and of the *ikons*, mostly in mosaic work, which adorn the walls and pillars of the temple. Strictly speaking, these are not worshipped, although the belief in images, to which miraculous powers are ascribed, or which have 'not been worked by human hands,' is not in its effect easily distinguishable from actual material adoration. The Russo-Greek Church rejects as idolatrous any carved or moulded representation of sacred or saintly subjects for purposes of worship, but holds that an Ikon painted, or produced in mosaic work, on a flat surface is not a violation of the Second Commandment.

Lavish use of malachite and lapis-lazuli has been made in the adornment of the Screen, and of the Sanctuary beyond the Royal Doors. Women are not admitted into this inmost shrine. It is supported by eight Corinthian pillars of malachite, which, like the lapis-lazuli, is not solid, but applied on copper tubes fitted over cast-iron cylinders. The stained window representing the Ascension, at the back of the high altar, was made in Germany, and is the only work of art within the church that is not Russian.

The view from the dome is extensive and instructive. First of all, we observe that from the so-called Admiralty, in which vessels are no longer built, remarkable for its tall gilded spire, surmounted by a ship under full sail, three great streets radiate like the ribs of a fan. The one nearest the palace is the Nevski Prospect, three miles in length, if the monastery of St. Alexander Nevski be taken as its terminus. This is the main thoroughfare of the capital, and with its two nearly parallel arteries governs the direction of most of the other streets. It is intersected by three canals that drain to some extent the city, and enable barges of light draught to distribute their freight, which is principally fuel. Light steamers also ply on these canals. Sir Samuel Bentham, a brother of Jeremy Bentham, was actively employed in Russia during a part of the reign of Catherine II., either as an agent of the British Government for building ships of war at Archangel, or as a naval commander, a lieutenant-colonel, an architect, and a general inventor in the Russian service. In one of his manifold capacities he had charge of the construction of the Fontanka Canal, the third of the canals before us. A new pile-driving machine which he devised, in order 'to put an end to the habitual skulking of the labourers,' greatly accelerated the progress of the work.

The first and second streets that run across the main thoroughfare are the Bolshaya (Great) and Malaya (Little) Morskaya (Naval) streets, the first being, like the Nevski, full of handsome buildings and shops. Turning in the opposite direction, we face the Vasili Ostrof, the largest island formed by the numerous branches of the Neva, and connected with the mainland by the handsome Nicholas Bridge and the floating bridge that leads from the Winter Palace to the colossal Exchange, recognisable by the two massive *Columnæ Rostratæ* in front of it. Beyond is another floating bridge that starts from the square on which stands the British Embassy, and abuts on the Fortress, to which we shall refer later. The last bridge, of stone and iron, establishes communication with the Viborg side, so called from its being the starting-point for a journey to the adjoining Grand Duchy of Finland, which has no through railway connection with the other parts of the Russian empire. In summer communication with the opposite side of the river is further maintained by the innumerable small steamers that have replaced the quaint-sterned ferry-boats which were formerly so prominently depicted in illustrations of St. Petersburg.

The Vasili Ostrof is, practically, the commercial quarter of the city. Off it are anchored, in mid-stream, the big steamers which, thanks to the Cronstadt Canal, are now loading grain, hemp, and flax, from the rough, flat-bottomed barges that have come from the innermost parts of the empire, to be broken up for firewood after discharging their duties as carriers of raw produce. The long granite quays are lined by other steamers that ply to Cronstadt, Sweden, or Finland. Of course we are speaking of the short summer months of the North. In winter the scene, so far as commercial activity is concerned, is one of comparative desolation, relieved only by the numberless sledges in which the inhabitants of either side of the ice-bound river are being silently but rapidly conveyed to and fro on *terra firma*.

In front of the Cathedral is the Park, which, within the last ten or fifteen years, has supplied an enjoyable shade to a once cobble-paved square that extended from the huge Senate and Synod houses on the left to the Winter Palace and the *État Major* buildings on the right. This was the site of the revolution in 1825, when the deluded soldiery shouted ' Constitutia,' under the impression that they were engaged in a pronunciamento in favour

PLAN OF ST. PETERSBURG.

of the Grand Duke Constantine, whose morganatic marriage to a Polish lady had, by his own consent, deprived him of the right of succeeding Alexander I., and placed the throne of All the Russias in the hands of his brother Nicholas, 'the Divine figure of the North.' Prominently standing out from its environment of trees and shrubs is the well-known equestrian statue of Peter the Great, erected by the great Catherine in 1782. The grand monolith of polished granite that commemorates the glory and the virtues of Alexander I. stands in front of the Winter Palace. Both of these remarkable monuments were designed and executed by Frenchmen; the first by Falconet, the second by Montferrand, the architect of the Cathedral from which we are looking down on those wonderful works.

The Nevski Prospect is the next point of attraction, although few travellers have sufficient systematic patience to make themselves acquainted with all its details on their first arrival. In summer the *drojkies*, and in winter the sledges, attract us by their peculiarity, in contrast with other European vehicles, while in their drivers we find ethnographical types on which we gaze with the interest we would bestow on a Hindu or a Chinaman in London. Their dress is almost a mediæval survival, and especially the summer head-dress, which is clearly a modernised descendant of the 'beef-eater's' hat brought to Russia by the adventurous Englishmen who discovered the sea-board of Muscovy in the sixteenth century. The indigenous hat for the same season is still almost the counterpart of the head-covering in which Paddy is wont to carry his 'dhudeen'; but it is now relegated to rural districts, although only ten years ago the *drojki* drivers of Moscow wore it generally, to the satisfaction of those who revelled in seeing Moscow in its primitive national aspect. The *Isvostchiks*, except to some extent the class who make it their special business to convey only those who are bent on pleasure, regardless of expense, are a very decent set of men, although a clear bargain as to the charge for a 'course' is necessary in order to avoid ultimate disagreement. The horses are active, wiry animals, under perfect control, and, strange to say, well acquainted with the sound of *Ptrru*, by which their eager course is at once arrested, as in Scandinavia. Stranger still, exactly the same sound is used in the island of Skye in stopping horses: and we may perhaps take the fact as a corroboration of the Scandinavian origin of early Russian civilisation. We are too far advanced in this century to see many *mujiks* clad in sheepskins, or in linen shirts covering trousers as far as the knees. No more striking change has come over the aspect of the country than the outward appearance of its cities and towns, and that of their inhabitants. In most of the rural districts, also, if not too isolated or distant from urban centres, the approximation to general European dress is evident, although disappointing to those in search of national peculiarities. Nevertheless, the summer dress of the peasant, essentially Asiatic or Indian, continues to predominate. It can be seen, as a revival, at some of the restaurants, or *traktirs*, at Moscow, which have not yet followed the example of similar establishments at St. Petersburg, where the guests are generally served by Tartar Mahomedan waiters in European evening dress.

The Kazan Cathedral, with its colonnade in imitation of St. Peter's at Rome, is soon reached on the right-hand side of the Nevski. Built between 1801 and 1811, it has internally the form of a cross, two hundred and thirty-eight feet in length by one hundred and eighty-two in breadth. A colonnade of granite monoliths, thirty-five feet high, extends in four rows from the four pillars that support the cupola; but, although architecturally grand, this arrangement somewhat crowds the interior, and adds to its conventional dinginess. However, the *ikonostas* is light and brilliant, for, like the balustrade in front, it is of silver, 'the zealous offering of the Don Cossacks,' who, during the campaign of 1812, retook from the French the church plate they had looted, and applied it to its present use.

There are many costly votive objects and military trophies in this cathedral, and the Emperor never fails to offer up his prayers here immediately on his departure from the capital and his return after a residence at some other imperial seat.

The Gostinnoi Dvor, or bazaar—so common to all Russian towns, and so decidedly Oriental in origin—claims our attention after visiting the Kazan Cathedral. There are also two other markets, the Stchukin and the Apraxin, in the street that turns off from the Nevski from the upper corner of the Gostinnoi Dvor. Crowds of purchasers fill the lanes and alleys by which those markets are intersected, and therefore a good opportunity presents itself of viewing national types of every grade. In the main bazaar, foreigners visit the excellent fur shops and those in which are sold Russia-leather slippers embroidered in silver or gold, cushions, hard, but of great utility on long journeys, and pretty sashes and ties deftly woven at Torjok. *Bric-à-brac* hunters revel in the Apraxin Dvor, but the prices asked are not those of the days before trading collectors had discovered this distant mine of wealth, and showed the native dealers that a European market was available for their goods. Those who have not visited St. Petersburg for any considerable number of years will be impressed by the development that has taken place in the local *bric-à-brac* trade. It used to be an intense pleasure to ransack the shanties we found full of incongruous odds and ends, and to secure from among the mass of rubbish a valuable or pleasing picture, or a bit of porcelain unchipped and bearing a genuine mark of note. Strings of pearls, precious stones of high value, were frequently picked up at the stalls, which were not quite unsuspected of exhibiting the produce of robberies. In fact, to this day, the market is a recipient of such articles, but the better vigilance of the police circumscribes and renders more difficult its nefarious operations.

Resuming our walk up the Nevski, the first building we notice immediately beyond the Gostinnoi Dvor is the Imperial Public Library, with a

VIEWS IN AND AROUND ST. PETERSBURG.

1. Kazan Cathedral. 2. The Admiralty. 3. The Church in the Hay Market. 4. Statue of Peter the Great. 5. The Winter Palace. 6. The Alexander Column. 7. The German Reformed Church. 8. The Palace of Peterhof.

statue to Catherine II. in front of it. Few libraries in Europe can compete with its riches, the number of printed volumes being over a million, and that of the MSS. about thirty-four thousand, in addition to nearly eighty thousand engravings and maps. The nucleus of this prodigious collection in a capital comparatively so new was the library of the Counts Zaluski, which had already become the property of the Polish State when Suvoroff captured Warsaw in 1794, and transferred its contents to St. Petersburg. Further acquisitions were subsequently made in Poland, the most valuable of these being the books and MSS. purchased by a Polish gentleman in France during the early part of the great Revolution. The MSS. consist of letters from kings of France to their ambassadors, secret State documents, and the correspondence of various sovereigns, the volume of English royal letters from Henry VII. to Charles I. being of especial interest to ourselves. They were taken from the Paris archives by an infuriated mob, and sold by improvised auction for anything they would fetch. The *Ostromir* MS., in the Slavonic character, and containing the Evangelistarium, bears the date of 1056 ; that is, it was written about seventy years after the introduction of Christianity into Russia. The Chronicle of Nestor, a monk at Kief, is brought down to A.D. 1116. A Greek *codex* of the four Evangelists, on parchment black with age, bears proof of its having been written in the ninth or tenth century. A still older Greek MS., the chief glory of this department, is the famous *Codex Sinaiticus*, a complete copy of the Greek Bible written in the fourth century, and discovered by Tischendorf in the Convent of St. Catherine, on Mount Sinai, in 1859. The unique collection of ancient Hebrew and Karaite MSS. is equally noticeable, twenty-five of them being of earlier date than the ninth century. There are also thirty thousand volumes in all languages, except the Russian, that relate to the history or geography of the empire. Early European printing (*Incunabula*) is exemplified in about eleven thousand volumes, from Gutenberg to the year 1521. Lastly, but more important to mankind than all the other treasures of the Library put together, is the complete series of the Bible printed in almost all the known languages and dialects of the inhabited parts of the globe. British missionaries and British religious societies have raised the major part of this grand and lasting monument to the glory of God and His Holy Word.

In this connection we may mention that, since the beginning of the reign of the Emperor Nicholas, the British and Foreign Bible Society has been engaged in the distribution of the Holy Scriptures in Russian, Finnish, and other languages spoken by the subjects of the Tsar, and that it maintains an agency at St. Petersburg as well as at Odessa.

Mr. N. Astafief, in his *History of the Bible in Russia*,[1] thus speaks of the influence of the Bible in Russia : 'What has the Bible as the Word of God been to our Russian people during the thousand years of its existence among them ? Has it not been "a light shining in a dark place ?" We call to mind the bright opening period of our national life which had its

---

[1] St. Petersburg, 1880.

birth under the influence of earnest instruction in the Word of God,[1] those glorious eleventh and twelfth centuries which so remind us of the first age of Christianity.[2] And then following this, in consequence of the desolation caused by the Mongols, the long, long period of darkness when the Word of God was a rarity in the country, once when men like Maxim the Greek,[3] or Ivan Theodoroff, the first printer,[4] or the learned brothers Lichud,[5] who endeavoured to carry the light of life into the thick darkness of ignorance and superstition which surrounded them, endured cruel persecution at the hands of the obstinate upholders of old errors, who had grown accustomed to them, ignorantly but honestly believing them to be truth. As one who sprang from the people and knew their needs, the patriarch Nikon (A.D. 1652), with his healthy spirit, understood the living significance of the Word of God, and with unconquerable energy he laid the foundation for its restoration, purifying it from the errors of copyists and from sophistical glosses. He himself fell, but the work begun by him as the daily need of the people did not come to nought. Others continued it, and at last, in the year 1663, appeared the Ostrojskaya Bible, printed at Moscow with some emendations, at first but few in number, in consequence of the opposition of the adherents of the old style. But a beginning had been made, and the revision of the Slavonic text, though slowly and with interruptions, went on. Peter the Great, who was deeply acquainted with and who highly valued the Holy Scriptures, supported in every way Biblical labours, and in A.D. 1710-11 cherished the thought of translating the Bible from the Ecclesiastical Slavonic into the Russian language of the day, for the sake of making it more readily accessible. The revision of the Slavonic text meanwhile went on in due course, and what could not be completed during the lifetime of Peter was finished by his daughter the Empress Elizabeth. Thanks to her energetic persistence, in 1751, the Slavonic Bible, with revised and emended text, at last appeared —the so-called "Elizabethan Bible." These Biblical labours did not remain without influences in quickening spiritual activity in society, but to the mass of the people the books of Holy Scripture remained inaccessible, because of their high price, and because of the little spread of education, owing to the want of popular schools. Both these obstacles were removed during the reign of Alexander I., who established a complete system of secondary and elementary schools, and called into existence the Russian

[1] Cyril and Methodius formed the Slavonic alphabet in order to translate the Scriptures into that language in 855-7. The first died 869 at Rome, the second in 885. The acceptance of Christianity by the Russians in the tenth century was bound up with the circulation of this Bible and the formation of schools to teach the people to read it.   [2] 1230 A.D.

[3] He came to Russia in 1518, endeavoured to revise the text by aid of the Greek MSS.; imprisoned 1525; died 1556.

[4] Of the Royal Printing Press, established at Moscow; but in 1564 Ivan was driven out, and the Press burnt, through the intrigues of the MSS. writers, who accused the printers of heresy.

[5] A.D. 1685; invited to Russia from Italy.

Bible Society,[1] which had for its object the circulation of the books of Holy Scripture as generally as possible, selling them at low prices and distributing them gratuitously; and at the same time it made a commencement in translating the Bible into the Russian language. At the present time the school system has received a wide extension amongst us, and alongside of this the circulation among the people of the Holy Scriptures at a price within the reach of every one, especially in their own native language, has made equal progress since the publication of the Russian Bible, A.D. 1876, by the permission of the Holy Synod.'

The Religious Tract Society has also largely helped recent efforts to spread throughout Russia the knowledge of the Gospel. Much has been done by the circulation of tracts and other Christian literature, and evidence has not been lacking to show that in Russia, as elsewhere, the 'glad tidings' of salvation by faith in the atonement of Jesus Christ enter the sinful and penitent heart, and by the blessing and aid of the Holy Spirit bring to it pardon and cleansing and peace.

On the opposite side of the square to which the front of the Public Library is turned, will be seen the Anitchkoff Palace, the residence of their Majesties when at St. Petersburg. It was built in 1744, for the Empress Elizabeth, by Count Rastrelli, the great architect of those days. On the bridge close to the palace are the two celebrated equestrian groups by Baron Klodt, and on the other side of it the former Beloselski-Beloserski Palace, now the property of the Grand Duke Sergius, and full of pictures and costly objects of art.

Now the activity of the Nevski begins to flag, and we come to the rough stone paving, over which carriages and *drojkies* have to rattle when off the wooden blocks laid down for them from the Palace Bridge to the Anitchkoff Palace and along the whole length of Bolshaya Morskaya Street. Past the Moscow Railway Station, at which the Nevski practically terminates in a huge and slovenly-looking square, the capital degenerates into an ordinary Russian town. Its rural suburbs are reached at the Monastery of St. Alexander Nevski, one of the most important in Russia, being a *Lavra*, or seat of a Metropolitan, inferior in precedence only to the *Lavra* of the Trinity at Moscow and the *Lavra* at Kief. It was founded by Peter the Great in honour of a canonized Grand Duke Alexander, who in a great battle fought on its site defeated the Swedes and Teutonic knights in 1241. The principal church, built in 1790, is decorated internally with Italian marble, Siberian agate, and Persian pearls. In a sumptuous shrine of massive silver weighing twenty-nine hundredweight lie the remains of St. Alexander, brought from the Cathedral at Vladimir by Peter the Great.

[1] Founded 1812; ended 1826. During its existence 290 auxiliary committees were established in all parts of Russia. The Scriptures or parts of them were translated into fourteen new languages used in the Russian empire. 1,000,000 copies were printed in twenty-six languages and dialects, of which probably 700,000 to 800,000 copies were distributed in Slavonic and Russian. In its first ten years the receipts amounted to 3,421,958 roubles.

Alexander's crown and the bed on which Peter I. died are among the most interesting objects shown in the Sacristy, which has also a large collection of mitres set in jewels, pontifical robes of gold brocade, an episcopal staff turned by Peter, and a great number of other valuables. Portraits of the founder of St. Petersburg and of Catherine II. are suspended on the two pillars opposite the Altar, behind which is a remarkable picture of the Annunciation by Raphael Mengs. Some of the *Ikons* are good copies after Guido, Rubens, and Perugino. Among the six other churches within the walls of the Lavra is the Cathedral of the Annunciation, founded in 1702. In its crypt are buried Natalia, sister of Peter I., Peter, his son, who died young, Suvoroff, Rumiantsof, and several other ministers of the brilliant epoch of Catherine the Great. On the mausoleum of the Naryshkins is inscribed the proud device, in Latin: 'From their race came Peter the Great;' his mother having been a member of that ancient noble family. Large sums are paid by the upper and richer classes for permission to repose in the adjoining cemetery, the Kensal Green of St. Petersburg. The monastery contains also a seminary, in which sons of the 'White Clergy' (as distinguished from the Monks) are prepared for the priesthood, and a theological college for instruction of a higher order to the more promising scholars selected for the vocation of tutors and professors in theological schools.

It is now time to leave the Nevski, and to glance at a few of the other places most worth seeing in St. Petersburg and its neighbourhood. The Cathedral of St. Peter and St. Paul within the fortress on the right bank of the Neva is conspicuous by its beautiful gilt spire terminating in an angel bearing a cross, the summit being 302 feet above the level of the ground. The foundations of the fortress were laid by Peter the Great in 1703, but the present grim stone work was executed in 1706 under the superintendence of an Italian architect. It is used as a State prison, of which the earliest notable occupant was Alexis, the eldest son of Peter I., who died in a sudden and mysterious manner in one of its dungeons 'after his examination on a charge of treason. Its guns are used for saluting purposes on imperial fête days, and also for giving notice of the rising of the Neva to inhabitants of cellars, and to the population of the lower parts of the city. Consecrated in 1733 on the site of a church coeval with the fortress, the cathedral was restored in 1757, after having been three times damaged by lightning. A tale of singular daring is connected with the repair of the angel and cross on the spire in 1830. With the aid only of a nail and a rope, a Russian *mujik* (peasant) climbed to the top, hanging gradually on to the raised edges of the copper plates with his fingers, although blood spurted out from under his finger-nails as he ascended.

Excepting Peter II., who died of small-pox when only fourteen, at Moscow, where he was buried, all the members of the imperial family have since the foundation of St. Petersburg been interred under the floor of this cathedral, the white marble tombs above marking the places of their sepulture. Close to the south door is the tomb of Peter the Great, and in the opposite aisle that of the Emperor Nicholas, whose martyred son and successor, Alexander II., the Emancipator of the Serfs, reposes alongside of him. Catherine II. lies to the right of the Altar Screen, which is of wood, superbly carved and richly gilt the work of four Russian carvers between 1722 and 1726. The ivory candelabrum, more than ten feet high, that stands in front of the *ikonostas,* was turned by Peter I. in 1724. An autograph of his found later within the centre ball recorded its dedication to Almighty God in gratitude for the benefit he had derived from the use of the mineral waters of Olonets, near Lake Ladoga

THE FIRST FLEET BUILT BY PETER THE GREAT AT VORONEJ.

The 'Grandfather of the Russian Navy,' a boat constructed by Dutch carpenters, on the Moskva river in 1668, is carefully preserved in a brick building near the cathedral. It was found by Peter the Great when yet a lad, at the country residence of his grandfather; and it was by sailing it under the direction of a Dutch shipbuilder that he acquired the nautical tastes which resulted in the construction of a fleet and the extension of the Russian dominions. Quitting the fortress by its eastern gate and making for the river-bank, we pass, almost at the foot of the floating Trinity Bridge, a small wooden church, with which traditions of Peter the Great are also strongly associated. It replaces a church which he erected between 1703 and

E

1710 in commemoration of the foundation of St. Petersburg and in which he was in the habit of singing as a chorister, and of reading the Gospels on the anniversary of the battle of Poltava, and on other great feast days.

Peter's cruelty and self-indulgence were strangely blended with his innate statesmanship and the devotional feeling he so frequently displayed in a practical manner. Next to his prejudice against beards, then typical of conservative Muscovy, was his hatred of lawyers. He said to Lord Carmarthen, his *cicerone* in London, whom he had asked who were the men in wigs and gowns bustling about Westminster Hall: 'Lawyers! I have but two in all my dominions, and I believe I shall hang one of them the moment I get home.' Within this church are several objects which belonged to the Great Reformer or were made by him. A short walk brings us to his cottage, the 'palace' which he built in 1703, and from which he superintended the building of his new capital; it contains only two rooms and a kitchen, their combined size being about 55 feet by 20 feet in breadth. The bedroom on the left, in which he also dined, has been converted into a chapel, generally crowded with worshippers, attracted chiefly by an Ikon of the Saviour, which accompanied Peter in his battles and effected the discomfiture of Charles XII. at Poltava! Among other relics of the sovereign who forcibly hurled Russia into the path of Western civilisation is a boat which he built, and the wooden bench on which he sat at his door. They are kept in the gallery that runs round the cottage, between it and the outer building by which the cottage and its interesting contents are preserved from decay. Those who take an interest in the life of Peter the Great should visit the three or four galleys of his period preserved in the 'Galley Haven,' in the estuary of the Neva.

The Anglican Church stands on the English Quay, once almost exclusively occupied, like the street in the rear of it, by British merchant princes—a race nearly as extinct as that of the mammoth. The church owed its origin, in 1753, to the 'Great Russia Company.' The present edifice, which has outwardly the appearance of only a private mansion, is the outcome of the work of reconstruction carried out in 1815 by Quarenghi, an architect to whom many of the finest edifices in St. Petersburg are due, Parliament having made a grant of £5,000, and the 'Russia Company' a contribution of £4,000 towards that purpose. In 1873 the interior was renovated, and unfortunately rendered very bare and cheerless-looking, notwithstanding the addition of stained windows, at a cost of £10,000, defrayed from the funds accumulated by the so-called 'British Factory,' in the form of a compulsory tax on British shipping, which at last became obnoxious to the tax-payers, and injurious to our trade. The capacious and valuable premises enjoy the boon of ex-territoriality, on the ground that the chapel, like our other Anglican establishments in Russia, is a chapel of the Queen's Ambassador. A boys' school, and an extensive circulating library for the benefit of

the two thousand British subjects who reside at St. Petersburg and its
vicinity, are also on the premises, and render complete the arrangements
made by our countrymen for the spiritual and moral welfare of the British
colony.

In summer all St. Petersburg is out of town; the migration to
suburban palaces, villas and cottages commences in the early part of our
June, and the return tide sets in towards the end of September. Nothing
can be imagined as more enjoyable than a Northern summer. Nature, more
or less dormant for nearly eight months, bursts suddenly into life, light, and
beauty, and rewards us amply for the frost and snow and the darkness

THE ENGLISH QUAY, ST. PETERSBURG.

through which we have passed. We hail with delight the warm sunshine,
the fragrance of the young birch trees, and the song of the nightingale,
even though we have enjoyed all the warm hospitality and the healthy sport
of a winter season at the capital of All the Russias. We may have skated
on the Neva and in the Yusupof Gardens, converted for the purpose into an
Arctic arcadia, become acquainted with the sensation of falling out of a high
window by going down *montagnes russes*—a refined and superior kind of
tobogganing driven in pleasant company in sledges drawn at wild speed by
three thoroughbred horses abreast, to festive establishments on the outskirts
of the city, shot bears, elk, and wolves with local sportsmen, and in fact
led a life of jollity without even getting an ear or a cheek frozen; and yet

E 2

the Elysian season will prove to be that of summer, and especially to those who have known many winters.

The more accessible villas are on the islands of the Neva, to which we drive a little before sunset, reaching the 'Point' of Yelagin Island in time to see the sun go down in golden glory. There is an imperial château on this island, with charming grounds and a delightful view. To the right the banks of the 'Little Neva' are dotted with picturesque *chalets* standing out from a background of sombre pines; and on the left we see within measurable distance the lofty gilt spires and domes of the capital glowing with the last red rays of the setting sun. At this witching hour the road to the 'Point,' which partly runs through Peter's Park, is almost as crowded with vehicles as the Epsom road on Derby day. The River Yacht Club is on Krestofski Island, and gives a considerable amount of life to the branch of the Neva on which its large establishment stands. In the ex-village of Novaya Derevnia, on the banks of the Little Neva, are the Livadia and Arcadia Gardens, while a more sober resort of evening pleasure will be found in the Zoological Gardens behind the fortress.

But we must now leave St. Petersburg, and make excursions by rail or steamer to some more distant summer residences; and we begin with Peterhof. Its palace, which overlooks the Gulf of Finland from an elevation of sixty feet, was built under the directions of Peter I., and although many additions and alterations have been subsequently made, its general character, and even its original yellow colour, are still perpetuated. The interior is replete with interest, for it abounds in beautiful tapestry, articles of *vertu*, tazzas of porcelain, malachite, and marble, as well as in pictures representing chiefly the naval victories of Orlof and other Russian generals during the reign of Catherine II. In one of the apartments is a collection of 865 portraits of beautiful young girls painted by Count Rotari for the Empress during a journey which he made for that purpose through the fifty provinces of Russia. No two are alike either in position or expression; but it is more than doubtful whether they are true to Nature or the ethnology of Russia, the stamp of the French school being very apparent on every canvas. In the study of Peter the Great hangs his portrait in mosaic, and its walls are wainscoted with some of his carvings.

Beneath the palace is the celebrated garden, laid out in terraces and walks, adorned with fountains and other ornamental water-works, little inferior to those of Versailles. The Samson, in the centre of the grounds, is a magnificent *jet d'eau* eighty feet high, and from it runs a boat canal that terminates on the shore of the gulf. We cannot, unfortunately, stop to describe the many other marvels of water-engineering here offered to our view, and we can only make bare mention of some of the buildings in the grounds: Marly, from which Peter I. was wont to contemplate his infant fleet moored off Cronstadt, plainly seen from its terrace, and the Marly Pond,

which he caused to be stocked with carp and chub, still summoned by a bell
to be fed with rye flour, in accordance with his directions; Monplaisir, a
summer-house in the Dutch style, also built in the reign of Peter, whose
bed, dressing-room, night-cap and slippers are exhibited in it; the Hermitage,
with a contrivance in one of its rooms by which dishes and plates are made
to descend from and ascend to the dinner-table through grooves in the
floor, in order to dispense with the presence of servants at intimate feasts;
the Pavilions on the Tsaritzyn and Olga Islands; the English Palace, built
in 1781, with a portrait, amongst many others, of Her Majesty Queen
Victoria; and Alexandria, in the lower garden, where the Emperor and
Empress reside in privacy when at Peterhof, full of fine pictures, and with
several cottages around it. From the roof of one of them the Emperor
Nicholas watched with a telescope the movements of the Anglo-French
squadron in front of Cronstadt.

By taking from Peterhof the good macadamised road to St. Petersburg in
a swift *troïka*, or carriage with three horses abreast, we have the opportunity
of seeing Michaelofski and Strelna, the properties, severally, of the Grand
Dukes Michael and Constantine, and we can terminate our drive and take
to the more prosaic railway carriage at Sergi. But we halt here awhile, to
visit the monastery of St. Sergius, founded in 1734, and more especially the
church that stands at the back of the grounds, and fronting the estuary of
the Neva. With its open roof, and its stalls of oak, it has an air of
elegance and comfort which few other Russian churches possess. It is,
moreover, celebrated for its monkish choristers, whose singing at vespers
(on Saturdays) is particularly fine and impressive. The sepulchral vaults
of many notable families are full of tokens that the dead have not been
forgotten by the living. Over one of the tombs are likenesses from life of
a mother bringing her children to the Saviour, who receives them, saying—
'Suffer little children to come unto Me.'

Our next trip must be either by rail *via* Oranienbaum, another ancient
imperial residence, or by steamer direct to Cronstadt, so well known to our
readers already, both as a place of busy trade and as a fortress defending
in an impregnable manner, so far as modern science can possibly effect such
an object, the sea-approach to St. Petersburg. We see, running along the
left of the natural and partly shallow channel followed by the steamer, the
great ship canal, seventeen and a half miles long, which since 1885 enables
steamers drawing twenty feet to proceed to the capital. By constant
dredging, a uniform centre depth of twenty-two feet is maintained in it, and
taken altogether, the canal is one of the most remarkable works of its kind in
Europe. Its result, however, is that Cronstadt will before long cease to be the
commercial outport of St. Petersburg, and become a purely military harbour.

The fortifications we have come to see were begun by Peter I. in 1703,
when he dispossessed the Swedes; but, needless to say, none of his wooden

walls remain. The formidable-looking stone forts date from the reign of Nicholas I. They have undergone considerable alteration and improvement since the days of the Crimean War, when, for reasons still unknown, Sir Charles Napier failed to take advantage of the passage through a channel on the northern side of the island discovered by a couple of his smaller ships. That channel is now effectively guarded by a substantial dam of stones, on which seven strong batteries have been raised. The southern defences are the strongest, and are formed by three lines of forts running

THE FORTRESS OF SCHLÜSSELBURG.

from west to east. The land defences, of recent date, consist of several parallel lines connected by many batteries and earthworks. In the town the canal which encircles the naval storehouses and workshops is bordered with granite, and by a tall iron railing begun in 1721. In the vicinity of the military harbour, the chief station in the Baltic for the Russian fleet, is a splendid steam factory, not inferior to Keyham in its mechanical appliances. The dry docks are capable of admitting some of the larger vessels of war. These are mostly built at St. Petersburg, and brought down to Cronstadt to be fitted. A very good statue of Peter the Great—whose genius created so much of what we have so far seen—stands on a square at the back of the middle harbour, near the governor's residence and the Summer Garden planted by Peter.

Tsarskoé Sélo, the favourite imperial residence, is second in some respects to that of Peterhof, since it has not the fountains and the cascades of its marine rival. But it is much larger in extent both as a town of private villas and as an imperial park. The latter, eighteen miles in circumference, is divided into the Old and the New Garden, both beautifully laid out and well wooded, originally by Catherine I., the consort of Peter, who had confined himself to building a small cottage, a hot-house, and a zoological garden on part of the ground now covered with palaces, pavilions, and a variety of other attractive buildings. The present aspect of this beautiful spot is, however, mainly due to the care bestowed on it by Catherine II. The Old Palace, built in 1744, in the *rococo* style of architecture, was restored and embellished by her. Originally the structural ornamentations, all the statues and the capitals of columns, were covered with gold leaf at a cost of more than a million of ducats; but, the gilding having worn off, the contractors engaged in restoring the palace offered £66,000 for the fragments of gold leaf, which the munificent Empress declined to accept, on the ground that she was 'not in the habit of selling her old clothes.' The dome and the cupolas of the Palace Chapel are now alone gilt.

Pavlofsk, three miles distant, is also a summer encampment of the Petersburgians, and at the same time the resort of those who are able to rush away from the capital for 'a mouthful of fresh air,' and to enjoy the music of the excellent orchestra that plays every afternoon, either outside or within the commodious Vauxhall attached to the railway station.

Schlüsselburg, formerly the Swedish fortress of Nöteborg, at the source of the Neva, is often the object of a day's excursion by steamer. Like the rest of Ingria, it anciently formed part of the dominions of Novgorod the Great, and passed for some time in the fourteenth century into the hands, alternately, of the Lithuanian knights and of the Swedes, who finally delivered it to Peter I., in 1702, after much contention. It has since been used as a State prison, and is now full of Nihilists and conspirators. In 1756, Ivan VI., son of the Empress Elizabeth, by whom he had been imprisoned (together with his father, the Regent Biron), originally at Dünaburg, and later at a lonely spot on the White Sea, spent the remainder of his life on this insular Bastille. He was killed in an attempt made for his rescue by an officer of the guard.

The town of Schlüsselburg, on the left bank of the river, which issues here from the Ladoga lake, forming rapids easily navigable, is a busy place of trade, being at the mouth of the famous canal that forms part of a fluviatile system that connects the Baltic with the distant Caspian.

CHAPTER IV.

THE NORTHERNMOST PROVINCES OF EUROPEAN RUSSIA.

THE 'Governments' of Archangel and Vologda form together an immense sparsely-inhabited plateau, sloping down to the Arctic Ocean, into which the region discharges its abundant waters. The province of Archangel alone has an area larger than that of Great Britain and France combined, while its total population is scarcely that of the city of Manchester. The long coast line, which commences at the Jacob River on the borders of Norway, finally settled in 1826, after a dispute that had lasted for five centuries, and guaranteed, together with the integrity of Sweden, by Great Britain and France in 1855, is broken by the gulf and the straits that give access to the White Sea.

This is the Murman (Norman) coast, to which attention is being more and more directed with reference to the possibility of establishing in one of its commodious and never-freezing bays, a Russian Naval Station, connected with the rest of the empire by rail. At present there is but one town (800 inhabitants) upon it, and only a few private whaling and fishing stations, active in summer. Kola, the town in question, was almost destroyed in 1854 by an English gunboat; but, as the seat of the civil administration of a wide district, it soon arose out of its ashes, and has now resumed its comparatively pleasant aspect in an amphitheatre of green, though woodless, slopes rising from a background of bluish-purple hills.

LANDING OF RICHARD CHANCELLOR AT HOLMOGORY, IN THE WHITE SEA, 1553.

(Reproduced by permission from the illustrated 'Niva,' St. Petersburg.)

The peninsula thus bordered on the one side by the Arctic Ocean, here somewhat tempered in its frigid severity by the Gulf Stream, and on the other by the White Sea, frozen during more than half the year, is known as Russian Lapland. The interior, constituting almost one huge mossy bog has been little explored except by the Lopars (Lapps) and the Saamy, or Samoyedes.

Eastward of Cape Kanin, on the opposite side of the Murman coast, right away to the spur of the Ural Mountains, which determines the frontier of Siberia and the limits of European Russia in the North, the coast is still more dreary and uninviting. It is here we begin to find, but in declining numbers, the Samoyedes, who, while wearing orthodox crosses round their necks, and delighting in the ringing of church bells when they have the opportunity, still more or less secretly worship their primitive idols of stone and wood. They hunt and fish over the vast hyperborean region that extends from the White Sea to some distance beyond the great Enisei River of Siberia, and to the foot of the Altai Mountains, which were the original home of this Ural-Altaic race. The Russian name of Samoyedes, literally 'self-eaters,' by which they are known to the civilized world, has the same signification as Esquimaux, namely, men who subsist principally on raw flesh.

There had been no maritime intercourse between Western Europe and Muscovy, which had inherited, politically, all these lands from Novgorod the Great, until the sixteenth century, when, by mere accident in 1553, the coast of the White Sea was reached by an adventurous expedition fitted out in London, by the chartered 'Mystery Company and Fellowship of Merchant Adventurers for the Discovery of Unknown Lands,' for the purpose of finding a northern sea passage to China and India. The design was conceived by Sebastian Cabot, a native of Bristol, although of Venetian parentage. Sir Hugh Willoughby, in the Bona Esperanza, of one hundred and twenty tons, was appointed commander, and under him were placed Richard Chancellor, in the Bonaventure, of one hundred and sixty tons, and Cornelius Durforth in the Bona Confidentia, of ninety tons. A severe storm in the North Sea separated the three vessels, Sir Hugh Willoughby with his own vessel and the Bona Confidentia ultimately reaching with much difficulty a bay near Sviaty Nos, on the Lapland coast, where he and his companions, sixty-five in number, were frozen to death. The Bonaventure alone escaped. On the 24th August, 1553, Chancellor cast anchor in the bay of St. Nicholas, at a village called Nenocksa, not far from the Korelian mouth of the Dvina, and ascertained from some fishermen that he had reached 'Russia or Muscovie.' Explaining, by means that remain unknown, that they were 'Englishmen sent unto these coasts from the most excellent King Edward VI., having from him in commandment certain things to deliver to their King, and seeking nothing else but his amitie and friendship, and traffique with his people, whereby they doubted not but that great commoditie and profit would grow to the subjects of both kingdoms.' Chancellor was kindly and hospitably received by the equally astonished natives. The engraving on page 57 represents him and his two principal companions—merchants named Burton and Edwards—being received in state by the Governor and other high authorities of the province, after he had obtained permission to repair to Moscow in the ambassadorial character which he had assumed, on the strength of an open Royal Letter with which each of the three vessels had been provided.

Ivan the Terrible, then Tsar and in the zenith of his glory as the capturer of Kazan and the Suzerain of Siberia, gave the three Englishmen a cordial and distinguished reception, and sent them back from Moscow in March 1554, with a letter to King Edward assuring him that his 'shippes and vessels may come as often as they please,' and requesting that one of His Majesty's Council should be sent to treat with the Tsar, 'whereby your country merchants maie with all kind of wares and wheare they will make their market in our dominions.' A new Company was thereupon formed in London by special charter, and in 1555 Chancellor returned to Moscow with a reply from Philip and Mary, then on the throne of England. A charter then granted by the Tsar enabled the Company to trade throughout his dominions without paying any taxes, and the Bay of St. Nicholas soon became an important place of commerce. Instead of getting the furs, wax, hemp and tallow of Muscovy from Flemish and Lithuanian traders by way of the Hanseatic towns, English merchants were now in direct and privileged communication with the country which supplied those valuable commodities; a later treaty with Queen Elizabeth secured to them the exclusive right to carry on the new trade in English ships, and even permission to seize and despoil of his goods the subject of any other Power who might attempt to reach India, Persia or China by way of Russia. The important right of coinage was also bestowed upon them.

It is not surprising that under such advantages the Company prospered, and obtained firm hold of all the most important centres of commercial Russia. With a head agency at Moscow, a Factory[1] at Holmogory (forty-seven miles above the mouth of the Dvina, not far from Archangel), and dépôts at Novgorod the Great, Pskof, Yaroslaf, Kostroma, Kazan and Astrakhan, they carried everything before them, and sold their goods at a profit which, according to native complaint, amounted to two and three hundred per cent. When Ivan the Terrible complained of these proceedings to the English Ambassador in 1569, they retorted that, on the contrary, they were fast being ruined by the execution of so many of their debtors. It is indeed true that the life of the early English settlers in Russia was not an easy one. They had to contend with civil commotions, pestilence and

[1] From *Factor*, an agent.   [2] 'Holmogory' is evidently derived from the Norwegian *Holmegaard*.

famine, and their agency house in Moscow was destroyed by the Tartars in 1571, when fifteen English men and women perished in the flames. Skilful negotiations, however, not only restrained the impatience of the Tsar, but also filled him with high hope. He desired to marry Queen Elizabeth, and meanwhile to enter into a treaty of mutual defence against common enemies. He desired the Queen to allow navigators and persons skilled in shipbuilding to come to Russia, and artillery and other warlike stores to be sent from England. Above all, 'it was to be ratified by oath between her and himself that either sovereign might take

ARCHANGEL.

refuge in the country of the other in case disturbances in their own realm should compel them to do so.' The matrimonial part of these proposals was politely rejected, but Elizabeth suggested the Tsar should marry Lady Mary Hastings, daughter of the Earl of Huntingdon, one of her maids of honour, who was not averse to the alliance. This would probably have been effected had not a special Muscovite ambassador reported unfavourably of her age (thirty) and of her personal appearance, her chief defects being 'red hair, a straight nose, and long fingers.' In the midst of this delicate negotiation, the boyars informed the merchants of the Company that 'their

English Tsar was dead.' Their exclusive privileges were therefore not renewed, and other nations, especially the Dutch, long jealous of the English monopoly, were in the succeeding reign permitted to participate in the commerce of the country. Next, in condemnation of 'the people who had put their Charles to death,' the English were relegated to Archangel; and, notwithstanding efforts made by the Earl of Carlisle at the Restoration, a renewal of their ancient privileges was never obtained.

Although the important trade thus established by Englishmen was thenceforth altered in its character, Russia proceeded to derive immense advantage from the opening of her seaboard to the commerce of all the maritime nations of Europe. Meanwhile, the English spirit of enterprise had not benefited Muscovy in this direction alone. Her first regular regiments were formed in the reign of Peter the Great's father, by Scottish and English officers, who, with about three thousand men, had passed into the service of the Tsar after the defeat and imprisonment of Charles I. The most famous of those officers were Thomas Dalzell (or Dalziel) of Binns, and William Drummond of Cromlix, who had great difficulty in obtaining the Tsar's permission to return to Scotland in 1665. Dalzell, whose nickname in his own country became 'Old Tom of Muscovy,' is spoken of in Kirkton's *History of the Church of Scotland* as a man whose 'rude and fierce natural disposition had been much confirmed by his breeding and service in Muscovia where he had command of a small army, and saw nothing but tyranny and slavery.' There were popular murmurs against the Muscovian rigour of Dalzell's military administration in Scotland, and he was railed against as 'a Muscovian beast who used to roast men.' Generals Dalzell and Drummond (created Baron Strathallan in 1685) were credited with the introduction of the 'thummikins,' a Muscovite instrument with which Covenanters were made to suffer.

A volume might be well filled with the exploits and services of our countrymen in Russia. Many of them were Peter the Great's ablest coadjutors in the extension and the reform of the empire he left to his successors, who profited in no smaller degree by similar aid. As in the case of the army, so in that of the navy of Russia, British officers were the first and foremost organisers and commanders. In the reign of Catherine the Great, and for a considerable time after, English admirals, captains, and lieutenants were engaged in creating her fleet, now the third, so far as numbers are concerned, in Europe. They won the earlier naval battles of Russia, although Orloff got the credit for them. Their names are, in fact, a legion, beginning, so far as eminent services are concerned, with Captain John Elphinstone, R.N., 'lent' to Russia in 1769, and who, aided mainly by Commander, subsequently Admiral, Greig, Captain Roxburgh, Lieutenants Dugdale and McKenzie, and some British volunteers, destroyed the Turkish fleet at Chesmé. Even in the reign of Alexander I., Cronstadt was

practically a colony of British naval officers and artificers in the service of
Russia. Nor was it the art of war alone that our countrymen taught
the Russians with such good and enduring results. Peter the Great's first
school of mathematics was under the direction of Farquharson, a Scotchman,
at Moscow. His chief physician was Erskine, a friend to the cause of the
Pretender, and a relative of the Earl of Mar, while the founder of the
Russian Medico-Chirurgical Academy at St. Petersburg was also a Scotchman,
Sir James Wylie.

We might add name upon name in proof that, excepting in ecclesiastical
matters, which not even the strong hand of Peter the Great was able
effectually to grasp while he was engaged in his great work of civil and
political regeneration, it is to British skill, learning, enterprise, and capital
that much of the present greatness of the Russian empire is due. No
disparagement to native genius, so undoubtedly abundant, is meant to be
conveyed by this assertion; any Panslavist who may be inclined to take
umbrage at it will do well to study the influence of Jews, Flemings,
Huguenots, and Germans on the more modern development of the equally
vast empire of Great Britain, whose foundations were laid by a conglomera-
tion of races. In further support of this view, we may instance the
astounding results attained in the United States of America by the immigration of multitudes with acquired skill, learning, and habits of industry; and,
in no smaller degree, by the blending of races, which, when strictly kept
within narrow bounds of nationality and consanguinity, are undeniably liable
to become individually effete. The colonies of Great Britain have long been
undergoing the same regenerative process, to their immense advantage.

Archangel, the starting-point of the modernisation of Muscovy, bears at
present little evidence of the importance it acquired in the sixteenth century.
The decline of the city dates from the reign of Peter the Great, who
removed its trade to the more accessible port of his new capital, in which
British merchants established themselves in great numbers. One of the
oldest houses still extant is the Archiepiscopal Palace, built in 1784, the
older building of timber having been destroyed by one of the many fires
that ravaged Archangel during the last century. The houses of the early
English merchants which stood in the Cathedral Square met with the
common fate. An Anglican church, erected at the beginning of the present
century, but no longer used, and the visits in summer of some fifty British
steamers to the port on the island of Solombola now alone attest outwardly the former importance of Archangel as a place of British trade.
There are plenty of other domes and spires, gilt or coloured, but none of
the Russian churches are of any antiquity, being not older than the last
century. The cathedral may be visited for the purpose of seeing the large
wooden cross preserved in it as the handiwork of Peter the Great after he
had escaped from a storm on the White Sea, and on which he made the

following inscription in Dutch: '*Dat cruys maken Captem Piter van a Cht.*, 1694.' In Western eyes, as the late Mr. Hepworth Dixon said in his *Free Russia*, 'the city is a magazine of oats and tar, of planks and skins.'

From the native point of view, however Archangel is the revered water-gate to one of the holiest places in Russia—the famed monastery of Solovetsk, to which some ten thousand pilgrims are annually conveyed in a steamer commanded and manned by monks. It was founded in 1429 by St. Sabbatheus, and began to grow in wealth and power from the year 1442, under Zosimus, one of its first abbots. About a century later the churches were rebuilt in stone, and between 1590 and 1594 the monks enclosed them within a wall of granite boulders, nearly three thousand feet in circumference, and supported at intervals by round and square towers, twenty to thirty feet high and twenty feet thick. Deeming themselves secure in their stronghold, the brotherhood refused in 1667 to receive the revised

THE SOLOVETSK MONASTERY.

liturgy sent by the Patriarch Nicon, and broke into a rebellion that lasted nine years. It fell at last by treachery, after a long siege, and many of the monks were put to the sword. A large number were executed later, or sent into exile, the remainder being kept in awe and submission by three hundred Streltsi.

The visitor is first shown the chapel erected over the spot on which Peter the Great, accompanied by his son Alexis, landed in 1702. On the sides of the gateway are models of the two small vessels in which they crossed from Archangel, and further on we come to an obelisk commemorating the harmless attack made on the monastery by the British White-Sea squadron in 1855, when the holy fathers walked in procession round the walls while the shells were flying over their heads. It is, however, the six churches of this fortified monastery that will chiefly interest him. Built of wood in 1438 and rebuilt of stone in 1558, the Cathedral of the Transfiguration contains the ponderous silver gilt shrines of Saints Sabbatheus and Zosimus, part of the relics of St. Philip, Metropolitan of Moscow, and an imposing *ikonostas*, put up in 1697. In the vicinity are two chapels (1753) containing the tombs of Germanicus and of other reverend fathers of local repute. The Cathedral of the Assumption was consecrated in 1557, and the Church of Nicholas Thaumaturgus in 1590. The remaining two churches enclosed by the walls were founded severally in 1596 and 1687, and restored or renovated in the eighteenth century. Outside the wall is the church dedicated (1667) to Onuphrius the Great, with a belfry 125 feet in height.

The artistic treasures of the monastery, its gold, silver, and precious stones contributed by Tsars and nobles, are carefully preserved in a special Sacristy. Among the objects of highest value are the sacerdotal vestments, ornamented with pearls of unusual size presented to the monastery in 1550 by Ivan the Terrible, who also gave the gold reliquary adorned with pearls and precious stones. In contrast with those gorgeous vestments is the plain linen chasuble of Zosimus. Nor are military trophies forgotten in this museum of otherwise sacred objects. There is the armour of the comrades of a monk, buried in this monastery, who was one of the most active of the patriots who expelled the Poles from Moscow in 1613; the sword of Prince Pojarski who, in alliance with a butcher of Nijni Novgorod, did good service in the same cause, and a large collection of ancient Russian and other weapons, and of military banners bearing the emblem of the cross.

Solovetsk was used as a political prison so recently as the reign of Nicholas. At its southern end the White Sea forms the Bay of Onega, at the head of which stands Kem, a settlement of the 'Old Believers,' who reject the innovations of Nicon, and who have since been very active as fishermen and seamen in the White Sea. It is also a place of political exile, as is indeed the whole of the region we have so imperfectly described in this chapter. The Lake of Onega, one hundred and fifty miles long and fifty miles broad, lies about half-way between Onega Bay and Lake Ladoga; on its western shore is Petrozavodsk, the capital of the province of Olonets, rich in copper, iron and mica. About forty-two miles north-west of Petrozavodsk is the Waterfall of Kivatch, equal in grandeur to the Imatra Falls in Finland, and Trolhätten in Sweden. Only a few Russian travellers have as yet seen it, although it has been immortalized in one of the best poems of Derjavin, once Civil Governor of Petrozavodsk. There is also abundance of bear and other shooting in this neighbourhood, and throughout the province of Olonets; but few scientific fishermen have as yet taken advantage of its wealth in trout, grayling, and char.

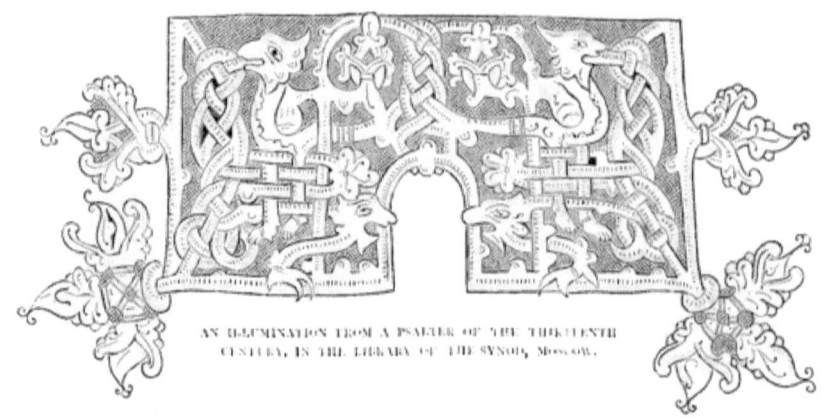

AN ILLUMINATION FROM A PSALTER OF THE THIRTEENTH
CENTURY, IN THE LIBRARY OF THE SYNOD, MOSCOW.

CHAPTER V.

MOSCOW: THE ANCIENT CAPITAL.

ON the way to Moscow a special excursion should be made by rail to Novgorod the Great, the cradle of the Russian empire. It is here that the Northmen under Röric established themselves A.D. 862, before they took their viking ships down the Dnieper to Kief. When, however, Kief became the seat of the grand ducal throne of the Scandinavian (subsequently called Varangian) conquerors, impelling them to internecine warfare for its possession, the citizens of Novgorod gradually acquired political power and independence, until from 1136 they assumed the right of electing or dismissing their prince at a *vetché* or witenagemote.

Trade with the Hanseatic towns, and water communication with the North and South of Russia, soon rendered the 'Lord Great Novgorod,' as the republic became styled, a central mart of great importance and prosperity. The city once covered an area forty miles in circumference. For a considerable period the Novgorodians were able to boast that no one could 'contend against God and the Great Novgorod;' but at last in 1478, Ivan III., the founder of Muscovite dominion, annexed their possessions to the Grand Duchy of Moscow; and, in order to destroy effectually their spirit of independence, removed 8000 boyars or nobles, and fifty families of the merchant class to his own capital, together with their *vetché* Bell, and

ONE OF THE PORCHES OF THE TROITSA MONASTERY.

F 2

countless treasures in gold silver, and precious stones. The ruin of the grand old city was completed in 1570, when even its monasteries and churches were sacked by Ivan the Terrible. Thousands of its inhabitants, who had contemplated a transfer of their allegiance to the Prince of Lithuania, were thrown into the River Volkhof.

The glory of the city survives only in its Cathedral of St. Sophia, constructed in 1050 by Byzantine artisans after the model of the famous St. Sophia at Constantinople, which is reproduced also at Kief. Later additions from the twelfth to the sixteenth centuries and complete restorations, in 1820 and 1837, have not deprived it of the distinguishing features of one of the oldest churches in Russia. The belfry tower dates from 1439, and the roof of the cathedral, with its figured cornice is a remnant of the work of the seventeenth century. Internally the cupola is supported by eight massive quadrangular pillars, which, with two similar pillars at the altar, supply the usual form of a Greek cross. In the galleries above are curious fresco representations of canonized princes and ecclesiastics; and traces of the same kind of painting (twelfth century) have been preserved in the apse, above the *thronos*, or seat of the Metropolitan, facing the altar, which is of oak.

CATHEDRAL OF ST. SOPHIA: NOVGOROD THE GREAT.

More ancient still, and probably of the same age as the cathedral, is the Byzantine mosaic work behind the altar. The *ikonostas* dates from 1341. The most ancient original *ikons* in it are those of St. Sophia (a Byzantine copy of the eleventh century) and St. Peter and St. Paul (brought from Khersonesus by St. Vladimir). Enshrined in silver or bronze are the remains of numerous saints, princely and clerical. The most ancient of these relics dates from 1030. Amongst the most venerated are those of St. Anne (d. 1050), daughter of King Olaf of Norway, and consort of Yaroslaf I. of Kief; their son Vladimir (d. 1052), founder of the Cathedral; of Nikita, Archbishop of Novgorod (d. 1108); of Mstislaf the Brave (d. 1180); and of John, Archbishop of Novgorod, who died A.D. 1186. The most modern of the saints expired in 1653, but the record of deceased Archbishops and Metropolitans of Novgorod is brought down to 1818 from A.D. 1223. Only two of the inscriptions over the numerous tombs of Novgorodian princes are now legible. They are dated respectively 1178 and 1218.

At the western or principal entrance to the cathedral are the exceptionally fine and interesting *Korsun* (Khersonesus) doors, still so called, notwithstanding that their Byzantine origin has long been disproved. They are of wood overlaid with bronze plates, bearing fifty-four inscriptions in Latin and Slavonic, a Magdeburg production of the twelfth century, although the Slavonic explanations were probably added later. The legend *Rigwin me fecit* over the head of a man in German dress, with tongs and a pair of scales in his hands, is alone sufficient attestation of the German and Roman Catholic character of the work, which is quite equal to that of the door of St. Zenone at Verona.

AN OLD CHURCH AT NOVGOROD.

There are several other churches within the walls of the Kremlin, or Acropolis, of Novgorod One of them has existed since the fifteenth century, like the tall tower close by, in which the Governor resided after the subjugation of the city by Ivan III. The archiepiscopal palace and the government offices are within the same walls, which were built in stone A.D. 1302, in place of wooden walls erected A.D. 1104. Rebuilt in 1490 by an Italian architect, they were renovated by Peter the Great in 1700. Close to the cathedral is the splendid bronze monument erected in 1862 to commemorate the thousandth anniversary of the existence of Russia, whether in the form of principalities, independent or confederated, or as the Grand Duchy of Moscow, by which those principalities were absorbed and ultimately welded at St. Petersburg into an empire. The life-size figures on the monument are emblematical of these several periods of Russian history.

But our object is to reach Moscow, and much as we should wish to say something of the other ancient towns that lie between the two capitals,

THE MONUMENT AT NOVGOROD COMMEMORATING THE THOUSANDTH ANNIVERSARY OF THE EMPIRE.

we must confine ourselves to a short mention of the famous New Jerusalem monastery, situated about fourteen miles from a railway station not far from Moscow. It was founded in 1657 by the Patriarch Nicon, who caused the neighbouring accidents of country to be named after various sacred sites in Palestine; for example, a river was converted into the Jordan, an artificial brook was made to represent the Kedron, a village close by was dignified with Nazareth, while a small chapel built on a mound was called Eleon. In order to render the analogy more complete, Nicon procured a model of the Church of the Holy Sepulchre at Jerusalem, and began, in 1658, to erect an exactly similar structure, devoting to it all his wealth and all the energy with which he had previously attacked the clergy for their intemperance and other irregularities. He also endeavoured to restore the Russian Church to Byzantine purity in matters of ritual, and in the pictorial representations of sacred subjects. His arrogance became so great that he exercised jurisdiction in civil as well as ecclesiastical matters, and in public documents assumed a title equal in dignity to that of the Tsar, his former friend, whom he fearlessly sermonised in the patriarchal cathedral. As a mark of dissatisfac-

THE PATRIARCH NICON.

tion, the Tsar absented himself from the cathedral on one of the great festivals of the Church; but Nicon was far from being daunted, and, relying on the speedy repentance of the sovereign, he publicly threw off his pontifical *sakkos* and mitre, laid down his crozier, and, attiring himself in the habit of a monk, withdrew to his retreat at the New Jerusalem. In spite of Nicon's protest that he was still a Patriarch, with the gift of the Holy Ghost to work cures, a Metropolitan was temporarily invested with the patriarchate, and replaced the primate even in the high ceremony of riding through Moscow on an ass, led by the Tsar himself, to typify Christ's entry into Jerusalem.

For six years Nicon was a recluse at New Jerusalem; but in 1664 his worldly ambition reasserted itself, and he made his appearance suddenly in the Cathedral of the Assumption at Moscow, arrayed once more in his pontifical robes, having been ordered, he alleged, in a dream, to resume his seat on the patriarchal throne. A council of the Eastern patriarchs convoked at Moscow disposed of his pretensions, and the Tsar was induced, although unwillingly, to banish him to a monastery in the province of Novgorod.

The monastery of the New Jerusalem was thus left uncompleted, and it was not finished and consecrated until some years later. In 1723, the principal tent-like cupola collapsed, and remained in that condition until 1749, when orders for its restoration were given by the Empress Elizabeth. Although the original plan of the church was in these circumstances somewhat departed from, yet internally it remains more like the edifice in which the Crusaders worshipped at Jerusalem than is that church itself since its destruction by fire, and its renovation in 1812. We cannot describe it more graphically than in the words of the late Dean Stanley : 'Externally, it has the aspect of an ordinary Russian cathedral, still further complicated by the addition of successive chapels built by, or in honour of, the various members of the imperial family in after times, down to our own day. But internally it is so precisely of the same form and dimensions as the church at the actual Jerusalem, that, intricate as the arrangements of that church are, beyond probably any other in the world, a traveller who has seen the original can

THE CHURCH IN THE MONASTERY OF THE NEW JERUSALEM.

find his way without difficulty through every corridor and stair and corner of the copy.'[1]

Our illustrations show the present outward form and the internal arrangements of this highly remarkable structure. Nicon is buried in the Chapel of Melchizedek, at the foot of the Golgotha, close to the corresponding spot in the actual church of the Holy Sepulchre where lie the remains of Godfrey of Bouillon. Over his tomb hangs the iron plate with a brass cross, which, as penance, he wore on his breast, suspended from

---

[1] *Lectures on the History of the Eastern Church.* London, 1869.

his neck by a heavy iron chain. In the sacristy are kept his hat, shoes, and sheepskin coat, the original wooden model of the church of the Holy Sepulchre, his portrait, and many other interesting objects.

Pilgrims come in vast numbers to the monastery, to assist at the Easter Eve service of the Russo-Greek Church, which is preceded on Good Friday by a ceremony that is not performed anywhere else in Russia. This is the Descent from the Cross. The body of our Saviour, embroidered on a cloth, is lowered by means of long strips of linen from the Golgotha Chapel, which is in an upper gallery, and after being laid on a bier in front of the altar screen, is anointed with ointment supposed to be identical with that used

PLAN OF THE CHURCH IN THE NEW JERUSALEM—AN EXACT COPY OF THE ORIGINAL CHURCH OF THE HOLY SEPULCHRE.

by Mary Magdalene, the original supply of which has been maintained by the continuous admixture of analogous ingredients.

Much interest also attaches to the *skit*, or hermitage, a four-storied tower from which Nicon watched the building of the church, and in which he wrote his *Chronicle of the Church of Jerusalem*.

In 1698 General Patrick Gordon defeated the rebellious Streltsi in the vicinity of the monastery, and finally freed Peter the Great from those ill-disciplined and even mutinous bands. Large numbers of them were decapitated by the orders and under the superintendence of Peter.

On reaching 'Our holy mother Moscow,' 'Moscow the white-walled,'[1] we are in the political and ecclesiastical centre of all that is truly Russian. We are at once struck by the busy life, the more or less irregular streets,

---

[1] Endearing epithets applied to the city by the Russian people.

crowded in summer as well as in winter with vehicles and pedestrians, and
in that respect so different from the ill-filled thoroughfares and squares of
St. Petersburg. The sheep-skinned *mujik* (peasant) and the wily, cloth-clad
kupets (trader) are here in their aboriginal
condition : the one driving long teams of rough-
looking waggons or sleighs, laden with every
variety of raw produce ; the other standing at
his shop door, and inviting passers-by to enter
and view his goods, the value of which he still
totals up on a Tartar *abacus*. The old *drojki*
—a sort of knife-board on four wheels—has
disappeared, together with its tattered and grimy
driver. In their stead are well-appointed carriages and swift *proliotkis* (a miniature victoria)
which rattle us over the long cobble-paved
streets that lie between the Nicholas Railway
Station and the Slavianski Bazaar or Hotel,
to which we are bound. We are received by
tall porters in national dress, that is to say,
long cloth coats which pretend to cover a shirt

GENERAL PATRICK GORDON.

of dazzling red silk, seen only at the neck, high boots of polished leather,
and a small round hat gaily adorned with peacocks' feathers.

It is not our object to describe hotels and the details of travelling in
Russia. Nevertheless, we cannot omit a passing reference to the comfort

OFFICERS OF THE STRELTSI.

THE STRELTSI OF 1613.

STRELTSI OF A LATER DATE.

and even the luxury of the accommodation now obtainable in all the
larger cities of Russia, and also to its relative cheapness, in these days
of a depreciated paper rouble. The Slavianski Bazar, and the Hermitage Restaurant, served by waiters in white shirts and trousers, will

bear favourable comparison with any other corresponding establishments in Western Europe.

A sketch of the history of Moscow must precede any description of its principal buildings. Chronicles record its existence as early as 1147. About a century later it was burnt down by the Tartars under Baati, the grandson of Chingiz Khan, who, with a horde of three hundred thousand men, devastated on that occasion the southern and central parts of what we now call Russia. Rising from its ashes, Moscow became, towards the end of the thirteenth century, the seat of a principality (or Grand Duchy) under Daniel, the younger son of Alexander Nevski, who was the progenitor of the subsequently mighty race of Muscovite princes. Kief had in 1158 lost its pre-eminence amongst the Russian principalities, and was succeeded by the city of Vladimir, which latter encountered a rival in Riazan; and it was only towards the middle of the fourteenth century that the Grand Duchy of Moscow became paramount, under Ivan I. It was he who built her first wooden walls, and gave to the space they enclosed the Tartar name of *kremlin*, or fortress. They were replaced in masonry A.D. 1367, and strengthened by a moat in 1394, after the sack of the city in 1382, when the Tartars left no building standing that was not constructed of brick or stone. By the early part of the fifteenth century, Moscow had regained the position of a flourishing capital, with many fine churches and monasteries; and the number of these continued to grow, notwithstanding great fires in 1536 and 1547, and the assault of the Crimean Tartars in 1572, when a considerable part of the city was reduced to ashes, and 100,000 of its inhabitants perished in the flames or by the sword.

Passing over other disasters by fire in 1611, when the Poles took possession of the city, and by the plague, which in 1771 greatly reduced the population—we come to the great tragedy of 1812, when the ancient city (which had ceased to be the capital in 1771) was fired by the orders of Count Rostopchin, its governor, in order to clear it of the invading legions under Napoleon. Their advanced guard, consisting of Polish and Prussian lancers, led by Prince Murat, took possession of the Kremlin on the 14th of September, 1812, and Napoleon made his solemn entry next day. This was the moment chosen for setting the city on fire, and for three days the flames raged with terrific fierceness. Napoleon withdrew to the Petrofski Palace, on the outskirts of the city, but returned to the Kremlin on the 20th September, after failing in an attempt to negotiate a peace. On the 19th October he left Moscow with an army consisting of 120,000 men, with 550 pieces of cannon, the remnant of the host of nearly half a million with which he had crossed the Niemen. What became of this small remnant of the *Grande Armée*, and of the plunder with which it left Moscow, has already been mentioned in the second chapter, and we can only refer to some of the incidents of the disastrous French occupation in our description of the churches and other buildings connected with its history.

Spread over a circumference of twenty-five miles, Moscow has now a population of three-quarters of a million. The Kremlin stands exactly in its

THE KREMLIN, MOSCOW.

centre, and, together with the walled *Kitai Gorod* (Chinese Town), which adjoins it, is the heart of the city and its chief attraction. Encircling these is the White City, anciently exempt from taxation, the Black or taxable part of the population having been located in the Earthen City beyond, so called from the wall of earth which formerly surrounded it, and which has since been converted into boulevards.

The Kremlin fortifications, rebuilt in 1367, were replaced between 1485 and 1492 by the high and stout battlemented walls and towers we now see; but which have been much restored and extended since they left the hands of the Italian architects by whom they were designed. They are 7280 feet in circumference, and are pierced by five gates, the principal of which is the Redeemer Gate, on the east face of the Kremlin. The tower over it was constructed in 1626 by an English clockmaker in a style (Gothic) discordant with the Italian battlements. A much venerated *ikon* of the Redeemer placed over the arch of the gate, and which was brought from Smolensk in 1647, has given to it the character of a *Porta Sacra*, and not even the emperor can pass through it without conforming to the old custom, once rigorously enforced, of uncovering the head. Peter the Great, who executed the Streltsi in front of it, two years after Gordon's victory over them, also made use of the gate as a point at which dissenters from the Orthodox Church were made to pay toll if they wished to preserve their beards.

Passing through it with bared heads, whether walking or driving, we approach the renowned tower or belfry of Ivan the Great, thus named after its architect (in 1600) John, or Ivan, Viliers. Under the guidance of one of the numerous *cicerone* who infest the basement, we ascend by some four hundred and fifty steps to the highest of the five stories of which it is composed, and proceed to enjoy one of the most striking and unique views in Europe. If the day be clear, and the season that of summer, our eyes are dazzled by the glitter of the gilded or star-bespangled spires and domes that surround us on every side, and tell of the existence of nearly four hundred churches, chapels, monasteries and convents. We trace the main streets and ancient circumvallations, and the eye ranges over a vast expanse of coloured house-tops, more or less embedded in trees. Close under the southern front of the Kremlin walls, with their quaint towers of glazed green tiles, flows the river which has given its name to the great city, notwithstanding its humble origin in one of the morasses of the neighbouring province of Smolensk.

Our attention is next directed to the bells, for which the tower is as famous as for its great height, which is three hundred and twenty-five feet to the top of the cross on its gilt cupola. The largest of these, named the Assumption, weighs sixty-four tons, and is, therefore, five times as heavy as the celebrated bell of Erfurt, and four times heavier than that of Rouen. It was re-cast after the partial destruction of the tower in 1812, when Napoleon and his marshals surveyed the city from it. The King of Bells, however, stands on a granite pedestal at the foot of the tower. Cast in 1733 out of the metal of a huge ancient bell, but weakened in its composition by the jewels and other treasures which the ladies of Moscow had thrown into the liquid metal with a pious intent, the Tsar Kolokol lost out of its side in 1737, by the falling upon it of some heavy rafters the large piece (seven feet high) that now rests against the pedestal, and which alone weighs eleven tons. The weight of the bell, minus the broken piece, is nearly two hundred tons, its height twenty-six feet four inches, its circumference sixty-seven feet eleven inches, and its maximum thickness two feet. The Tsar Alexis and the Empress Anne appear upon it in relief figures, and on the scroll below are representations of the Saviour, the Virgin Mary, and the Evangelists, all surrounded by cherubim.

Another monster of which the Muscovites

ON THE BELFRY: THE IVAN VELIKI TOWER, MOSCOW.

are proud is the Tsar Pushka of the Kremlin, a cannon of enormous size, weighing forty tons, cast in 1586. It guards the corner of the arsenal, the entire front of which is decorated with cannon taken during the retreat of the French.

The Great Palace, imposing in aspect, is unfortunately not ancient in age or in style. It stands on the spot upon which, from the earliest times, the Moscow princes and tsars built their habitations, originally of wood, and later of brick. These suffered destruction at the hands of Tartars and

Poles, and were not unfrequently destroyed in the many accidental conflagrations to which the Kremlin has been subjected. The present edifice replaced, in 1849, a palace built by Catherine II. which the French burned down after Napoleon had left it. Incongruous as is its exterior, from the old mixture of various periods and forms of architecture which it exhibits, the great beauty and grandeur of the state apartments within render the Bolshoi Dvorets a residence fully befitting the mighty Autocrat of All the Russias.

A great episode in Russian history is illustrated on an immense

THE GREAT BELL.

canvas in the gallery at the top of the noble staircase that leads to those apartments. Dimitri, Prince of Moscow, is seen defeating the Tartars at Kulikova, on the banks of the Don, in 1380. The first of the series of magnificent halls is dedicated to the military order of St. George. It measures two hundred feet by sixty-eight feet, while its height is no less than fifty-eight feet. On the shining white walls are inscribed in letters of gold the names of the individuals of all ranks and of the regiments decorated with the order, which was founded by Catherine II. in 1769, and is bestowed only for distinguished acts of bravery or success in the field.

We must, however, leave the modern and magnificent for the antique and more interesting parts of the palace, setting aside perforce the Winter Garden, the Picture Gallery, the chapels, and a host of private apartments. At the end of a gallery, into which open rooms allotted to maids of honour of the imperial court, is the Zolotaya Palata, or Gold Hall, dating probably from the early part of the fifteenth century, but restored in the style of the seventeenth century in the reigns of Paul I. and Nicholas I. From the

THE GREAT PALACE, MOSCOW.

seven recesses and seats along the walls, and which are taken to represent the seven councils, it is supposed to have been an audience chamber of the patriarchs and metropolitans ; but it is on record that in a chamber similar to this in character the Tsaritsas of Moscow received the boyars, the clergy, and foreign ambassadors on great occasions.

In the Granovitaya Palata, a large square building, with its fronts cut

G

into facets, and which we cannot avoid observing from the palace yard, we find a true restoration of an audience chamber built by Italian architects for the Tsar of Moscow in 1491. Its high arches rest on a central pillar, around which is stacked the imperial plate when an emperor is crowned. Here on the richly gilt throne of silver the monarch sits in his coronation robes, and dines with the sovereigns and princes, the nobles, the superior clergy, and the diplomatic personages who have taken part in the great ceremony.

Attached to the palace is the ancient (restored) building called the *Terem*. Its two lower stories were built in the early part of the sixteenth century, and the two upper ones were added in 1636. The rooms are all very small, and yet it was in the *Terem* that the first Romanoff sovereigns gave audience to foreign ambassadors. The Earl of Carlisle was received in it in 1664.

The Treasury, which forms the right wing of the palace, is the depository of a vast number of historical objects and of treasures hereditary in the reigning house. Ancient armour and weapons, German and Russian, fill the first two rooms.

The Round Room is full of thrones, crowns, and other regalia. The most ancient of the thrones is that of the last Christian Emperor of Constantinople, brought to Moscow in 1472 by Sophia Palaeologus on her marriage with Ivan III. Its ivory is beautifully carved with representations of the labours of Orpheus and the legend of Thrace. Three thrones of Persian workmanship, studded with diamonds, rubies, turquoises, and pearls, belonged, severally, to Ivan the Terrible, Boris Godunof, and Alexis. Most curious, however, is the double throne of vermeil made in Germany for the coronation of Ivan and Peter as the joint successors of Theodore III. (1682); on lifting the drapery at the back, an aperture is seen through which Sophia, their sister, who had been charged by the Streltsi with the control of State affairs, prompted Ivan, who was both mentally and physically incapable of governing, and who in 1689 resigned his share of the government to Peter I., then only seventeen years of age.

Among the crowns we single out the jewelled cap of Vladimir Monomachus, originally twelfth-century work, which all the Emperors of Russia have assumed at their coronation, in token of the ancient descent of their vast power. It is in fine gold filagree work, resting on a broad border of dark sable, and surmounted by a plain cross terminating in large pearls at each extremity. A topaz, a sapphire and a ruby—all of large size—spring from the dome of the cap on gold stems, while upon the cap itself are four emeralds, four rubies, and twenty-five pearls of Ormuz. A good specimen of Moscow work of the middle of the sixteenth century is seen in the Crown of Kazan, bestowed by Ivan the Terrible, after he had conquered the Tartar kingdom of Kazan, upon Simeon, a Tartar Khan, whom he converted to Christianity, and elevated to the dignity of a vassal Tsar. The ornaments and the entire decorations are Oriental, and the elegant gold arabesques of a decidedly Persian character. Many large jewels adorn it, and the top is surmounted by an enormous topaz. Next to it is the tiara-shaped crown, or cap of maintenance, made for Peter I. A diamond cross rises from the immense uncut ruby on its summit, and no fewer than nine hundred diamonds adorn the body of the cap, in addition to numerous rubies and emeralds fixed on pliant stems. Some of the orbs are of great magnificence, especially the one reputed to have been sent to St. Vladimir by the Emperors Basilius and Constantine, A.D. 988, but in reality made for Ivan III. in the fifteenth century. It is studded with fifty-eight diamonds, eighty-nine rubies, besides a great number of emeralds and pearls. The two *barmi*, or collars, part of the regalia of the Russian sovereigns up to the time of Peter I., cannot escape notice. They are both of Byzantine workmanship, in the most beautiful style of Greek art. The plaques of coloured enamel, attached to a strip of brocaded silk, represent the principal episodes in the life of David, and are divided by the four symbolical figures of Byzantium: the eagle, the lion, the griffin, and the unicorn.

THE CROWN OF MONOMACHUS.

The furthest room is a museum of gold and silversmiths' work, mostly of the seventeenth century, and with only a few objects of the fourteenth and fifteenth centuries. In a separate case are some specimens of English work, presented to the Tsar of Moscow by the Stuart sovereigns. Among the old state carriages preserved in a room below is a coach which Queen Elizabeth sent, together with eight horses, to the Tsar Boris Godunof. Its panels are ornamented with allegorical allusions to a crusade the Tsar had proposed to make against the Turks, but in which good Queen Bess refused to join. We thus see in this relic the record of a very early phase of the great 'Eastern Question.'

Moscow abounds in churches, and we must preface our description of the more notable cathedrals with a few observations on the origin of the architectural features of those edifices, generally classed as Russo-Byzantine.

As a matter of fact, no churches of the early Christian age survive in Russia in the material or the integrity of their original forms. It is even doubtful whether in Central Russia, Moscow included, ancient churches of a Byzantine type in all its purity ever existed. An abundance of timber caused them to be built of wood, which at the same time lent itself more easily to the construction of tent or cone-shaped pinnacles, subsequently reproduced in stone. If we examine closely the older ecclesiastical architecture of Russia Proper still extant, we shall arrive at the conclusion that when stone or brick buildings began to predominate over constructions in timber (in the fifteenth century), Byzantine influence was already very feeble, and that the Italian architects called in by Ivan III. succumbed to the Oriental taste of the Russians, adapted their work in accordance with it, and created a special type of ecclesiastical architecture in a mingled Italian and Persian style, non-existent in Byzantium. Their Russian disciples varied again that style according to their own taste, under the influence of Georgian as well as Persian forms, with a later combination of the Polish, essentially Italian, style of construction. Indeed, a careful study of the Russian churches built between the fifteenth and seventeenth centuries will show that in their architectural details they are Italian rather than Byzantine, the characteristic features of the latter style surviving only in the outlines of their apses.

The Uspenski Sobòr, or Cathedral of the Assumption, in the centre of the Kremlin—the most venerated pile in Russia, since its sovereigns continue to be crowned in it—was built in 1479 on new foundations by an Italian architect named Fioraventi, who, according to Russian chronicles, gained the prefix of Aristotle 'on account of his cunning.' It was considered a wonderful structure, its grandeur, height, size, and brightness being features previously unknown in national architecture. Nevertheless, as Dean Stanley correctly observed, it is in dimensions what in the West would be called a chapel rather than a cathedral. Its five domes, including the central cupola, were covered with copper-gilt plates only in 1684. They are supported internally by pillars covered with frescoes on a gold ground, similar to that of the walls. Grim representations of martyrs moderate the glitter that would otherwise have given more light to the interior. Among the many tombs in the cathedral the silver shrine of Philip, Metropolitan of Moscow 1566–1569, is an object of more than ordinary interest, for it is that of a prelate who had the courage to rebuke Ivan the Terrible publicly for his atrocities. For this offence he was dragged from the altar at which he was officiating, and ultimately put to death.

The Cathedral of the Archangel Michael, separated from the Assumption by a small paved square, dates from 1509, when the original edifice of 1333 was rebuilt by a Milanese architect. It has been restored several times, especially after 1812, when the French used it as a storehouse. Nevertheless, the interior is extremely interesting, having been perfectly restored to its ancient appearance of a mausoleum of the Rurik and Romanoff dynasties from Ivan I. to Peter the Great. The only emperor buried in it is Peter II., with whom the male line of the Romanoffs became extinct in 1730. No fewer than forty-seven princes of those families repose in the tombs that literally fill the cathedral. Frescoes on the walls, against each sepulture, record their names and features. Next the altar lies Ivan the Terrible, notwithstanding his numerous offences against the canons of the Church. His tomb is covered with a black pall, to denote that he died a monk, the monastic vow having been administered to him on his death-bed, under the mistaken belief that it could save his erring soul.

Close by is the Cathedral of the Annunciation, rebuilt in 1489, restored after a fire in 1547, and thoroughly renovated in 1867. Many of the *ikons* within it were acquired at the sacking of Novgorod the Great by Ivan IV., who also covered the nine domes with gold.

In the old residence of the Patriarchs, part of the Synodal Buildings within the Kremlin, is a large and curious collection of ecclesiastical vestments, ornaments and vessels, the most interesting of the latter being a long-necked vase, overlaid with mother-of-pearl, *cloisonné* in gold, and called the Alabastron. Notwithstanding its Persian form and distinctly Russian workmanship, it is held to be the original receptacle of the chrism obtained from Constantinople on the introduction of Christianity into Russia, and purporting to have been a portion of the ointment used by Mary Magdalene. A few drops only are annually used in the preparation of the 'sacred oil' with which orthodox children are anointed at their baptism, and Russian emperors consecrated at their coronation. The Metropolitan of Moscow, assisted by his higher clergy, prepares a new supply of the *mir* every two or three years at the season of Lent, and causes it to be distributed among the bishops of the several dioceses. A great variety of gums, balsams, essential oils and spices are added to the necessary quantity of oil and white wine, the entire compound being then hallowed by a drop or two of the contents of the Alabastron. The most venerable of the robes that hang in numerous glass cases is the *sakkos*, or dalmatic, of the Metropolitan Peter, made in 1322; but the richest one is that of the Metropolitan Dionysius (1583), covered with rubies, emeralds, and diamonds—an expiatory gift of Ivan the Terrible after the murder of his son. Of the seven mitres, in another room, the most ancient belonged to the Patriarch Job (1595). The 'great mitre,' out of four that belonged to Nicon, is diadem-shaped, and studded with precious stones of great value. We cannot stay to point out all the many cinquecento *panagias*, or portable pyxes, and other precious ornaments of fine workmanship which the sacristy of the Patriarchs offers to our view.[1]

---

[1] They are well described in Mr. Maskell's *Russian Art*, already quoted.

Much treasure of a similar kind is preserved in the sacristies of the churches within the Chudof Monastery and the Ascension Convent, that stand side by side at the Redeemer Gate, by which we issue from the Kremlin. We are now in the great Red (or beautiful) Square, where we

CATHEDRAL OF ST. BASIL, MOSCOW.

are at once struck by the eccentric appearance of the Cathedral of St. Basil the Beatified.

Our illustration of it justifies the description given of the edifice by Theophile Gautier: 'It is without doubt the most original monument in the world; it recalls nothing that one has ever seen, and belongs to no known style. One would imagine it to be a gigantic madresore, a crystallised colossus, a stalactite grotto turned upside down; a thing which has neither prototype nor similitude. It might be taken for a Hindoo, Chinese, or Thibetan pagoda. In looking at this impossible church, one is tempted to ask if it is not a whimsical will-o'-the-wisp, an edifice formed of clouds fantastically coloured by the sun, which the movement of the air will presently cause to change in form, or vanish into nothingness.'

Ivan the Terrible, after conquering Kazan, built on this site (anciently a cemetery in which was buried Basil, 'a prophet and miracle-worker, idiotic for Christ's sake'), with the treasure he had taken from the Tartars, a wooden church dedicated to the Intercession of the Holy Virgin. It was rebuilt in stone A.D. 1555, in commemoration of the additional acquisition of Astrakhan, by an Italian architect whose name remains unknown, but whose eyes were certainly not put out, as legends assert, in order that he should not produce another structure of equal merit. Seven years later, side chapels were added to it, and the edifice, such as it is after subsequent alterations, was not completed until the end of the sixteenth century, when it became known by its present name. It was pillaged and defiled by the Poles early in the seventeenth century, and in 1626 a fire which broke out in the dome of one of its chapels spread over the whole of Moscow. Again, in 1668, the great fire that devastated the Kitai Gorod destroyed all the cupolas of Basil the Beatified. In 1737 another great conflagration destroyed the church, with its domes and eighteen chapels and all the vessels and treasures within it. Restored seven years later, and again thoroughly renovated in 1784, in strict accordance with ancient drawings, Napoleon, in 1812, found it in its present form, and ordered 'that Mosque' to be destroyed.

Fortunately for later visitors not of iconoclastic temperament, his orders, in the confusion and danger of the French occupation of Moscow, were not carried out, although the edifice suffered to the extent of being robbed and used as a stable. It has now eleven domes, each different in colour and design, surmounting as many separate places of worship, connected by a labyrinth of passages.

In one of the lower chapels Basil, the tutelary saint, reposes in a costly shrine little in harmony with the equally venerated emblems of his austerity, in the form of heavy iron chains and crosses which he wore for penance. Another chapel is famed for the relics and the penitential weights of cast iron of 'Ivan the Idiot,' who acquired also the epithet of 'Big-cap,' from the heavy iron head-piece on which he was wont to carry buckets of water as an exercise of charity; this *curio* disappeared in 1812. The Protestant reader must bear in mind that idiocy is a form of mendicancy very common in Russia, and the innate compassionate feelings of the people are

much moved by it. Another common, perhaps more painful, appeal to charity
consists in the exhibition of sores resulting from accidents by fire, and it is
not unusual even to see beggars going about barefooted in winter. It must,
however, be admitted by any recent visitor to Moscow that the accounts
given by previous travellers as to the great number of mendicant men and
women, monks and nuns to be seen in the streets of the city, in the porches
of its churches and chapels, and at the neighbouring monasteries, is no

A PEASANT COLLECTING MONEY FOR A CHURCH OR MONASTERY.

longer correct. The
same observation may
be made with regard to
the appearance of the
civic population, which
is certainly better-
dressed and more Euro-
pean-looking than even
fifteen years ago. Also,
like most other cities and
towns in Russia, Mos-
cow has gained much
in recent years from a
more imposing style of
building, from the im-
provement of its princi-
pal streets, which are
now better kept and
lighted, as well as from
the planting of trees in
squares and boulevards.
The thoroughfares in
and about the Kitai
Gorod are scarcely re-
cognisable by one who
has not seen Moscow
for some length of time.
A striking feature in
these improvements is the erection of arcades or *passages*, in which ladies
can do their shopping without discomfort either in the heat of summer or
the excessive cold of winter. A couple of years more, and the old Gostinnoi
Dvor (Great Bazaar) on the Red Square will be replaced by a building more
worthy of the site, and of the monument in front of it, erected (1818) in
memory of Minin and Pojarski, the butcher and the boyar who drove the
Poles out of Moscow in 1612.

Apropos of markets, we must not fail to mention the *al fresco* mart

under the walls of the Kitai Gorod, of which we give an illustration. The assemblage is of a decidedly un-inviting character, in odour as well as in appearance, and the rawest material of Muscovy is well represented in it. It suffices to view the animated scene of sale and purchase in every possible description of merchandise, whether

THE OLD CLOTHES MARKET, MOSCOW.

honestly or otherwise acquired, at a respectful distance, on the outskirts of the surging, busy throng.

One of the most remarkable of the modern buildings in Moscow stands at the end of the square opposite the Cathedral of St. Basil. Indian and Persian in design, this huge edifice of red brick is a museum in which the history of the human species in what is now Russia is in course of being illustrated by specimens of workmanship, implements, arms, &c., at the various epochs of man's existence, from the earliest age down to modern times. A room decorated with frescoes, and ornamented in a style of coeval art, represents each such epoch, so far as it can be defined. In the first three apartments are relics of the Stone and Bronze Ages, in the shape of mammoth tusks, stone arrowheads and tools, and models of interments in the mounds that are found scattered over South Russia. Savage man is seen on a huge fresco, worrying to death with stones and sticks a mammoth taken in a pit-fall. The next room brings us to the end of the Bronze Age, and we shudder at the ghastly frescoed representations of an interment at Bulgar on the Volga. A chief lies dead in a boat, and his wives, horses and dogs are being slaughtered preparatory to the burning of the boat and its contents. Early Arab geographers give graphic accounts of those sacrificial rites, with details which will not bear reproduction here. The 'Babi,' or hideous idols of stone in human form, found in great numbers in the province of Ekaterinoslaf, represent the state of religion in the Iron Age of Russia. After this come objects illustrating the Helleno-Scythian period. Christian monuments not later than the tenth century, with copies of contemporaneous frescoes found in catacombs. Frescoes copied from the walls of St. Sophia at Kief and from those of other Russian churches, and typical of Russian ecclesiastical art down to A.D. 1125, are in two rooms full of early Slavonic objects. When completed, this unique and comprehensive museum will rival in fame and interest the Kremlin and all thereunto belonging.

The adjoining gate is the principal entrance into the Kitai Gorod, and between its two arches we find the Iverskaya Chasovnia, or chapel dedicated to the Iberian Mother of God, whose *ikon*, here deposited, was brought from Mount Athos in 1648. This is the most venerated image in Moscow ; the Emperor always stops to pray before it ere he enters the Kremlin, and the popular belief in its miraculous powers is so great that a very large sum is annually realised from the donations of worshippers, rich and poor, and from the visits paid by the *ikon* to the houses of the sick, and from its attendance at the weddings of the affluent, and at frequent ceremonies of blessing a new house or public edifice.

Another secular building of high interest is the Romanoff House, in Varvarka Street, within the Kitai Gorod. Some of its stone walls are alone of undoubted antiquity ; but, ravaged by fire, and sacked by the French, it was rebuilt in 1859 in the style of noble Muscovite dwelling-houses of the sixteenth century, it being on record that Michael, the first Tsar of the present dynasty, was born on this spot, in a house of the same kind. The boyar's apartments, above the cellars, kitchen, and offices, consist of a vestibule, a room for female servants, a nursery, and a large room called the Chamber of the Cross, in which priests offered their congratulations on great Church holidays, and the household assisted at matins and vespers. As in the Granovitaya Palata, or banqueting hall of the palace, the family plate was exhibited on great occasions in this apartment, which has also many secret recesses for the concealment of treasures. An oratory, and a small study, in which are shown two brass ink-bottles like those used in the days of Chaucer, complete the arrangements of this storey. Above is the

THE ROMANOFF HOUSE.

Terem, built of wood, and including the bed-chamber, adorned with rich carvings in wood, a reception-room panelled with stamped leather, and affording a charming view of the city from its windows. The turret on the west is surmounted by a vane in the form of a griffin, bearing the offensive and defensive weapons of the Romanoff coat-of-arms—a short sword and a shield.

The principal sights of the Kremlin and the Kitai Gorod are now exhausted, and we go farther a-field. We are attracted towards the grand Temple of the Saviour, whose huge gilt dome (ninety-eight feet in diameter) and attendant belfry-cupolas shine pre-eminently over Moscow. Founded in 1839, to commemorate the deliverance of the city from the French, it was completed only in 1883, at a cost of two millions sterling, spent exclusively on native material and labour. 'God with us,' is the inscription over the entrance to the principal portico, supported by thirty-six marble columns. Being of white sandstone, the stone from which Moscow derives one of her most endearing popular appellations, it is as dazzling in summer as the sheen of the dome and the four cupolas that surmount this otherwise inelegant and bare-looking block, *haut reliefs* and other ornaments notwithstanding. But the interior of the casket is magnificent and elegant beyond all description.

THE SUKHAREF TOWER.

The dark, highly-polished 'Labrador' marble, quarried near Moscow, brings into relief the gold with which the walls and pillars are abundantly decorated.

Outside the precincts we have now visited, the Sukharef Tower claims our attention, not only as a conspicuous object, but as an edifice with which, almost exceptionally, the activity of Peter the Great is connected in the ancient capital of the empire he created. In 1695, moved by his enthusiasm for naval matters, he caused this structure to be built in the form of a vessel, the tall tower, in a mixed Lombardic and Gothic style, and two hundred and thirteen feet high, representing the mast, and the surrounding galleries the quarter-deck, while the extremities were meant to resemble the bow and the stern of a contemporaneous flag-ship. Structural accretion has destroyed all trace of such resemblances, and after serving as the location of a naval school, the direction of which was entrusted by Peter I. to a Scotchman named Farquharson, the main building has been used as a pressure tower or reservoir in connection with a supply of water, introduced in 1829 from a source twelve miles distant, and within recent years perfected by the application of British capital, which, like the military and naval enterprise of our countrymen in more ancient days, has played no unimportant part in the development of the Russian empire.

There are monasteries in numbers all about Moscow well worthy of being mentioned, if not described; but it is almost superfluous to say that a host of other buildings and institutions of high interest must remain un-

CHURCH OF THE NATIVITY AT IZMAILOF, NEAR MOSCOW.

CATHEDRAL, POKROFSKI VILLAGE, NEAR MOSCOW.

CHURCH OF ST. NICHOLAS, AT MOSCOW.

CHURCH OF THE VIRGIN OF KAZAN, MOSCOW.

FOUR CHARACTERISTIC RUSSIAN CUPOLAS.[1]

recorded in our pages. From the Donskoi, Danilofski, and Simonof monasteries delightful views of Moscow and its multitudinous cupolas are obtained; their churches and sacristies being also well worthy of inspection.

[1] The superposition of the cross on a crescent so often seen on Russian cupolas is not emblematical of triumph over Mohammedanism, for the device was used ages before the expulsion of the Tartars from Russia. It typifies the connection between Mary, the mother of our Lord, and the cross, she being represented in ancient Greek pictures with her feet resting on a crescent.

The well-known Sparrow Hills afford, however, the finest view of the ancient capital, which Napoleon first beheld from their summit. Standing on this slight elevation of the left bank of the Moskva, which we reach towards the hour of sunset, on a glorious northern summer's day, we can well realise the feelings of the French invaders when they caught sight of the Kremlin walls and the glistening domes before us, and exultingly shouted, 'Moscow! Moscow!'

Another favourite trip by carriage or tramway is to the Petrofski Park and Palace. It was built between 1775 and 1800, and was occupied by Napoleon after the Kremlin had become too hot for him.

RUSSIAN PEASANTS NEAR KUNTSEVO.

Izmailovo, a village about six miles from the centre of the city, is an ancient domain of the Romanoff family. In the seventeenth century the Tsars had a well-stocked menagerie as well as an aviary at this residence, of which, however, nothing remains except the church, rebuilt in 1679. In the palace, on an island of the lake, Peter the Great studied the art of war, and it was here also that he discovered in a shed the 'Grandsire of the Russian Navy,' a boat now preserved at St. Petersburg. Kolomenskoe, on the Moscow-Kursk Railway, is another ancient seat of the Tsars in the vicinity of Moscow.

One of our pleasantest drives on a recent occasion was to Kuntsevo, about six miles off, and situated in pretty woodland scenery dotted with villas. The estate came to the Naryshkin family from the Tsar Alexis, son-in-law of the boyar Cyril Naryshkin, who was also the father of Peter I.

The mansion is of a somewhat later period, and is of little interest, but the inscription on a granite pyramid near the conservatory is worth recording: 'On the 4th July, 1818, Frederick William III., King of Prussia, having viewed Moscow from Kuntsevo, thanked her for saving his kingdom.' At so short a distance from Moscow, which is so rapidly becoming modernised, we are glad to find a primitive Russian village still occupied by stalwart specimens of the true Slavonic type of Moscow, unimpaired by contact with town life and factory labour. Our illustration, engraved from a photograph taken on the spot, shows not only the character of the contemporaneous dwellings of the inhabitants of the central part of Russia, but also that of one of their agricultural processes. Here, within a few miles of Moscow, we find Russian 'peasant proprietors' threshing corn with the Biblical flail! The instrument is used throughout the rest of Russia, except in the southern provinces, where the corn of the peasantry is generally threshed by the equally ancient method of the tramp of bullocks. A large and increasing quantity of agricultural machinery is sold at the two capitals to the larger landed proprietors, farmers, and German colonists; but the serf holds doggedly to his primitive plough and flail, and to his extremely rude methods of husbandry, which are naturally detrimental to the quality and the quantity of Russian agricultural produce.

One of the most remarkable of the holy places in Russia is within easy reach of Moscow by rail. Few travellers fail to devote a day to an inspection of the Troitskaya-Sergiéva Làvra, or Monastery of the Trinity, the Canterbury of orthodox pilgrims. It was established in 1342 by Sergius, a nobleman of Rostof, and twelve brethren. To the blessing he bestowed on Prince Dimitri is ascribed the great victory gained on the Don over the Tartars. Lands, and treasure in gold, silver, and jewels, were consequently bestowed on the monastery, and the claim of its abbot—the pious, simple, and self-denying Sergius—to canonisation, after his death in 1392, was rendered all the stronger by the appearance to him (as recorded in the annals of the Russo-Greek Church) of the Virgin Mary and the Apostles Peter and John, A.D. 1388.

Laid waste by the Tartars in 1408, the monastery was re-established fifteen years later, when its principal cathedral was erected. Thirty minor monasteries were later attached to it, and such vast estates that by the middle of the eighteenth century more than 106,000 male serfs, representing a population of at least 500,000, owed fealty and quit-rent to St. Sergius. In 1608 the monastery was besieged, but unsuccessfully, by 30,000 Poles. The same enemies appeared before its walls a few years later, when Ladislav of

Poland disputed the rights of the newly-elected Michael Romanoff. These are the last incidents in the military history of the monastery. The walls, nearly a mile in circuit, completed in 1547, were repaired by Peter the Great, to whom in his youth they had afforded shelter against insurgent Streltsi. Of the twelve churches which it contains, the most ancient and the most venerated is the Cathedral of the Trinity, which stands on the site of the original edifice raised by Sergius. The entrance is level with the ground, and we enter a portico full of stalls, at which monks sell *ikons*, pictorial crosses, tapers, oil, and a variety of other articles of ecclesiastical use or character, the life and doings of St. Sergius being the principal subjects represented in pictures and photographs, and on coarse enamel and deft wood-carving. Dingy, not over clean, and somewhat unsavoury from the presence of way-worn pilgrims, of whom 100,000 repair annually to the

THE TROITSA MONASTERY.

monastery, the interior is rendered attractive only by the costliness and the interesting nature of its contents. In the archbishop's stall we find a representation of the Last Supper in solid gold, the figure of Judas being alone of brass. Close to the *ikonostas*, burdened with jewelled *ikons*, is the shrine of the tutelary saint, weighing nearly one thousand pounds in pure silver, the gift of Ivan the Terrible, whose name recurs so frequently in Russian history, as much in connection with atrocious crimes as with prodigal acts of piety. The 'incorruptible' remains of St. Sergius are exhibited in it, certain small parts of the body being left uncovered, for the applications of the kisses of the orthodox faithful. In a glass case inserted in the altar screen are seen his pastoral staff and other paraphernalia.

The Cathedral of the Assumption, with nine cupolas, typifying the nine celestial hierarchies, and built in 1585, is larger, but curious chiefly for its frescoes, painted in 1609. Peter I. was concealed under the altar when the Streltsi were seeking to wrest him from his sister Natalia, and a large two-headed eagle in wood commemorates his escape. Boris Godunof, usurper of the throne of Muscovy, is buried at the western entrance. We cannot but admire the elegant belfry, designed by Count Rastrelli, to whom so many important edifices in Russia are due, which was completed in 1769. It is nearly three hundred feet in height.

Of the other sacred edifices we need only notice the church of St. Sergius Radonejski, which contains a library of four thousand old books and manuscripts. A copy of the Evangelists in it is attributed to the early part of the thirteenth century.

A detached building contains the sacristy, an object of paramount curiosity to pilgrims, pious or mundane. Its treasures are mostly of not earlier date than the seventeenth century. Chief among them is a resplendent copy of the Gospels, given by the Tsar Michael in 1632. The binding is beautifully ornamented with floral and arabesque patterns in enamel work, and emblazoned with a large cross in rubies of fine colour, contrasted with emeralds and sapphires of great size and beauty. We are to some extent prepared to see a large collection of imposing ecclesiastical garments, jewelled crosses, and other ornaments, but the extraordinary richness of those at St. Sergius seem to be worth all the treasures in the cathedrals and monastic establishments at Moscow put together.

About a mile and a half from the monastery is the *Skit*, or Hermit's Cell of Gethsemane, founded by the late Metropolitan Philaret as a retreat from the cares of his high office. The interior of the church is remarkable for its simplicity, after the profuse gorgeousness of the churches we have just viewed, and we are still more impressed with its austerity when we descend to the neighbouring catacombs, in which vows of perpetual seclusion are being fulfilled by human beings in the garb of monks, who have elected to breathe the pure air of heaven perhaps only once a year. In some catacombs beyond, effectually walled in, recluses hardly ever leave their subterranean cells. Female worshippers are admitted once a year into the church at Gethsemane, dedicated to the Ascension of the Virgin Mary. The sight is a strange one on a hot day in August, and in reality far from pleasant. Not a hand can be raised in the densely-crowded edifice to wipe a streaming brow, while the ardent worshippers look and feel as if they had emerged from a steam bath, in which their thin linen and cotton clothing had not been removed.

A short distance beyond is the Bethany Monastery, established in 1783 by Plato, an equally renowned and learned Metropolitan of Moscow. He is buried here, next to the house in which he lived, and over which, in those less tidy days, he caused to be inscribed the significant admonition, 'Let not him who comes in here carry out the dirt he finds within.'

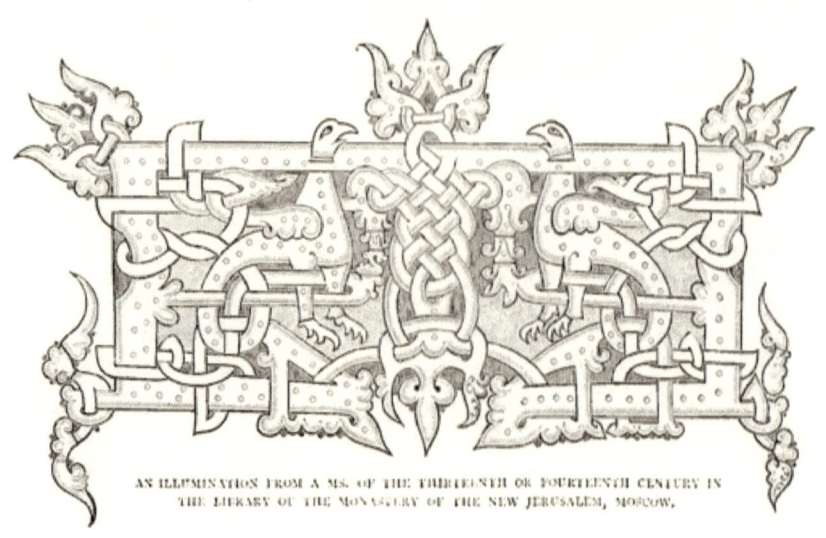

CHAPTER VI.

A VOYAGE DOWN THE VOLGA.

WE are bent on descending the Volga, not because we are inspired by the popular Russian robber-song *Vniz po Matushki, vniz po Volgé* (Down the Little Mother, down the Volga)—a song with which the present generation of middle-aged Muscovites were made familiar in their childhood as a song inciting to deeds of daring, and to the exercise of untrammelled liberty—but because we desire to see the celebrated fair of Nijni Novgorod, and the great cities on the main water-artery of the Russian empire. Ptolemy and other ancient geographers mention, but with little accuracy, the Rha (great river) or Volga, as flowing through the country of the Scythians and Sarmatians. The Huns, Khazars, and Bolgars subsequently formed powerful states on it, but were gradually subdued and absorbed by the 'Great-Russian' race, after the foundation of the powerful Russian principalities of Suzdal and Murom (eleventh century) and the removal, in 1158, to Vladimir of the paramount throne, established by the Northmen at Kief, under Rurik. In the thirteenth century came the Tartars, and after their power had been destroyed in the sixteenth century, Central Asia and China sent fresh masses of nomads (Bashkirs, Kalmucks, and Khirghizes) to the banks of the Volga. These were in their turn subdued by means similar to those which have brought the modern Russians to the frontiers of Afghanistan and Persia. 'The task,' observes a Russian writer, 'commenced by the armed bands of

KAZAN.

Suzdal has been completed by the detachments of Cherniayef and Scobelef."

But although thoroughly Russianized, so far as language, administration, and to a great extent, religion, are concerned, the banks of the Volga, on its course of 2320 miles, from a small lake near the town of Valdai, to the great inland Caspian Sea, still afford rich materials for the study of the aboriginal races by which they were held, particularly the Mordva, the Chuvashi, and the Cheremyssi of Finnish or Ugrian origin.

Few travellers have the patience to embark on the great river at Tver, where it first becomes navigable by small steamers, or even at Yaroslaf, the depôt in the sixteenth and seventeenth centuries of the English goods imported at Archangel, and now a great centre of manufacturing industry. One of the finest specimens of Russian architecture is the Church of John the Baptist, at Yaroslaf, while another sacred edifice in it is adorned with two leopards, in honour of our own country. Tradition says it was built (in 1652) with the proceeds of gold which a Russian trader had discovered in a cask sold to him as containing paint, by an English merchant, who waived his claim to the treasure, and desired that it should be employed in the service of the Almighty or in some benevolent object. We could, if so inclined, take the river higher up than Yaroslaf, namely at Rybinsk, to which a branch line runs from the Moscow Trunk Railway. This is one of the most important commercial entrepôts of the empire, especially for grain, its position in that respect dating from the middle of the last century, when by means of canals communication was established between the Volga and the Neva. About 5000 craft and 100,000 labourers find employment on the artificial waterway which thus connects the Caspian with the Baltic.

But most travellers are content to make the easy railway journey from Moscow to Nijni (the lower) Novgorod, at the time when the celebrated fair is being held. So much has already been written about that great cosmopolitan gathering that it would serve no useful purpose to devote much space to a description of it. A recent visit confirms an impression long since formed, that, like everything else nationally peculiar in Russia, the inevitable process of assimilation that results from modernized intercommunication by rail and telegraph is rapidly depriving Nijni Novgorod of its older mercantile features. We certainly found in 1888 the same huge stocks of iron (most of it under water, in consequence of a severe flood), of tea, now chiefly sea-borne, of cotton, brought in larger and larger quantities from Central Asia, of furs and skins brought from the northernmost parts of the empire, of textile goods manufactured chiefly in the provinces of Moscow and Vladimir, and of gaily-painted chests and other articles so extensively produced by the 'village industries' of Russia. The formerly itinerant Bokharian, Persian, or Armenian, has, however, now taken refuge in the modern arcades which protect his customers and himself from rain, oppressive

heat, and blinding dust. The wares exhibited in those galleries are as a
rule German, cheap and inferior, and we might fancy ourselves at Leipzig,
or at any other continental mart. Even the multitude of stalwart Tartars,
more Turkish than Mongolian in features, and who are always mentioned in

VIEWS IN NIJNI NOVGOROD.

descriptions of the fair, appear
to be dwindling in numbers.
Nor are the craft they are
engaged in unloading so quaint
and mediæval-looking as they
were only a few years ago, before the great develop-
ment of steam transport and trim iron barges, propelled by the use of
petroleum refuse as a cheap, abundant, and commodious substitute for wood
as fuel.

Beggars exhibiting repulsive sores to the superstitiously charitable, who
fear to withhold their donations lest their mercantile transactions be influenced by the evil one are likewise types that are fast disappearing under

the active and enlightened administration of General Baranoff, the present
governor of the province, which takes its name from the city and its fair.
Shelter and food are abundantly provided for the absolutely indigent, while
the poor are fed at a nominal charge per meal. Count Ignatief, of
Panslavist celebrity, is the honorary patron of one of several night refuges,
in which six to seven hundred of the poorer labourers find a resting-place;
and glad enough are they to take advantage of the wooden ledge and the
cast iron cylinder offered to them as a substitute for mattress and pillow.
Their clothes, such as they are, supply some of the needed softness for
body and head, and the small amount required as covering during the hot
nights of July and August. At another of these refuges, supported by a
benevolent merchant named Bagroff, rye bread is supplied gratis to the
miserable 'casuals.' Near the 'Siberian Line' that skirts the Volga are
several soup-kitchens well worthy of a visit. For the sum of five copecks
(about 1½d.) labourers are supplied in them with an ample dinner consisting of
soup and black bread *ad libitum*, and of about one pound of *kasha*, or
buck-wheat porridge the staple food of the Russian masses. The average
consumption of bread alone is one and a half pound per man, but it is not
at all rare to find a labourer capable of disposing of three pounds. No
spirits or ale are allowed, but tea is available throughout the day, at a
charge of three copecks, or less than a penny. The financial deficit on these
charitable arrangements is made good out of the revenue yielded by the
fair.

Among the masses of goods stacked on the banks of the Volga and the
Oka, its first great tributary out of thirty-seven others, or piled on board
the floating part of the fair, our sorely tried olfactory nerves will soon
discover the masses of dried or salted fish that have been brought from the
rich fisheries on the Volga and Caspian, for the consumption of the fast-
keeping orthodox. This alone is a trade of colossal proportions, and we
shall see as we descend to the Caspian, how important a part it plays in
the occupations of the population on the lower course of the Volga. We
are travelling towards the source of the supply of caviar that delicious
délicatesse which no one can properly appreciate until he has tasted it almost
fresh from the sturgeon. We make our first real acquaintance with it at
Nijni Novgorod, at one of the many restaurants to which the pangs of
hunger after a long stroll will inevitably bring us.

Under the guidance of an officer of the civil service, specially deputed
by the obliging governor, on the strength of old acquaintance, to show us
all the holes and corners of the fair, we visited some very curious places of
nightly entertainment for all sorts and conditions of men, from the peasant
upwards. It was a novel spectacle to see a Russian *mujik* sitting in a
merry-go-round, not in the open air, but in a room of large dimensions,
with a bottle of beer beside him, and a cigarette in his mouth. Here again,

we could see the process of European assimilation at work, although in one
of its painful and demoralizing phases. However, there was not much, if
anything, to shock the student of national life. There was no disorder and
no brawling; but our accompaniment by detectives in plain clothes through
the Kunavino quarter was sufficient proof that the tranquil surface exhibited
to us was in a certain measure delusive.

There is no doubt that in this respect we were under deep obligations
to the enlightened official who had supreme charge of us, and he will, it is
to be hoped, not take it amiss if we record our gratitude towards our good
friend, Mr. Andrei Alexandrovitch Titof, of Rostoff Yaroslavski, who may
already be known to some of our readers as a learned archæologist and
consummate *connoisseur* in matters of Russian ecclesiastical lore and art.

The old walled city of Nijni Novgorod has in itself strong claims on
the intelligent traveller. It was for the purpose of arresting the incursions
of the 'godless Bolgars,' inhabiting the country now known as the province
of Kazan, that the Prince of Suzdal took, in 1219, their city of Oshel, near
the mouth of the great Kama, a tributary of the Volga, and founded a
strong settlement at the confluence of the Oka with the Volga, which he
named Novgorod—the 'New Town of the Low Countries.' We pass over
the common episodes of Tartar invasion and princely internecine strife, and
come down to the great turning-point in its history, namely, the removal to
it of the ancient Fair of Makarief, so called from a privilege granted in 1641
to a monastery dedicated to St. Macarius, still prominently extant about
seventy miles lower down the great river. In the same century, 'Nijni'
became conspicuous as the place at which a company of Holstein merchants
built the first war vessel ever launched in Russia under a charter for opening
a trade with Central Asia, Persia and India, by way of the Caspian, in
imitation of our countryman, Anthony Jenkinson, who had already, in 1558,
crossed that sea in a ship that bore the red cross of St. George.

The Kremlin walls we see towering on the cliffs of the right bank of
the Volga were built in 1511 by a Venetian, who incorporated in them two
towers which dated from the fourteenth century, the Dmitrofskaya and the
Tverskaya. They were, however, much reduced in height and circumference
after a great fire. Although restored in 1620, the Cathedral of the Archangel, which they enclose, is substantially a structure of 1227, and consequently
of high interest. The neighbouring unsightly Church of the Transfiguration
dates its existence from 1834, and is remarkable only for its octangular,
Tartar-looking belfry on the opposite side of the street. Altars on either
side of the *ikonostas* are dedicated to the patron saints of Minin and Pojarski,
the deliverers of Moscow, to whom a monument in the form of a granite
obelisk was raised opposite the cathedral in 1826 by 'grateful posterity.'

Out of the forty odd churches outside the Kremlin, we need only
indicate the Rojdestvenskaya, distinguishable by its eccentric colouring and

peculiar architecture.
It was built in 1710,
by Count Gregory
Stroganof out of a
portion of vast riches
acquired by gold-
mining in Siberia.

Of the monasteries
at Nijni Novgorod, the
most ancient is the
Annunciation, on the
banks of the Oka,
not far from the float-
ing bridge, and which
existed, according to
some authorities, in
1229, when it was
ravaged by Purgas,
Prince of the Finnish
or Mordva tribe.
Critics trace its erec-
tion to 1371, by the
Metropolitan Alexis,
who probably pre-
sented to it the *ikon*
of the Holy Virgin,
attributed, as in all
cases of swarthy
representations, to
Korsun, or Khersonese
workmanship. A
Greek inscription on
it testifies that it was
painted in A.D. 993,
and it must therefore
be the most ancient
holy image in Russia.
Before proceeding on
our voyage, we walk
or drive to the *otkos*,
or terrace at the
extreme end of the
city, overlooking the

THE KREMLIN WALL, NIJNI NOVGOROD.

Volga from its junction with the Oka. We see a far-reaching alluvial plain, dotted here and there with forests, and are impressed by the monotony of the landscape, and our own personal insignificance in relation to the great works of the Creator.

Our good fortune has secured to us a commodious berth on board the Novoselski, so called after His Excellency Nicholas Novoselski, the founder of the steamship company, and the originator of several of the greatest and most successful enterprises in Russia. We are favoured to the extent of sleeping on board during our stay at Nijni, and of finding a charmingly jocose and eminently intelligent and communicative commander in the person of 'Sea Captain Felix Alexandrovitch Pietroschiewich,' as inscribed autographically in our note-book. Few were the languages in which he could not convey either his serious or his merry thoughts. Those of the latter description were appropriately garbed in the American-English of 'Frisco,' to which this real salt-water tar had traded during the greater part of his life, in the service of the Russo-American Company, extinguished some years ago by the cession of the Aleutian Islands to the United States of America. He was a real cosmopolitan, an aboriginal of the coast of Croatia or Dalmatia (evidently the scene of his nativity), with the cuteness and droll levity of a Yankee, and all the blunt outspokenness of a Russian Slav with a *shirokaya natura*, or wide, expansive mind and habit.

Subsidised for the carriage of mails and exiles, criminal and political, the Caucasus and Mercury Company are in a position to offer superior advantages in relation to other steam-ship companies on the Volga, in the matters of punctual speed, tolerable accommodation, and culinary requirements. A majority of our party had travelled from Australia, and confessed unreservedly that they had never been better taken care of than by the merry commander of the Novoselski. The steamer was one of the many American-typed vessels that have supplanted the earlier pioneers of the Volga. Our cabins were below, our saloons above them, and over all was the spacious top deck, on which we paced or settled ourselves comfortably whenever the great heat of the sun was tempered by a kindly breeze or moderated by a welcome cloud. The absence of smoke and of attendant soot was soon explained by the fact that the steam by which we were propelled owed its origin, not to wood or coal fuel, as when we travelled on the Volga some fifteen years before, but to the refuse of petroleum, now so abundantly supplied from Bakù on the Caspian. There is not one of the five hundred Volga steamers of all kinds and dimensions—American river-craft with propellers, or stern wheel iron steam barges and tugs—that now uses any other description of fuel. Led by the attentive captain to the engine-room, we found it in charge of a couple of men, one being the engineer, the other the 'stoker.' The more appropriate name of the latter should be the 'trimmer,' for his duties consisted solely in setting alight, by means of a rag saturated with naphtha and ignited by a lucifer match, the jet of petroleum refuse conveyed under each of the four boilers and set free by the turn of a cock, the closing of which, on the other hand, sufficed to arrest at a stopping place the further generation of steam. The petroleum is scattered into spray as it issues from the supply-pipe, and made to burn furiously over the bottom of the boiler by a jet of steam issuing from the same nozzle, divided for that purpose into two parts.

There were few races in Europe or Asia that were not represented among the five hundred passengers embarked in the Novoselski, and sub-
sequently increased to nearly seven hundred, notwithstanding occasional disembarkations. The Asiatics and the lower classes, including priests, soldiers, and peasants, were huddled together on the second deck, each passenger more or less snug at night on mattresses and felt rugs. Persians, Bokharians, and Tartars formed camps of their own, distinguished by their cleanliness and their stores of pillows and warm coverings. They slept in rows and batches, apart from their more lowly Christian companions, who were not, like themselves, merchants in cotton madder, silk, or turquoises. The Russian *kupets*, or trader, was accompanied by his samovar, or tea-urn, to which he had frequent recourse with the aid and companionship of his *prikastchi* or clerk. All had more or less a well-to-do appearance, including some soldiers

A RUSSIAN TRADER WITH HIS TEA-URN.

of a crack regiment of guards on furlough, and excepting only a village priest, who, more than usually indigent and untidy in his outward appearance, was very soon put on shore, on the ground of not having paid his fare. We were travelling by one of the best mail steamers, the fair of Nijni was yet scarcely on its decline, and the rougher classes of the Russian population were consequently in a minority.

All sorts and conditions of men and women above the trader stratum of Russian society were assembled in the saloon cabin. There was but little talk among them during the daytime, which was spent in eating and drinking, sleeping, and gazing on the busy activity at numerous places of call,

The scenery, until we approached Simbirsk, was too monotonous to attract much attention, and we soon get accustomed to the strings of barges that were being towed up the Volga through its shallow, winding, and often shifting channels. It was after the ladies had retired, the night become dark and the atmosphere cool, that sociability commenced. The economical condition of the country, and especially of the Volga provinces, was then discussed with a freedom that would astonish those who had been led to believe that in such matters Russia is a country of mutes. It is so far the reverse outside the precincts of hotels and restaurants, over which the secret police is supposed to keep close watch, that a foreigner acquainted with the language is often placed in a condition of some embarrassment, the criticisms which he cannot help hearing being generally very strong against the present state of affairs and the powers that be.

With these fellow-passengers, representative of different sections of society, and entertained and instructed by the vigorous discussion of political and social questions, we dropped down the Volga at the rate of nineteen miles an hour, and next day touched at Cheboksary, a town of 5000 inhabitants, on the right bank of the river. This is the 'town of towns' of the Chuvash race, and it is equally interesting as the capital of a barren district in which another ancient Finnish people—the Cheremyssi—are evidently living out their last days. There are not more than 100,000 of them left in the district. The unfavourable climatic conditions under which they have so long struggled, the barrenness of the soil they occupy, the unremunerative character of the simple industries that are known to them, and the unsanitary state of their dwellings, which are not supplied with chimneys, have contributed to this result, accelerated as it has also been by the prevalence of *goître* and other diseases. The abnormal number of idiotic and deaf and dumb children is another symptom of the moribund condition of the Cheremyssi. Although nominally Christian, they are in reality more than half pagan, and have contributed greatly towards keeping alive among the population of the middle course of the Volga the customs and superstitions of remote ages. There is indeed no part of Central Russia where these have been better preserved. To this day, on the outbreak of murrain among cattle, the old women of a village sally out at night unclad, and, dancing frantically round each hut, belabour unmercifully any one who may come in their way during their weird operations, and whom they pursue with wild cries as an impersonification of death. Every year also the young girls of the northern forested region of the Volga beat, under similar conditions, the bounds of newly sown fields, to protect them from drought and destructive insects.

At Kazan we find a very different population. It is Russian, with a strong admixture of a handsome and vigorous Tartar element ; for this is the ancient capital of a Mongol kingdom which flourished between 1438 and 1552, when Ivan the Terrible, with an army of 150,000 men, subdued it, slaying all the troops of the Tartar Tsar. A stoppage of four hours enabled us to visit the city in a carriage that had been ordered by telegraph, and in it we rattled, half smothered in dust, along the high causeway, five miles in length, by which the city is connected with the river bank. It was under partial repair, and we were astonished to find that the material used for that purpose was rich stable manure! Similar waste may be observed over a great part of Russia, especially within the zone of black earth, where the sweepings of stables are thrown into ravines, under the rude and obstinate belief that the land is not in need of any stimulant or restorative.

We pass the Admiralty suburb, in which Peter the Great built a flotilla for the Volga and the Caspian, and to the left of the causeway our attention is directed towards a pyramidal monument raised on a small mound over the bones of the Muscovites who fell at the capture of Kazan, while far away to the right we see the mosques and minarets of the Tartar suburb. The city retains some of its ancient appearance only in its Kremlin walls (of 1508), and in its Sumbeki Tower. The latter is an object of great reverence to the ten thousand Tartars of Kazan. It is supposed to have been originally the minaret of the mosque (demolished in 1552) in which the Khans or Tsars of Kazan were buried. The site of their graves, on the west face of the tower, is visited on Wednesdays and Fridays for devotional exercises by crowds of pious Tartars, who thus keep alive the memory of their ancient rulers.

The most interesting of the churches within the Kremlin is that of the Annunciation, built in 1562, after the model of the Assumption in Moscow. Its altar marks the spot on which Ivan IV. planted a cross after he had stormed the city. In the church of a convent close to the Kremlin walls is the original *ikon* of the 'Virgin of Kazan,' to which the deliverance of Moscow from the Poles in 1613 was attributed. Although adorned with a diamond crown presented by Catherine II., the costliness of its ornamentation is insignificant compared with that of the copy we have seen in the Kazan Cathedral at St. Petersburg.

Chief among the numerous public institutions of Kazan is its University, founded in 1804, and attended by about six hundred students, chiefly of surgery and medicine, although Oriental languages were formerly the principal objects of study at this seat of learning. As at most other Russian universities the students have the benefit of a Lector of the English language.

Hurrying back to our steamer, parched and grimy, we refreshed ourselves voraciously with the delicious fruits—melons, pears, apples, grapes—of which we bought a small sack full for a few coppers at the long row of stalls displayed close to the landing-stage. And glad we subsequently were that we had made so good a provision, for the heat became so intense that until the sun went down we supported ourselves principally on caviar and

water-melons, washed down by cool cups
of Badminton, manufactured out of
Caucasian or Bessarabian wine, to the
wonderment of our less experienced
fellow-passengers, who preferred sipping
hot tea.

The tanks being filled by means of
a hose with a supply of oozy petroleum
refuse, and after embarking a fresh
contingent of travellers, the Novoselski
sped again down the muddy waters of
the Volga. At about fifty miles from
Kazan, the Kama River, itself the
recipient of the waters of five hundred
and seventy-four affluents, over a course
of 1160 miles joins the Volga, bringing
to it a vast number of vessels and rafts
laden with salt, iron, and other produce
of the interior of Siberia. Numerous
villages and groups of storehouses on the
riverbank tell us that we are passing through
the great corn-producing districts
of South-eastern Russia, and we
reach one of the chief centres of
the grain trade at Simbirsk, a city
of the seventeenth century, perched
on a cliff 560 feet above the level
of the river. It suffered greatly
in 1670 from
the robber
bands of
Stenka Razin,
a rebellious
Cossack of
the Don; but
nevertheless
its fortress
ultimately
arrested the
victorious
march of the
insurgents.
A century
later the whole

TARTAR MOSQUE AT KAZAN.

of the country at this part of the Volga joined another rebellion, under Pugatchef, also a Don Cossack, who personated Peter III. (suffocated some ten years previously) and seriously threatened to wrest Moscow from Catherine II. It required an army to subdue the rebels, and the Empress breathed more freely after Pugatchef had been brought to her in an iron cage.

Here begins the only really pretty part of the Volga: its right bank rises in cliffs of curious formation, with thickly-wooded hills beyond, while the opposite side of the river is one continuous cornfield or grass meadow. An ordinary map of Europe shows the Samarskaya Luka, or bend formed by the Volga between Stavropol and Samara. This is the magnificent estate of Count Orlof-Davydoff, whose late father devoted to its cultivation and improvement the knowledge he had gained in Scotland, as a student at the University of Edinburgh and as a practical admirer and copyist of all good things that were British. There is nothing of interest in Samara, which, with a population of 65,000, is the capital of a rich agricultural province of the same name. It bears no evidence of being inhabited, like Simbirsk, by noble landlords, for its buildings are mean except in the main thoroughfare, which is about the only one that can boast of what is called paving in Russian towns. Clouds of dust hang over or pervade its broad streets, except when a copious shower has converted them into the deepest and blackest of mud, through which men and cattle have to trudge until the sun has reasserted the supremacy of dust.

We had long watched our approach to the shining silver domes of the red brick cathedral and belfry of Samara, and had imagined that its surroundings would be in keeping with such imposing resplendence. Although this did not prove the case, yet it is a city of great commercial importance, and being connected by rail with Moscow on the one hand and Orenburg on the other, much of the trade and intercourse of Russia with Central Asia passes through it. The memories of Kalmuck and Cossack ravages in the seventeenth century have long been extinguished, and only a few remnants remain of the walls of the fortress by which the inroads of Cossack robbers and nomadic tribes were eventually arrested. Next in celebrity to the trade of Samara in grain and tallow is the supply of *kumyss*, or fermented mares' milk, which the adjoining steppes offer to those who are afflicted with diseases of the lungs and kidneys. Its efficacy has for some time past been recognised in England, and we can say from personal experience that, whatever may be its alleged curative properties, mares' milk, that sparkles like champagne, is far from being a repulsive beverage even to the sound and healthy.

Pretty landscapes open out after the steamer leaves Samara and passes the Sulphur Hills. A village on the right bank has been named after Ermak, the conqueror of Siberia, who had previously, like so many other

Cossacks, been a Volga pirate. Other villages of piratical origin dot the
banks until we reach the Cavern Hills, containing the largest deposits of
asphalte in Europe, next to those of the Abruzzi in Italy.

Near Syzran, our next great station, the broad Volga is spanned for
the first and as yet the only time by a railway bridge, magnificent in
design and execution. It enables trains to run uninterruptedly from St.
Petersburg to Orenburg, the principal goal of the migrating peasantry.
Beyond are the prosperous domains of the Old Believers, or dissenters
from the Russo-Greek Church, one of whose principal settlements is
Khvalinsk, a town situated at the foot of a hilly background, with patches

AN ANCIENT PIRATE RAID ON THE VOLGA.
(From a contemporaneous print.)

of limestone that have the appearance of snow. Within the district are the
hermit cells of Cheremshansk, the Palestine of the seceders to the
Austrian Confession, so called from the fact of their having been permitted
to return from Austrian Poland, where they had taken refuge when being
persecuted by the Russian Church. This still denies the apostolical
succession of their bishops as stoutly as it does that of our own Anglican
prelates.

We are not long in reaching, at Ekaterinenstad, an ethnographical and
religious centre of a widely different character. From the mouth of the
Irghiz River begin to stretch the neat and thriving German colonies

planted by Catherine II., with the object of improving the condition of agriculture in Russia. That result has so far not been attained beyond the boundaries of the colonies, whose Russian neighbours adhere doggedly to their primitive modes of husbandry, while the Lutherans keep themselves

A COSSACK OF THE VOLGA.

entirely aloof socially, and retain strongly their prejudices against the Russo-Greek religion, and particularly against intermarriage with those who profess it. In the provinces of Samara and Saratof these colonists number at least 300,000.

I

Built on undulating ground within an amphitheatre of bare and frowning hills, Saratof is a handsome and important city of 112,000 inhabitants. It was a thriving place so far back as 1635, but it was subsequently ravaged on several occasions by Kalmuck Tartars. The robber bands of Stenka Razin then held it until 1671, and in the eighteenth century it was pillaged by the rebel Cossacks of Bulavin and Nekrasof (1708). The redoubtable Pugatchef bombarded it from the Falcon Hill, a neighbouring bluff 560 feet high; and to this long list of disasters must be added the ravages of the plague in 1807, and visitations of cholera in 1830 and 1848. Surviving all these misfortunes, Saratof is now a highly prosperous emporium of trade in wheat, tallow, linseed, tobacco, and other agricultural produce. Its many fine public and private buildings, its

A TARTAR LADY OF THE VOLGA.

broad and paved streets, and the exceptional advantage of waterworks constructed with the aid of British capital, render it the most European-looking city on the Volga. There was evidence and promise of still greater improvement, and it may be hoped that the citizens will not much longer delay the lighting of their streets with gas. They have reason to be proud of the Museum of Art with which the city has been endowed by Professor Bogoliubof, a celebrated painter, whose gallery of pictures, Russian and foreign, it contains.

From Saratof the Volga takes a direct southerly course for a considerable distance, with a breadth of nearly three miles. The bluffs on the right bank are mostly perpendicular, and are occasionally intersected by ravines. Each prominent cliff has a name of its own, and in some cases notoriety is connected with robber deeds, mostly of the Stenka Razin period. Another large German colony, with an extensive trade in grain, is passed on the left bank, a couple of hours after leaving Saratof; but the most important stopping-place is at Kamyshin, a town which was founded and fortified in 1668 by Colonel Thomas Baillie, one of the numerous British officers then serving the Tsar of Moscow. Its fortifications proved very useful in the suppression of piracy. Like all the other towns on the middle and lower courses of the Volga, its history is one of bloodshed. In 1700, instigated by the Don Cossacks, the citizens rose in rebellion against the reforms of Peter the Great, and murdered all those who shaved in compliance with his orders. Pugatchef took the town, and hanged all its inhabitants in 1774, after which Catherine II. caused it to be repopulated.

We can now only mention, among other large and thriving villages trading in wheat and in salt, raised in Elton Lake, the little town of Dubofka, with 13,000 inhabitants, formerly the capital of the Volga Cossacks. Although the railway that now runs between the Volga and the Don (the only two great Russian rivers of which the waters are not naturally or artificially connected) has diminished the importance of the place, yet its former prosperity is to a great extent maintained by its steam mills, potteries, and tanneries.

Almost buried in fine sand, which flies about in clouds like the indigenous mosquitoes, Tsaritsyn (the Tartar Sari-chin, yellow sand), with a population of 36,000, looks as if railway and steam communication had roused it too early from the slumber of a Russian provincial town. Ragged children and squalid pigs roam about in most of its dirty unpaved streets, and it is only the new large storehouses on the river bank, and the fine shops and warehouses in the central square, that attest the great and growing commercial importance of the place. This is further apparent from the presence of a great number of Jews, to whom, whatever Jew-baiters may say to the contrary, the south of Russia owes much of its material development. A short railway, connecting the Volga with the Don, carries large quantities of salted and dried fish (a species of *corigonus*) from the Caspian, and a considerable amount of timber to Kalatch on the Don, where the goods are shipped for Rostof, at the head of the Sea of Azof. Not less important is the petroleum or kerosine trade of Tsaritsyn. Nobel's Town, in the immediate vicinity, so called after the enterprising Swede who started the industry, and justly acquired the title of the 'Naphtha King,' is well worth seeing. The oil stored on the river bank in the long rows of iron cisterns belonging to the Nobel and other companies is brought from Bakù on the Caspian in iron vessels, and delivered at Tsaritsyn into naphtha-cars, which can be seen travelling in vast numbers over the rail net-work of European Russia.

At Sarepta, our next stopping-place but one, we find ourselves suddenly in a bright patch of German civilization. This is a neat, stone-built, and prosperous colony of Hernhuter (*Brüderunität*), or Moravian Brethren, founded in 1770 on communistic principles, which were subsequently abandoned, having proved in practice to be inconsistent both with real liberty and with modern progress. In addition to agriculture, the colonists pursue a variety of industries, of which the most important is the preparation of mustard. Sarepta mustard is used all over Russia, and gives our well-known 'Colman' but little chance of competition. A strong balsam is also made here out of mustard seed, and our passengers rush on shore to obtain a supply of the healing and invigorating cordial.

I 2

The Volga now makes a sudden bend to the east, and, after parting with the range of hills that had so long accompanied its right bank, flows through a vast uniform steppe, declining gently towards the Caspian, and forming the province of Astrakhan. To our left the country appears unpopulated, although when explored it will be found dotted over with Kalmuck encampments or *kibitkas*. A little further down on the same side we come upon a short line of railway abutting on the Boskunchak Lake and saltworks, on the border of the Kirghiz steppe. The right bank is comparatively lively, for we pass villages (locally called Vatagas), and Cossack

MODERN TARTARS OF THE VOLGA.

settlements, in which the principal occupation is fishing. Kalmytski Bazaar is the chief settlement of the Mongolian Kalmucks, subject to Russia since 1655, but who, between the fourteenth and seventeenth centuries, ruled supreme over almost the whole of Central Asia. Subduing the Nogai Tartars, they at one time, in alliance with the wild Bashkirs, held the lower course of the Volga in such force as to be able to threaten Russian towns so distant as Penza and Tambof. At the place we have mentioned remains their chief temple, which many travellers are induced to visit, in order to witness the religious rites of that once mighty Tartar race. Beyond is Tsitrakhan, the capital, in the twelfth century, of the kingdom of Astrakhan, founded by the Kipchak Tartars, known in their later invasions of Muscovy as the 'Golden Horde.'

In four and a half days from Nijni Novgorod we end our voyage at Astrakhan, the later capital of the Tartar kingdom, which Ivan the Terrible conquered in 1554. It is now half Asiatic, half cosmopolitan. There is not another town in Russia, and perhaps in the world, in which such a medley of races is concentrated. The Russians predominate numerically, to the extent of about seventy-five per cent. out of a population of 70,000 ; but it is the Kalmucks, the Tartars, the Persians, the Central Asiatics, and the Armenians who are most *en évidence* to the European eye, on account of their respectively peculiar dress and features. The forest of masts which bursts on our view as we approach the vast harbour between the main stream and the Bolda branch of the intricate Volga delta will be found on closer inspection to belong to a variety of quaint craft well worthy of the artist's pencil.

The history of the city has already been foreshadowed in our frequent reference to Cossack rebels and marauders, who in 1665 checked by their depredations the trade which by permission of the Tsar Alexis the Duchy

AN ASTRAKHAN BOAT.

of Holstein established with the countries on the opposite side of the Caspian. The last local rebellion occurred in 1706, and six years later Peter the Great reached Astrakhan with a large force, and after the capture of Derbent and the acquisition also from Persia of Bakù and the provinces of Gilian, Mazanderan, and Astrabad, not only made secure the possession of Astrakhan, but gave to Russia the sovereignty over the Caspian Sea.

If we land at the pier of the Caucasus and Mercury Company in Astrakhan, we find ourselves within the precincts of the 'Admiralty and

Port,' founded by Peter I. but transferred as a naval station in 1867 to Bakù, owing to the silting of the estuaries of the Volga. Here, in a small house built for the great Reformer, are kept the yacht and the boat in which he sailed, as well as models of ships, a collection of old arms and specimens of the tools used during his reign in shipbuilding. The most striking edifice in the city is the Cathedral of the Assumption, completed in 1710. The sacristy has one of the richest collections in Russia of vestments and mitres. A Persian mosque stands in the principal street, which is intersected by the Varvazzi Canal, deepened by a Greek of that name in 1817, but excavated originally in 1744, as a precaution against the inundations to which the city is liable.

In autumn, winter, and spring, thousands of labourers flock to Astrakhan to take part in its rich fisheries, in the salting and drying of the fish, and in the preparation of caviar. At least forty thousand men and women find such employment at the Volga fishing stations, and no fewer than twenty-five thousand men are engaged in the five thousand and odd vessels and boats that pursue the same industry on the Caspian. At Astrakhan the most valuable product of the Volga is the sturgeon (*Acipenser sturio* and *Acipenser huso*) and the smaller sevriuga (*Acipenser stellatus*). The average annual catch of these three descriptions of sturgeon is respectively 300,000, 100,000, and 1,500,000. They are mostly taken—partly in nets, partly on ground lines—in those branches of the delta which are too shallow for navigation.

The gear used is of the strongest; for the sturgeon, although averaging thirty pounds in weight, run up to nineteen feet in length, and to a weight of 800 and even 1600 pounds. Their extirpation has been proceeding at a rapid rate for many years past, and the time is evidently approaching when measures will be adopted by the Government for the preservation of so important a source of wealth. It is at present very difficult for any fish to escape the ground-lines with closely set hooks, generally unbaited, with which the many small channels of the Volga delta are practically barred. Nor have the fish any repose even in winter, for they are then harpooned in shallow places through openings in the ice. The larger fish are drawn on shore and cleaned on the spot, while those of more convenient size are dealt with in the boats, or hauled up to high landing-stages, whence they are carried to store-houses, to be soaked for about twelve hours in brine, and then stored in an ice-cellar.

Isinglass is produced by a process of drying from the inner part of the spinal marrow of the sturgeon, and a fine fish-glue is obtained from its bladders. The roe yields caviar, of which thirty thousand barrels are despatched yearly from Astrakhan alone. We may observe in passing that the Russian name for this delicacy is *ikra*, caviar being a corruption of the Italian word *caviale*, which, again, is only an attempt to reproduce the sound of the word *kaviar*, by which the Turks and Tartars knew it ages before its appearance in Southern Europe. After the fish has been cut open, the roe is taken out and divided into two qualities, the best being converted either into pressed or 'grainy' caviar, while the inferior is merely salted and packed in small barrels for consumption by the less wealthy classes. The higher sort is passed through sieves that retain the membrane in which the roe is contained, and packed in tins or barrels with a small quantity of dry salt; the rest is left in strong brine until it is ripe, *i.e.*, until it can be taken out by the hand in balls, after which, when its superfluous moisture has been drained off, it is packed in bags made of the bark of the lime tree (bast) and put under a strong press. The commoner sort of caviar replaces bread

DOG SLEDGE WITH FISH, ASTRAKHAN.

in the daily *menu* of the labouring classes on the Volga; but the 'grainy' quality, of a semi-transparent greyish colour, and with no taste of fish or salt, is reserved for the tables of the affluent, and can seldom be found in perfection beyond St. Petersburg, so far as the rest of Europe is concerned.

Fishing in the delta of the Volga is also pursued on a large scale by pelicans. Spying, with the aid of sentinels, a school of small fish, they form a semicircle, and gradually enclosing it in a shallow bight, swoop down in thousands to gorge themselves on their artfully-earned prey. It is a tradition among the fishermen of the Volga that these clever birds disgorge the fish they have pouched, and, laying them down on the sand, make a fair division of the total catch, the sentries being also in due proportion rewarded for their vigilant services.

ILLUMINATION FROM A MS. OF THE FIFTEENTH CENTURY IN THE LIBRARY OF THE MONASTERY OF THE
RESURRECTION, OR NEW JERUSALEM, MOSCOW.

CHAPTER VII.

SOUTH RUSSIA.

COMING from the north, the first town of any importance in Southern
Russia is Kursk, three hundred and thirty-five miles from Moscow
in an almost direct line, the railway passing through the cities of Tula (the
Russian Birmingham) and Orel, the centre of a rich agricultural district
connected by rail, on the west, with Riga on the Baltic, and on the south-
east with Tsaritsyn on the Volga. Authentic records attest the existence of
Kursk in 1032, and in 1095 it was held by Isiaslaf, son of Vladimir
Monomachus, from whom it passed alternately to the Princes of Chernigof
and of Pereyaslavl. In the thirteenth century it was razed to the ground by
the Tartars. In 1586 the southern frontiers of Muscovy were fortified, and
Kursk became one of the principal places on that line of defence against
the Crimean Tartars and the Poles. Its disasters and sufferings as a military
outpost ceased only towards the end of the seventeenth century, after Little
Russia (the more southerly districts watered by the Dnieper) submitted to
the Tsar Alexis.

We are now almost in the heart of the *Chernozem*, or black soil country, so called from the rich black loam of which its surface is composed to a depth of two and three yards and more. These vast plains were known to Herodotus, Strabo, and other ancient geographers only in their present *steppe*, or flat and woodless condition. It is a great relief to the eye to see at last a handsomely-built city like Kursk, perched, relatively to the surrounding flatness, on an elevation, and almost smothered in the verdure of numerous gardens. There is, however, not much to see within it, for even the churches are mostly not older than the second half of the eighteenth century.

The more southerly part of the province of Kursk is in the *Ukraine*, or ancient border country. Its semi-nomadic population obtained in early days the designation of Cossacks. This word is not Slavonic, but Turkish; and

PLOUGHING ON THE STEPPES.

although it long denoted in Russia a free man, or, rather, a man free to do anything he chose, it had been used by the Tartar hordes to designate the lower class of their horsemen. From the princes of the House of Rurik these southerly districts passed into the possession of Lithuania, and, later, into those of Poland. Little Russia was another arbitrary name anciently given to a great part of what has been also known as the Ukraine. No fixed geographical limits can be assigned to either of these designations, and especially to the Ukraine of the Poles or the Muscovites; for as the borders or marches became safe and populated, they were absorbed by the dominant power, and ultimately incorporated into provinces. Little Russia is, in fact, a term now used only to denote the Southern Russians as distinguished principally from the Great Russians of the more central part of the empire.

There is a strongly-marked difference in the outward appearance, the mode of life, and even the cast of thought of these two branches of the Slav race. The language of the Little Russian, or *Hohol*, as he is contemptuously called by his more vigorous northern brother, is a cross between the Polish and the Russian, although nearer akin to the Muscovite than to the Polish tongue. Ethnographically, also, the Little Russians become gradually fused with the White Russians of the north-west (Mohilef and Vitebsk) and with the Slovaks of the other side of the Carpathians. The *Malo-Ros* (Little Russian) is physically a better, though a less muscular, man than the *Veliko-Ros*, or Great Russian. He is taller, finer-featured, and less rude and primitive in his domestic surroundings. The women have both beauty and grace, and make the most of those qualities by adorning themselves in neat and picturesque costumes, resembling strongly those of the Roumanian and Transylvanian peasantry. Their houses are not like those of other parts of Russia—log huts, full, generally, of vermin and cockroaches ; but wattled, thatched, and whitewashed cottages, surrounded by gardens, and kept internally in order and cleanliness.

Their lives are altogether more happy, although their songs, full of deep feeling, and not without a vein of romance are, like those of all Slavs, plaintive and in the minor key. The men sing of the daring exploits of their Cossack forefathers, who were not freebooters like the old Cossacks of the Volga, but courageous men engaged in a life-and-death struggle with nomadic hordes, and later with internal enemies, Poles and rebels. The greater refinement of the women of Little Russia is attributable to the comparative ease of their lives in a fertile country, with a climate more genial than that of the more northerly parts of the empire. There the Great and the White Russians had to contend with a soil much less productive, with swamps which had to be drained, with thick forests which had to be cleared, with wild beasts which had to be destroyed or guarded against, and with frost and snow that left scarcely four months in the year for labour in the field.

The upper classes of South Russia, enriched by the cultivation of large and fertile estates, and favoured in their social development by long contact with the ancient Western civilisation of Poland, exhibit a similar superiority over the bulk of their compeers in Great Russia. Except, however, in the case of the larger landed proprietors, the every-day life of the Southern Russian bears a strong resemblance to that of the Irish squireen. There is a strong tinge of the same *insouciance* as to the material future, and an equal propensity to reckless hospitality, to sport (principally coursing), social jollification, and to a great extent to card-playing. Indeed, there are well-appointed country seats in the South of Russia in which the long summer days are entirely spent in card-playing, with interruptions only for meals. There are horses in plenty in the stable, and vehicles of every description to which they can be harnessed; but 'taking a drive' through endless cornfields along natural roads or tracks, parched, cracked, and dusty one day, and presenting the next a surface of black mud, offers but few attractions to the ladies, and vehicular locomotion is therefore resorted to only as a matter of necessity, on journeys to estates or towns often fifty to one hundred miles distant. Country life, indeed, has no great attractions in any part of Russia

A PEASANT GIRL OF 'GREAT RUSSIA.'

Proper, and ever since the Emancipation of the Serfs and the accompanying extinction of the power and authority of the proprietary classes, absenteeism has been largely on the increase, to the advantage solely of the principal provincial towns, and of certain capitals and watering-places in Western Europe. Thus, while Kursk and Kharkof owe much of their riches and progress to the immigration of landed proprietors from the northerly and eastern districts of the 'Black Soil Zone,' Kief is the resort of the more princely landlords of the south-western districts, strongly and favourably affected by Polish culture.

In Kief we see the 'Mother of Russian towns,' planted by Northmen on their way from Novgorod the Great to Byzantium which they reached by descending the Dnieper and crossing the Black Sea in 200 viking ships. About A.D. 882 it became, as we have previously mentioned, the seat of the paramount throne of the Variag (*Varægr*) principalities. Its close intercourse with Constantinople, after the conversion of Vladimir to Christianity, and his marriage with the sister of the Emperor of Byzantium, contributed so much to its prosperity and importance that in the 11th century no fewer than four hundred churches stood within its walls. From that time also Kief has continued to be the Jerusalem, the Canterbury of the Russian empire. Conflagrations, intestine commotions, wars, and Tartar sieges in 1240, 1496, and 1500, swept away the grand monuments of Christian antiquity which the city once possessed. Traces of them are to be found only in the much-restored Cathedral of St. Sophia, and in the ruined stonework of the gilt gate which Boleslas the Brave in the 11th century opened with a sword (now in the cathedral at Cracow) that was long after used at the coronation of the Kings of Poland. The original Scandinavo-Slavic character of the great city was lost during the occupation of the provinces of which it was the capital, first by the Lithuanians (from 1320), and then by the Poles until 1667, when by a treaty with Poland Muscovy regained the Ukraine on the left bank of the Dnieper, together with Kief. It was only at the second partition of Poland (1793) that all the districts which now constitute the 'South-western Provinces' of Volhynia, Podolia, and Kief (of which Kief is the seat of administration) passed finally under the Russian sceptre.

But interrupting here for awhile our description of the city, we proceed to give, as concisely as the subject will permit, an account of the great event which made it glorious and memorable to all ages, viz., the conversion of the Russian people to Christianity nine centuries ago.

Partly from motives of policy, Olga, Regent of Kief, had embraced Christianity at Constantinople about the year 955; but it was left to her grandson Vladimir to establish the Christian religion in his dominions, and to become the founder of the Russo-Greek Church. Nestor, who lived between 1050 and 1116, gives a very circumstantial account of the conversion of Vladimir in A.D. 988, and a very interesting epitome of it exists in the late Dean Stanley's *Lectures on the History of the Eastern Church*, from which we shall here quote a few passages. In the year 986 envoys from the different religious bodies of the then known world came to Vladimir, at Kief, to induce him to abandon pagan worship. The first to arrive were Mussulmen from the Bolgar kingdom on the Volga, who urged him to believe in their religion and to honour Mahomet. To the question ' In what does your religion consist?' they replied that they believed in God, and also in what the Prophet taught: circumcision, abstinence from pork and wine, and after death life in a harem. The rude prince would not, however, accept the prohibitions, and above all, the prohibition of drinking. 'Drinking is the great delight of Russians,' he said; 'we cannot live without it.'

Next came the representatives of Western Christendom, which was then fearfully expecting the end of the world, under a general feeling of despondency, the Papal See having at that epoch, says the late Dean Stanley, 'become the prey of ruffians and profligates.'

They came from the Pope to tell him that their religion was the true one: 'We fear God, who made the heaven and earth, the stars and the

INTRODUCTION OF CHRISTIANITY INTO RUSSIA.

moon, and every living creature, whilst thy gods are of wood.' On learning that the law of the Latin Church commanded fasting, and eating and drinking only in honour of God, Vladimir told them to 'go home,' with the objection: 'Our fathers did not believe in your religion, nor did they receive it from the Pope.' Some Jews, who explained their belief, the requirements of their law, and their dissidence from Christians and Mahometans, were also dismissed in a summary manner. They had been led to confess that they had been dispersed for their sins throughout the world. 'What,' said Vladimir, 'you wish to teach others; you whom God has rejected and dispersed? Do you wish, perhaps, that we should suffer the same?'

A 'Philosopher from Greece' came last. He derided the religion and the practice of the Mahometans, condemned the celebration of Mass by the Roman Church with unleavened bread—the point on which the two greatest Churches of the world had been torn asunder—and explained why the 'Germans and Greeks' believed in Him whom the Jews had crucified. He triumphed over the other envoys by exhibiting to Vladimir a tablet on which was painted the scene of the Last Judgment. The prince was impelled to exclaim, 'Happy are those who are on the right; woe to the sinners who are on the left!' But he would not consent to be baptized until he had been more fully instructed about each religion. For this purpose he sent wise men 'to examine the faith of each and the manner of their worship.' These reported in A.D. 987 that the Mahometans 'prayed with their heads covered, and that their stench was insupportable;' while of the German and Roman Churches they represented that although they were better than the Mussulman mosques, they had 'no ornaments nor beauty.' It is curious to find in this objection such early evidence of an innate human yearning to combine the beautiful and the impressive with religious worship. There is no record of any adornment in the rude temples of the Pagan Northmen and Slavs, and even their idols were coarsely hewn out of wood or stone. This yearning appears to have been fully satisfied at Constantinople, at that period celebrated for the splendour of its ceremonial both of Church and State. It was in the Church of St. Sophia, then all gorgeous with gold and mosaics, that the Russian emissaries witnessed a service which had purposely been rendered more than ordinarily magnificent. They were struck by the multitude of lights and the chanting of the hymns; but what most filled them with astonishment was the appearance of the deacons and sub-deacons issuing from the sanctuary with torches in their hands and with white linen wings on their shoulders, and at whose presence the people fell on their knees and cried, *Kyrie eleison !*[1] They were told by the wily Byzantines that these were angels who had come down from heaven to mingle in the service; and wanting no further proof of the trueness of the Greek religion, which surpassed all others in the grandeur of its form of worship, they hastened back to Kief.

Vladimir did not long hesitate to act on the recommendations of his envoys. But he first besieged the rich city of Khersonesus in the Crimea, founded by Heraclean Greeks, and then made as a condition, both of not subjecting to a similar fate the Byzantine capital and of his immediate conversion to Christianity, a marriage between himself and Anne, the sister of the Emperor Basil Porphyrogenitus. This sacrifice was made, and Vladimir was baptised A.D. 988 in the Church of the Holy Mother of God, at Khersonesus, now replaced by a splendid cathedral[2] in commemoration of the nine hundredth anniversary of the conversion of the Russian people to Christianity. This was effected wholesale. Under the stern orders and

---

[1] *Lectures on the Eastern Church*, p. 300.   [2] *See* p. 147.

threats of the prince, all the men, women, and children at Kief were bathed in the waters of the Dnieper; some sat on the banks, some plunged in, others swam, whilst the priests procured from Constantinople read the prayers. Perún, the huge wooden idol, was dragged over the hills at a horse's tail, scourged by twelve horsemen, and cast into the river. We may well agree with Nestor that it must have been 'a sight wonderfully curious and beautiful to see.'

From this centre the Christian religion spread gradually over Russia, by the example, influence, or command of the lesser princes of the Rurik line. Both the late Dean of Westminster and the late Count D. Tolstoi, the author of *Romanism in Russia* (the eminent Minister of the Interior, recently deceased), point out the prominent fact in this conversion, namely that, almost exceptionally in Europe, it was effected without the agency of missionaries. Gaul, England, and Germany were Christianized respectively by a Martin, an Augustine, and a Boniface, but there was no corresponding apostle in Russia except Vladimir, on whom the Russian Church has conferred the same title as that of Constantine the Great: *Isapostolos*, or 'Equal to an Apostle.'

A NUN COLLECTING MONEY FOR A CONVENT.

It would lead us too far to describe, however faintly, the development of the Russo-Greek Church through the four periods into which its history is divided. Suffice it to say that it was consolidated between the beginning of the fourteenth century and the middle of the seventeenth, subjected to gradual changes in matters of liturgy, principally by Nicon, whose doings we sketched on our way to Moscow, and reformed to a certain extent during the reigns of Peter I., Catherine II., and more recent sovereigns. It remains essentially Eastern, and in close connection with autocracy. From the Roman Catholic Church it differs strongly on many points. It does not, of course, recognise the spiritual supremacy of the Pope; and in respect of matters of faith and doctrine, it denies that the Holy Ghost proceeds from the Son, rejects purgatory, predestination, indulgences, and dispensations; holds the necessity of complete submersion of the body at baptism, except in the case of danger to life and under other urgent circumstances; and affirms, in regard to the Eucharist, whilst admitting the doctrine of transubstantiation, that the holy bread must be leavened. Another important distinction is that, on the secular or 'white' clergy, marriage is obligatory, although a second marriage is forbidden to a widowed priest. The Russian Church also retains the Gregorian Calendar.

As regards the Anglican Church, some of the principal points of doctrine are unreconcileable with those of the Russo-Greek faith, and another great stumbling-block against official communion between these two Churches continues to be the denial by the Russian Synod of the apostolical succession of the Anglican bishops. But even if these points were conceded, it is difficult to see what practical harmony and co-operation could be established between the Churches for any useful purpose. Many generations will have to pass before the Russian clergy attain a high level of culture. Their almost entire material dependence on the rude, uneducated masses with which they are socially blended militates against their worldly regeneration. Their position in the social scale is well exemplified in the following anecdote. Not very many years ago a young Englishman was staying at the country house or mansion of one of the greatest and most highly-educated noblemen in Russia. To his surprise, the lady of the house said to him one day she had a great favour to ask, and after much genuine hesitation on the part of the lady, she divulged that she would like to ask the village priest to dinner! And yet he was no ordinary rural 'pope,' compelled to do his own tilling and harvesting, or associated with his parishioners in their love of *vodki*; but a man of orthodox learning, well informed also on lay matters relating to his own country, scrupulously clean, and clad in a handsome cassock of mauve silk. The Englishman, who happened to know Russian, took a seat beside him, and the interest he took in the 'little father's' observations was so great that it was mistaken for an excessive politeness, for which he was profusely thanked by the hostess, who declared that his kindness to the priest was much more than she had expected even from his known amiability!

The services of the Church are conducted in the old Slavonic, into which the Scriptures were translated after Cyril and Methodius had introduced the semi-Greek alphabet, which is still used with some modifications. This was an advantage which Pagans converted by the Latin Church were not permitted to possess, and which accounts, in some degree, for the propagation of Christianity in Russia without the aid of missionaries. Time has, however, so much modified the Russian language, that the ancient Church Slavonic is now practically almost as different as Latin is to the vernacular of Roman Catholic countries the purest in ethnological descent.

We cannot compress even a superficial reference to the services of the Russo-Greek Church into fewer sentences than those used by Mr. Maskell in his oft-quoted work :—

'The ceremonial of the Greek Church is excessively complex, and the symbolical meanings by which it represents the dogmas of religion are everywhere made the subjects of minute observance. During the greater part of the Mass the "royal doors" (in the altar screen) are closed: the deacons remain for the most part without, now and again entering for a short time. From time to time a pope or popes pass throughout the church, amongst the crowd, incensing the holy pictures in turn; the voice of the officiating priest is raised within, and is answered in deep tones by the deacons without. Now from one corner comes a chant of many voices, now from another a single one intones. . . . Now the doors fly open, and a fleeting glimpse is gained of the celebrant through the thick rolling clouds of incense. Then they are closed again suddenly. To a stranger, unable to follow and in ignorance of the meaning, the effect is bewildering.'

The religious music of Russia 'has a peculiar charm of its own, far above the barbarous dis-cords that are to be heard in Greek and other churches of the East at the present moment. There is a sweetness and attractiveness in the unaccompanied chanting of the choir, in the deep bass tones of the men mingling with the plain-tive trebles of younger voices which is indescrib-able in its harmony. It is unlike any other; yet underneath lies the original tinge of Orien-talism, the wailing tones of all barbaric music. No accompaniment, no instrumental music of any kind, is permitted. Bass voices of extraordinary depth and power are the most desired. It is said that the tones now used in the Russian Church are comparatively

A SOUTH RUSSIAN WOMAN.

modern. They have long been written in the modern style with five lines in the treble clef, not as in the Gregorian, in four lines on the tenor or bass clef.'

Next to a coronation at Moscow, the most gorgeous ceremony of the Russian Church is that of Easter Eve, when as the clock strikes twelve the officiating priest announces that 'Christ is risen,' on which each member of the crowded congregation falls on his knees, crossing himself and responding

K

sotto voce, 'Yea, verily He has risen.' The choir bursts out simultaneously
in the beautiful Easter hymn of the Church; every bell in city, town, or
village rings out its merriest peals, and no one who has not been in Russia
can realize the impressive effect of the ringing of so many bells, as a rule
the largest and sweetest in tone of any in the world. The churches are on
this great occasion bathed in light from chandeliers, lustres, and huge
candelabra, the congregation adding no small amount of illumination from the
wax taper which each worshipper, prince or pauper, is bound to carry in his
hand. Friends, irrespective of sex, then give to each other three kisses, with
the paschal salutation, 'Christ is risen,' and, as a matter of fact, continue to
do so for some time after Easter Sunday, until the salutation has been
exchanged with each friend or acquaintance. As soon as the service is over,
the people rush back to their homes, to 'break the fast' which a majority
of them have kept, more or less strictly, for the previous forty days. Bread
and a kind of conical cake made of curds, both consecrated beforehand, and
hard-boiled eggs dyed mostly red, will be found even in the lowliest cottage,
while the tables of the higher and middle classes groan also with viands
and refreshments of a more solid kind. Wine, beer and *vodka* continue
to flow throughout the country for several days, with the result that this
sudden break from subsistence on fish, dried mushrooms, and groats mixed
with hempseed oil, to inordinate indulgence in meat and drink, tells heavily
on the public health after Easter is over.

The exchange of dyed or painted eggs at the time of paschal salutation is
a general custom throughout Russia, and so are the games played with those
eggs; such as rolling them down a hollowed-out piece of wood raised at one end
by a stand about twelve inches high. The victory is to the owner of the egg
which rolls furthest on the smooth floor, and he can also win the competing eggs
which his own well-directed egg may touch while rolling. Another favourite
Easter-tide game is the testing of the relative strength of eggs. Those with
the hardest point crack the weaker shells, and therefore win the wager—
which may be the damaged egg or a small coin. It is curious that the
existence of very similar games with eggs 'on Pace-egg day,' or Easter
Monday, has recently been reported from Northumberland.[1] No less curious
is it to know that a competitive tapping of dyed eggs at Easter-tide prevails
also in some parts of Sweden and Norway.

It is now, however, time to return to Kief. Picturesquely perched on
steep elevations of the right bank of the Dnieper, the ancient Borysthenes,
which falls into the Black Sea after a course of more than 1000 miles
(being therefore one of the greatest rivers in Russia), the city is divided into
the Old Town, the Pechersk, the site of the famed monastery of that name,
and the Podol, or Town on the Cliff. The latter is the commercial quarter,
and is regularly laid out with broad streets worthy of the handsome houses

---

[1] *St. James's Gazette*, April 27, 1889.

which line them. The best part of the city, containing the principal official and other residences, and shaded with fine old trees, is between the Pechersk quarter and the Old Town, enclosed within earthen ramparts; the latter was anciently the site of the Pagan Pantheon from which Perùn (or Jupiter)[1] was ignominiously dragged by Vladimir, who, in the place of Perùn's temple, erected a Christian church dedicated to St. Basil. This edifice is only nominally extant, for it was reconstructed in the twelfth century and again in 1695, and thoroughly restored in 1826. Here also is the great Cathedral of St. Sophia, founded in A.D. 1017, destroyed two centuries later by the Tartars, restored between 1385 and 1390, repaired in the seventeenth century, and renovated once more in 1850. Its original form—a reduced copy of the Church of St. Sophia at Constantinople—has been much altered by repairs and additions, and the ancient structure has in reality been preserved only in the centre of the existing mass, where we also find internally some remnants of the work of Byzantine artists. Some of their beautiful mosaics have been preserved on the altar walls and in places on the wall-supports and the arches. Above the Metropolitan's stall are figures in mosaic of Byzantine prelates of the third and fourth centuries, and in a lower tier, divided from the upper by wide bands of ornamentation in similar work, is a superbly executed representation of the Lord's Supper. Another remarkable figure in mosaic is that of the Virgin Mary, on the convex surface of the hemispherical vaulting above the Metropolitan's stall. Equally interesting are the Greek frescoes on the wall-supports and partly in the upper galleries, which in early ages contained chapels. All these were discovered in 1843 under the whitewash which had been applied to them while the cathedral was (1590–1633) in the possession of the Uniats (Catholics, *ritus Græci*), whose priests are depicted on the pillars that support the dome, wearing the Catholic tonsure and with shaven chins. These effigies bear witness to the attempt made by Roman Catholicism to wean the Ruthenian or South Russian peasantry from the Russo-Greek Church, and they have survived the results of those labours, for the Uniat Faith or Church exists no longer, its adherents having been re-united to the Russo-Greek Church by official conversion and 'administrative measures.'[2]

The tomb of Yaroslaf, the founder of the cathedral, stands in a chapel dedicated to St. Vladimir. This, with the relics of a Metropolitan who was decapitated by the Tartars in 1497, is among the principal treasures of St. Sophia.

The Tithes Church, which, although consecrated only in 1842, is erected on the site of a sacred edifice bearing the same name, built A.D. 989 by Greek artists and artisans, is considered to be an exact reproduction of the original, the most ancient *basilica* in Russia of the Byzantine style. Its mosaic floor in front of the principal altar belonged to the original church.

---

[1] The Lithuanian Perkùn.

[2] The Uniat Faith is spreading among the Slavs of Austro-Hungary and the Balkan peninsula.

In the ruins of the latter were found the tomb, with only the head, of St. Vladimir. These are now deposited under a block of grey marble within the new church.

For a view of the Podol quarter we must repair to the terrace of the Church of St. Andrew, built in the elegant proportions of the style of Louis XV., in 1744, and standing on the spot on which St. Andrew, the Apostle of Greece and of Scythia, planted, according to an ancient legend, the first cross seen in Russia, predicting that on hills about 'shall hereafter shine forth the grace of God; there shall be a great city, and God shall cause many churches to rise within it.' To the right we now see the gilt domes of the Bratski Monastery, with a handsome cathedral built by Mazeppa for the use of the Uniats, and an Orthodox Ecclesiastical Academy, which was formerly a Jesuit College; while on the left are the shining cupolas of the huge Ascension Convent for Women. Early in spring, when the Dnieper assumes in front of Kief the dimensions of a vast lake, the view from St. Andrew's terrace is more than ordinarily striking.

It is easy among such surroundings and such memories to realise the spectacle of the great gathering of the prelates and priests of the Russo-Greek Church and of the Eastern Churches in close communication with it, that took place at Kief in July, 1888, on the occasion of the celebration of the nine hundredth anniversary of the conversion of the Russian people to Christianity. Even the Archbishop of Canterbury was present in the spirit, for his grace addressed a letter of congratulation, sympathy, and goodwill to the Metropolitan of Kief, in which also regret was expressed that, owing to an assembly in London of the Universal Episcopate of the Anglican Church, it had been found impossible to send 'a bishop to Kief to represent the Church of England.'

We have left to the last our mention of the most interesting sight in Kief, and one for which the city is well worth visiting. This is the Pecherskaya Lavra, or Monastery, the first in rank in Russia, and the most ancient in origin (1055), enclosed within the immense fortress that crowns the hill of the Pechersk quarter of the city. Approached from the east, the gilt and coloured domes and spires of the monastery, brought into strong relief by the massive fortress walls and bastions, have a strikingly picturesque effect, and at once arrest attention from almost every part of Kief. We mention *en passant* that the huge arsenal which the fortress shelters supplies all the troops in South Russia with arms, while its barracks are capable of accommodating thirty thousand men. Kief is the most important strategical point in the South of Russia, and is intended to serve as a basis of operations.

The monastery is entered by a gate ornamented with frescoes of St. Anthony and St. Theodosius, the first two abbots. Its principal cathedral, with seven gilt cupolas, is reached by a fine avenue of trees, flanked by the cells of the brotherhood. The belfry alongside is more than three hundred

feet high; internally, however, the style of architecture is neither elegant
nor imposing, and the ancient stalls of the monks perpetuate its somewhat
Roman Catholic appearance. The richly-decorated ceiling is scarcely seen
even by the light of the innumerable tapers which are kept constantly
burning by pilgrims who come from every part of the empire, and who are
certainly not fewer than two hundred thousand in number each year. So
many sacristies have already been described that we must pass over the
treasures of the Pechersk Monastery, in the shape of *ikons*, chasubles, church

THE PECHERSK MONASTERY AT KIEF.

vessels, and pectoral crosses of great value and religious interest. An object
of special veneration is the true head of St. Vladimir, which the cathedral
claims to hold in a side chapel, although the veritable tomb which contained
it is undoubtedly in the Tithes Church of which we have spoken.

The monastery owes the principal part of its celebrity and of its
revenues to the neighbouring catacombs of St. Anthony and St. Theodosius,
excavated in the limestone of the high river-bank. They extend a
considerable distance in passages blackened by the torches of visitors, and

on either side of which lie saints in open coffins, with palls of cloth and silk worked in gold and silver; their mummified hands are so placed as to be able to receive the devotional kisses of the pilgrims, who individually apply for the intercession of the saint most renowned for removing some distinct besetting sin. In one cell are the remains of eleven 'martyrs,' who voluntarily and at one and the same time immured themselves in it, and took food, until they died, through the small windows from which we turn away with a shudder. Nestor, the annalist, lies in the first catacomb, and St. Anthony, its founder, at the extreme end of the gallery. We are shown his small chapel and the cell in which he passed the last fifteen years of his life without breathing the fresh air. The catacombs of St. Theodosius, to the south of those of St. Anthony, are on a smaller scale, and as they contain only forty-six bodies (the others have seventy-three) of departed saints of a secondary order, they are not held in equal veneration. Nevertheless, we find here also the remains of ten monks who had immured themselves in order, as they believed, to gain the kingdom of heaven. One 'martyr' is exhibited who, in fulfilment of a vow of continence, died from being buried almost up to his neck for some months; and in that posture his body still remains.

Other ancient catacombs have recently been discovered under the city itself, but their origin and history have not yet been ascertained. Numerous human remains and coffins have been found in them, and the Christian character of the interments is evidenced by the pectoral crosses that have also come to light.

What a contrast between these primitive works of man and the achievements of the skill and labour of the nineteenth century, typified in the two grand bridges by which the Dnieper is spanned close to Kief! The Nicholas Suspension Bridge, 6755 feet in length, is considered to be a noble monument of engineering art. It was built between 1848 and 1855 by an Englishman, Mr. Charles Vignolles. In proximity to it is the splendid girder bridge constructed by a Russian engineer, over which the railway passes.

Kharkof, to the east of Kief, with a population of 160,000, is the principal seat of trade in South Russia, being a centre from which the products and manufactures of Northern and Central Russia are spread throughout the provinces to the east and south, down even to the Caucasus.

Sugar, largely produced in this part of Russia from beetroot and 'bounty-fed,' and corn, brandy, wool and hides from the central provinces, are largely sold at the five fairs held each year at Kharkof, which has also reason to be proud of its university with upwards of six hundred students, and of its connection by rail with the shores of the Baltic and those of the Black and Azof Seas. In 1765, Kharkof became the capital of the Ukraine, after having been a Cossack outpost town since 1647, when Poland finally ceded the province to Muscovy. Anciently, this was the camping-ground of nomadic tribes, particularly of the Khazars, and later the high road of the Tartar invaders of Russia, whether from the Crimea or the shores of the Caspian. In the province of Kharkof are found those remarkable idols of stone which we have seen in the Historical Museum at Moscow, and a vast number of tumuli, which have yielded coins establishing the fact of an early intercourse both with Rome and Arabia.

Poltava, also a place of extensive trade, principally in wool, horses, and cattle, is familiar to us in connection with the defeat of Charles XII. by Peter the Great in 1709. The centre of the field so disastrous to the

THE BATTLE OF POLTAVA.

Swedes is marked by a mound which covers the remains of their slain. Two monuments commemorate the victory.

At Ekaterinoslaf we are again on the great Dnieper. It was only a village when Catherine II., descending the river from Kief in a stately barge accompanied by Joseph II. of Austria, King Stanislaus Augustus of Poland and a brilliant suite, raised it to the dignity of a town bearing her own name. On that occasion she laid the first stone of a cathedral which was not destined to be completed on the imposing scale she had projected, and which has been reduced to one-sixth in the edifice that was consecrated only in 1835. The town consists of only one row of buildings, almost concealed in gardens and running for nearly three miles parallel with the Dnieper. Catherine's Palace, a bronze statue which represents her clad in Roman armour and crowned, and the garden of her magnificent favourite, Prince Potemkin, constitute the 'sights' of Ekaterinoslaf, the more striking feature of which, however, is its Jewish population, huddled together in a special quarter between the river and the bazaar. A considerable number of them pursue the favourite Jewish occupation of money-changing, and the Ekaterinoslaf Prospect is dotted with their stands and their money-chests, painted blue and red.

We now follow the route taken by Catherine II. in 1787, and descend to Kherson, at the delta of the Dnieper. In commemoration of her visit, she caused to be inscribed in Slavonic over the Cathedral of St. Catherine : 'Dedicated to the Saviour of the human race by Catherine II.' By her directions, Prince Potemkin, the founder of the town, was buried in this cathedral in 1791, but her son, the Emperor Paul, ordered the remains to be exhumed, and to be buried in a hole under the floor of the crypt, from which they were again disinterred in 1874, and restored to a more fitting abiding-place, marked by a tombstone of white marble, on which are recorded his principal achievements.

Within a high circular wall near the Church of the Assumption is a simple obelisk, with a sun-dial on one face and a portrait-medallion on the other. An inscription on it in Russian and Latin tells us that 'Howard died on the 20th January, in the year 1790, in the 65th year of his age— Vixit propter Alios. Alios Salvos Fecit.' The great English philanthropist died and was buried in a village about four miles north of Kherson. In the month of November, 1789, he set out from Kherson on horseback to visit a lady at some distance on the banks of the Dnieper. Being lightly clad, he caught a cold, on which typhus fever supervened. The monument over his grave is a block of marble surmounted by a sun-dial, according to his last wish, and the inscription is : 'Johannes Howard, Ad Sepulchrum Stas, Quisquis es, Amici, 1790.'

A drive over forty miles of steppe, somewhat relieved in its monotony by numerous ancient tumuli, brings those who do not proceed by steamer to the great naval station and commercial port of Nicolaef, at the junction of the Ingul with the Bûg. It was the site until 1775 of a Cossack *setch*, or fortified settlement and in 1789 it received its present appellation in commemoration of the capture of Otchakof from the Turks on the feast-day of St. Nicholas. Destined from the first by Potemkin to be the harbour of a Russian fleet in the Black Sea, temporarily neglected by the naval authorities, Nicolaef re-asserted its claim to that proud position after the fall of Sevastopol. It owes much of its present affluence to the sound administration of Admiral Samuel Greig, son of the admiral of Scotch parentage who, with the aid of some equally gallant countrymen, won for the Russians the naval battle of Chesmé in 1769. Next to Odessa, Nicolaef is the handsomest town in New Russia, as this part of the country was called after its conquest from the Turks and Tartars. Its large trade, mostly in grain, has been greatly promoted by the railway, which now connects this important harbour with Kharkof and other rich agricultural centres.

Of the six ports on the neighbouring Sea of Azof, Taganrog, where

A NOGAI TARTAR.

Alexander I. died in 1825, is the most considerable, although steamers have to anchor at a considerable distance from it, owing to the shallowness of the roadstead. The annual value of its exports of corn, wool, tallow, &c., is about five millions sterling, and, as at Nicolaef, British shipping is chiefly employed in the trade. Much of the produce shipped here comes from Rostof on the Don, the chief centre of inland trade in the south-east provinces of Russia, and one in which many industries (especially the manipulation of tobacco grown in the Caucasus and the Crimea) are pursued. A short distance above this great mart is Novocherkask, the capital of the 'Country

A RUSSIAN SHOEMAKER.

of the Don Cossacks,' anciently the abode of Scythians, Sarmatians, Huns, Bolgars, Khazars and Tartars. The present population dates from the sixteenth century, when renegades from Muscovy and vagrants of every description formed themselves into Cossack or robber communities. They attacked the Tartars and Turks, and in 1637 took the Turkish fortress of Azof. Until the reign of Peter the Great the powerful and independent Cossacks were not much interfered with, but from 1718 they were gradually brought under subjection to the Tsar, whom they powerfully assisted in subsequent wars. The town was founded in 1804, and is adorned with a bronze monument to the famous Hetman (Ataman or chief) Platof, leader of the Cossacks between 1770 and 1816. It is usual to bestow on the Russian heir-apparent the title of 'Ataman' of the Don Cossacks. The last investiture with the Cossack *bâton* took place in 1887, when also the reigning Emperor confirmed, at a 'circle,' or open-air assemblage, all the ancient rights and privileges of the warlike Cossacks of the Don.

Odessa on the Black Sea is the *Odessus* of the Greeks, the *La Ginestra* of the Genoese, and the *Hadji-Bey* of the Turks. It was not until 1791 that the fortress of Hadji-Bey and the whole of the Turkish provinces of Otchakof were annexed to the Russian empire, in virtue of the Treaty of Jassy. Catherine II. employed the Neapolitan De Ribas and the Frenchman De Volante (both in her military service,) to construct a town and harbour, which, peopled mostly by Greeks and Albanians, received in 1795 its present modernized name of Odessa. Various privileges and immunities were later granted to the city, but it owes its present prosperity chiefly to the talents and energy of the Duke Emanuel de Richelieu, a French *émigré*, who became its first governor in 1803. Eleven years later, when he was succeeded by Count Langeron, also a Frenchman, the population of Odessa had grown from nine to twenty-five thousand. It is now 240,000, thanks in a great measure to the privileges of a free port, enjoyed by the city between 1817 and 1857. Prince Woronzoff, who in 1823 took up his residence at Odessa as Governor-General of New Russia, carried on with great vigour and enlightenment the works of construction and improvement initiated or contemplated by his foreign predecessors. Under such advantages we are not surprised to find that Odessa has developed into a handsome city of South European aspect, and with an export trade now valued at ten millions sterling. Its splendid harbour, rendered secure by a breakwater designed by Sir Charles Hartley, is annually visited by at least fifteen hundred steamers, of which one-half are under the British flag. Their crews have the advantage of an institute and reading-room, established in 1875 by Consul-General Stanley, and under the patronage of H.R.H. the Duke of Edinburgh.

Formerly enveloped in clouds of fine dust, devoid of any vegetation beyond a few shrubs and sickly acacias, and dependent for its supply of water upon rain-tanks and a few brackish springs, Odessa has now an atmosphere pure and bright, trees and gardens of great beauty, and ample means of quenching thirst—thanks to the expenditure of over a million pounds sterling by the British Odessa Waterworks Company, Limited, whose suffering shareholders are still wailing over the unprofitable (to them) investment of so much hard cash. The water is brought from the Dnieper, thirty miles distant, through thirty-inch pipes, after being carefully filtered.

The combination of Russian, Greek and Jewish sharpness that prevails at Odessa has not on the whole been favourable to the employment of foreign capital. The Greek element has, however, only a secondary influence in the administration of local affairs, although it prevails in the great export trade of the city. Nor is the power of the Jews so considerable as it once was. In fact, it is likely to disappear under the 'baiting' to which the members of that community are periodically subject. This culminated, not many years ago, in a notice put up by a certain chartered body in the sea-bathing establishment of which it contrived to dispossess the municipality. The notice was in the following words: 'No dogs or Jews are allowed to bathe here.'

It is much to be desired that a more sober and correct view in regard to the Israelite community at Odessa should supervene, and that due allowance should be made for the disabilities under which the Jews have so long struggled in Russia, as they did in days long gone by in England and in other countries to which they resorted, with no small advantage to the states in which they were permitted to become free citizens and loyal subjects.

ILLUMINATION FROM A MS. OF THE TENTH OR ELEVENTH CENTURY IN THE IMPERIAL PUBLIC
LIBRARY, ST. PETERSBURG.

CHAPTER VIII.

THE CRIMEA AND CAUCASUS.

THERE is no portion of the surface of the globe more adapted to a homogeneity of mankind than the Russian empire, from the circumstance of its extension over an almost boundless expanse of level territory; and yet, although so many diversities of the human race are brought into near contact, all subject to similar rule and government, still do many continue to live, it may be said, apart, speaking their own tongue and observing their own customs and religion, as we shall discover in our journey over the Crimea and the Caucasus—the subject of this chapter.

The Crimea has a special interest for Englishmen of this generation, from its having been the battle-field of the last war in which England has been engaged with a great European power, while many of its incidents must be fresh in the memory of the middle-aged. In those days the Crimea was a somewhat distant land; whereas we may now pack up our traps and set foot at Sevastopol on the sixth day after leaving Charing Cross, for Russia's network of railways, even though studiously strategic, is being energetically proceeded with throughout the empire.

Like that part of the Russian continent with which it is connected by the narrow isthmus of Perecop, the Crimean peninsula, consisting of about nine thousand square miles, is one vast steppe, largely teeming with corn, except where the Tauric range, extending over a distance of forty-five miles,

MOUNT ST. PETER, CRIMEA.

and rising to an altitude of three thousand to four thousand feet, ensures to the inhabitants on the declivities that slope to the sea a climate suggestive of the Riviera, with vegetation varied and prolific beyond description.

Starting from Balaclava, at the west extreme of the range, by the Woronzoff (carriage) road, we first pass through the Baidar valley, the possession of which afforded so many good things, even some of the luxuries of life, to our beleaguering troops. Here the Tartar villages lie embosomed in the midst of truly lovely scenery, with luscious pastures, brooks, copses, and cornfields with green hedges, reminding one much of an English land-scape. From this valley the road leads over a spur towards the Baidar Gate, at which point there suddenly bursts on the view one of the grandest sights that it is possible to conceive, offered by a combination of mountain, cliff, and beautiful region in close proximity to the sea. In front rise the bold precipitous heights lorded over by the majestic Ai Petri (St. Peter), sturdy pines and junipers looking like tufts of verdure as they overhang the perilous brinks, while here and there from fissures in the rocks strike forth again the pine and juniper or the beech. Lower down, where the irregular declivities project into the sea, shaping the most fantastic of sea-boards, the road is constructed through a wealth of vegetation, the indigenous trees comprising the Tauric pine, juniper, yew, oak, elm, maple, ash, poplar, and the fir and beech which attain a very large size. The cypress and magnolia are beautiful in their development, and the banks are seen covered with the crocus and violet, lilies of the valley, and sweet-pea, the peonia, veronica, geranium and orchids.

The first genuine Tartar village is Kikeneis, embedded in the midst of sumptuous cultivation; and as we proceed, we from time to time pass masses of gigantic blocks of granite thrown up at various periods by the convulsions of Nature. Alupka, the seat of the late Prince Woronzoff, where two *Wellingtonia gigantea* planted in 1869 by the Prince and Princess of Wales are shown, and Mishor, are within a few miles of each other, and beyond is Gaspra, a place to which three ladies repaired, in the reign of Alexander I., for the purpose of converting the Tartars to Christianity. One of those ladies, the Countess Guacher, was better known, under different circum-stances, as the Countess de la Mothe, who was publicly whipped for being concerned in the affair of the diamond necklace of Marie Antoinette. The residences of the Grand Dukes Michael and Constantine, and of the Emperor, at Livadia, are seen from the road, none attractive in their architecture, but all surrounded by perfectly fascinating scenery.

At Yalta we are in the most fashionable watering-place in the South of Russia, its comfortable hotels and luxurious clubs attracting the wealthy from all parts during the bathing-season, which begins in April and continues to November. Excellent carriages and good saddle-horses facilitate excursions up the smiling valleys, horsemen being enabled to visit the interior of the peninsula by crossing the passes above Derekyuy or Uchan-su. Yalta is the westernmost point of the wine-growing district, which includes Massandra, Partenite, where is a church of the eighth century, Gurzuf, and Alushta at the eastern end of the range, from which village the carriage-road turns sharp away from the coast, and leads direct to Simpheropol, the capital. The Russians are very proud of the wines grown on these shores, but *connoisseurs* prefer the wines of France and Germany. The yield, including the produce

YALTA.

of Sudak on another part of the coast, amounts annually to about three million gallons, and consists of Bordeaux, Burgundies, Hocks, Madeira, and some sweet wines.

From the earliest times have nations fought for, and disputed, the possession of this narrow strip of territory—classic as the scene of the wanderings of Ulysses—because of the golden harvests to be gathered from over the hills, and of its own even temperature. History asserts that the

Cimmerians were the first inhabitants of whom so little is known; that
they were succeeded by the Tauri; replaced, seven centuries before the birth
of Christ, by Grecian colonists, who supplied their barren mother-country,
during several centuries, from what had become known as the 'granary of
Greece.' Then came the Huns, who were succeeded by the Goths, the
earliest Christian settlers, and they held possession until the proud Republic
of Genoa sent forth her galleys laden with men and arms to seize, if
possible, upon so fair a land. In 1265 the Italians occupied Theodosia,
then known as Caffa, and subsequently every other point of vantage along
the coast, forming settlements, appointing consuls or governors, establishing

INKERMANN.

an extensive and powerful hierarchy, and at the same time constructing
those splendid defences at Sudak, Theodosia, and Balaclava, of which
enough remain to excite the admiration of every passing traveller.

Visitors who throng to the south coast for the benefit of sea-bathing
travel by rail to Simpheropol, the chief town, and thence continue their
journey either by way of Sevastopol, or take the carriage-road already
alluded to, to Alushta; but the more favoured route is *via* Odessa, where
fine bi-weekly steamers convey passengers to Eupatoria, Sevastopol, Yalta,
Theodosia, and Kertch, continuing the voyage to the ports of the Caucasus.
It was near Eupatoria that the British and French forces landed, on
14th September, 1854, not to evacuate the peninsula until July, 1856, during

L.

which period were fought the decisive battles on the Alma and Chernaya, at Balaclava and on the heights of Inkermann, and the fortress of Sevastopol was evacuated after a lengthened siege and bombardment. The country between Eupatoria and Sevastopol has been compared by travellers to that around the Dead Sea, owing to its sterile and uninviting aspect, but the Saki mud baths in those parts attract numerous patients suffering from rheumatism and diseases of the skin.

The Bay of Sevastopol, four miles in length and nearly one mile at its widest part, is one of the securest harbours in the world, having an almost uniform depth of ten fathoms. The handsome town which stood on the slope of the hill and extended to the water's edge, was completely destroyed during the war, and has only of late years commenced to recover from its calamities, for it has again been decreed a naval, military, and commercial port and station, while the railway gives an immense impetus to export trade. The hotels are good, and guides are obtainable for visiting the sites of the several camps, batteries, and battle-fields, which, in a few years, will be inaccessible to the traveller, by reason of those localities becoming enclosed within the proposed new lines of defence. As the warriors fell during the siege, they were laid within small enclosures inside the divisions and batteries of attack and defence in which they were serving, so that when the land was evacuated by the contending parties it was seen to be dotted with numberless cemeteries, of which one hundred and twenty-six were inside the British lines. The Russians and French early availed themselves of facilities afforded for removing their dead to grounds specially set apart for the purpose, and raising to their memory mausoleums which remain objects of veneration, even to the destructive Tartar herdsmen, who persisted, year after year, in inflicting every kind of damage upon the memorials of our own dead; until at length the reproaches of travellers of all nations and creeds stirred to action a small body of Englishmen, supported by the Prince of Wales; with the result that all our soundest monuments have been removed from the scattered enclosures to the largest cemetery, called Cathcart's, after the gallant officer of that name who fell at Inkermann; the walls of the old enclosures are levelled, and the graves covered with two to three feet of earth, so that in a few years the very sites will be forgotten.

> ' After a length of time the lab'ring swains,
> Who turn the turf of those unhappy plains,
> Shall rusty piles from the ploughed furrow take,
> . . . . . .
> Amazed at antique titles on the stones
> And mighty relics of gigantic bones.'

Quite near to Sevastopol stood the ancient city, Khersonesus, founded by Grecian colonists seven centuries before Christ, and of whom it is recorded that they preserved their independence, and owed their prosperity and high state of civilisation during the space of one thousand years to the free institutions they enjoyed, and to competence for self-government. This city became a dependency of the Eastern empire, continuing, however, to enjoy its own municipal institutions, until taken by siege by the Russian Prince Vladimir, who restored it to the empire as one of the conditions of his receiving the Emperor's sister in marriage. Vladimir embraced Christianity and built the church, the foundations of which are to be seen in the crypt of the cathedral lately completed. Strabo men-

THE CATHEDRAL OF ST. VLADIMIR, RECENTLY COMPLETED AT KHERSONESUS.

tions Khersonesus as being a flourishing city in his day, and describes in exquisite detail the features of its neighbourhood and of the adjoining coasts, so that the student is able to verify with extraordinary minuteness the graphic delineation of that most exact of geographers, and fix with tolerable accuracy upon the sites so delightfully illustrated by honest Herodotus.

Eight miles from Khersonesus, says Strabo, is Symvolon-limen. In the *Odyssey* it is mentioned as the port of the Læstrigons, but we know it as Balaclava, now so familiar to English ears! A beautifully secure landlocked harbour, the delight of the ancients, of the Genoese, and of England too, since it was the only port of debarkation for all our *matériel* of war, and the sole safe haven for our shipping. Some of the Genoese defences of the fourteenth century remain, but nearly every vestige of the British occupation has disappeared. The inhabitants, as everywhere else on the shores of the Black Sea, are Greeks, here engaged in the pursuit of fishing and salting their gains for import—the sea at this part abounding in turbot, haddock, mackerel, bream, etc., and a species of pilchard. The road from Sevastopol to Balaclava almost skirts, on the left, the plain which was the scene of the famous cavalry charge under Lord Cardigan, now marked by an obelisk; and a branch road to the right leads to the Monastery of St. George, founded in the tenth century, that lies ensconced amidst luxuriant gardens and vineyards reaching to the sea, its inviting situation presenting a very different aspect to the sterile surroundings north of the cliff by which it is sheltered. The apartments that were occupied by Florence Nightingale during the war are shown by the monks with unaffected satisfaction, for the remembrance of that lady is respectfully preserved.

Sevastopol is thirty miles from Bakhchisarai, the last capital of the Khans, and one of the largest towns inhabited entirely by Tartars, stricter Sunnites than their co-religionists on the south coast, but equally removed from the fanaticism of Mahometanism. For instance, they are, as a rule, monogamists, and although the females are not in the habit of holding intercourse with others, they do not wear the *yashmak*, or veil, nor do they hesitate to receive aliens in their houses, should occasion arise. In their cleanly cottages the women's apartments are on an upper story, entirely apart from those of the men, the cooking department and guest-chamber being on the ground floor, the latter freely decorated with an abundance of towels embroidered in gold, silver, or silk, and well furnished with mattresses and pillows of every hue, because the larger the display, the more affluent are supposed to be the circumstances of the inmates. In the houses of the *murzas*, or nobles, the floors are covered with expensive Turkey carpets, upon which are spread reclining mattresses and bolsters in satin or velvet, and coverlets richly embroidered in gold.

These Tartars are very indolent, and never think of learning a trade; they work in their gardens and orchards from the end of May to the third week in August, during which period it is agreed among them that no festivities shall take place, and for the rest of the year they remain idle. They are hospitable, and at all times willing to welcome the belated or worn-out traveller. Their children are fair to look upon; nevertheless the females do not retain their good looks in adult age, whilst the practice of dyeing and uniting their eyebrows with a straight dark line, and staining their finger and toe-nails, and occasionally their teeth, is certainly not to their advantage.

When a Tartar is engaged to be married, he goes about for three days with a handkerchief over his head, so placed as to conceal his face, for he is a man 'with shame;' and the bride during that same period remains screened off in a darkened room, quite ready to sob if spoken to by anybody. On the wedding day, the bride, closely veiled, takes her place at her mother's side in a carriage, a pile of gaily-coloured handkerchiefs being on the seats in front, one of which is given by the mother as a wedding favour to any friend who may approach to offer his congratulations; that friend ties the kerchief round his left arm, and joins the procession as it moves along, slowly and silently, the relatives in other carriages following that in which is the bride. Should the procession pass through a village, the people turn out and stretch a rope across the road, as is the custom in the Vosges, and compel the bride to pay her 'footing;' but there is no spirit in the proceedings, no fun, no cheering, no—not one merry shout! And when the bride finally alights at the door of her future home, she is seized by a crowd of women who are in waiting, and dragged or even carried into the house and delivered to the 'happy man,' after which exciting, but still noiseless scene, the guests immediately disperse as silently as they had assembled.

A TARTAR BRIDE AND BRIDEGROOM.

Bakhchisarai is famed for its leather-work, useful and ornamental, with which it supplies the entire peninsula, for the Tartar continues to be very conservative in his tastes, remaining perfectly indifferent to every description of improvement introduced from without, whether in manufactures or in agriculture; and so we continue to see the same kind of shoes or slippers, belts, cushions, horse-trappings, etc., as have been in use amongst this people during many centuries. The Tartar does not despise even the old flint-lock gun, and prefers his native cutlery, now also manufactured at Bakhchisarai, but formerly made at Karasu-bazar, a place which, in its prosperity, used to turn out as many as 400,000 sword blades annually, chiefly for use in the Khan's army, but also for export to the Caucasus.

The great attractions of Bakhchisarai are the places of interest within easy distance, such, for instance, as Chufut-Kaleh, 'Jews' fortress,' on the summit of a rock, said to have been a stronghold since 460 B.C., and the cradle of the Karaïm, a sect of Israelites opposed to the Talmudist Jews, by whom they are looked upon as heretics. The Karaïm reject all tradition and Rabbinical writings, adhering solely to the Old Testament, whence

their designation, Karaim, or readers—readers of Holy Writ—the plural
of Kara, a reader. They esteem the high moral teaching of Jesus Christ,
in whose crucifixion, they assert, they took no part, accusing more
especially the Pharisees of having shed innocent blood; but they look for
the coming of the Messiah from the house of David, and for the rebuilding
of the Temple. The Karaim are energetic and industrious, and hold the
largest part of trade in the Crimea, where they number about 5,000. Their
precept is: 'If thou canst not do as much as thou wouldest, desire that
thou mayest do as much as thou art able to perform.' The Karaim date

BAKHCHISARAI.

the foundation of their sect from the period of the Maccabees, in the second
century B.C., when traditional lore was introduced to the prejudice of the
books of Moses; but, according to the Rabbinists, who form the larger
section of Jews, their reputed founder was one Anan-ben-David (Hannassy),
of the race of Betzur, in the eighth century of the Christian era. Anan
erected a synagogue at Jerusalem, which has been ever since the great
centre of the Karaim, who acknowledge his successors as their head. Such
of the Karaim as are scattered about the south of Russia speak the
Tartar; those in Turkey hold intercourse in Greek, and in Egypt their

language is the Arabic. It is computed that there are from 50,000 to 60,000 Karaim in various parts of the globe.

At the foot of the 'Jews' fortress' is the Valley of Jehoshaphat, a cemetery of great antiquity, in which every Karaim would wish to be buried, and wherein is pointed out, with pride, the grave of Isaac Sangaris (A.D. 767), who converted the Khazars to Judaism. The countless tomb-stones are very varied in form, some being in the shape of a sarcophagus, others like coffins or kysts, but the more remarkable are finished off with head and foot stones. High up, the rock itself is pierced with a number of excavations provided, like others at Katch-kalen, Cherkess-kerman, etc., with reclining places, corn-pits, water-tanks, chimneys and other conveniences formed out of the solid rock; originally, in all probability, together with many similar localities, the dwellings of the wild Tauri. The more numerous of these cave habitations are at Tepe-kerman, but the more remarkable are near the summit of Mangup, where one chamber measures twenty-one feet by seventeen feet. The citadel of Mangup was the principal defence of the Goths; and of the residence of their prince, within its limits there still remains standing a wall, believed to be of the fifteenth century.

A KARAIM JEW.

Near Bakhchisarai are two pillars of calcareous rock of striking appearance, a *lusus naturæ*. The Tartars say that there was once a woman who fled her village, desiring to become a Christian: that her daughter pursued her to bring her back, when suddenly the would-be apostate was turned to stone for wishing to desert the true faith, whereupon the daughter, amazed at the sight, herself became petrified!

Travelling in the Crimea, as in all steppe country, is dreary work, for in summer and autumn the beds of the larger water-courses—they cannot be called rivers—are almost arid, not presenting even the appearance of those verdant meandering lines exhibited by the prolific orchards on the banks of such smaller streams as the Alma and Belbek, orchards from which Russia is annually supplied with a large variety of most excellent apples and pears to the value of something like £200,000. In these streams are taken trout, roach, and dace, and salmon are speared at their estuaries, cray-fish being also abundant, but chiefly in pools and ponds. The bird of the steppe, the bustard, attains a large size and is in great demand, but he is profoundly shy of his mortal enemy, man, who has to stalk him with rifle and bullet; unless he prefers milder sport—such as quails, pigeons, snipe, and partridges, all plentiful enough in season, as are many kinds of waterfowl on the coast, especially to the north-east and north-west.

When the wretched village Stary-Krim, in the east of the peninsula, was a capital, called Solghat, that could count 100,000 men on a war footing, the viceroy resided at Ak-mesjid, now Simpheropol, the chief town and seat of government. It has become the neutral ground of Russian, Greek, Israelite, Armenian, and Tartar traders, and of gipsies, who meet here periodically over and over again, but as if they had never met before, deporting themselves with perfect indifference towards each other, scarcely exchanging a nod of recognition as they jostle one another in the crowded market-place or bazars, and avoiding all mutual intercourse, but each bent on driving the hardest possible bargain with his neighbour. Occasionally, a German colonist makes his appearance, more reserved than the rest, but he is straightforward in his dealings, not boisterous, setting value upon time, and if not respected he is at least feared. To this town, the chief and central mart, roads converge from every part of the peninsula, its caravans of double-humped camels, where the railway has not yet been introduced, being in constant communication with the south coast and Kertch, the city and fortress at the extreme eastern point of the Crimea, where we must now hasten as being our port of embarkation for the Caucasus, of which there is so much to say, having regard to its extent and the interest ever excited by that fascinating land.

ENTRANCE TO THE TOMB OF A SCYTHIAN KING, NEAR KERTCH.

Kertch, as elsewhere in the peninsula, has a remarkable history, extending over something like twenty-four centuries, from the time when it first received a name that of Panticapæum to the day when a handful of the allied forces effected a landing in 1855, to occupy and to hold! A unique feature in its neighbourhood are the countless barrows that extend in every direction—dismal-looking hillocks, the silent and imperishable monuments of an ancient, great, and wealthy people, who, after they laid their dead, thus piled the earth over them. These tumuli or barrows vary in size, and when, some years ago, one of the largest, measuring one hundred feet in height and one hundred and fifty feet in diameter, was explored by direction of the Russian Government, it was discovered to be the tomb of a Scythian king, verifying in every particular the account left to us by scrupulous Herodotus, who relates that when a king died, his wife and attendants were strangled and his horses killed, that they might be laid in his tomb, together with himself, his weapons, golden vessels, etc. It has been already noted on page 33, that visitors to the superb Kertch gallery at the Hermitage, St. Petersburg, will find therein, carefully preserved, the remains of the king and queen, of attendants, of horses and their trappings, and the vessels of gold, silver, electrum, and bronze, that were recovered out of this very sepulchre. But besides the tombs of kings, those of victors, warriors, and priestesses have been brought to light, recognized by the golden wreaths that had adorned their brows, and a profusion of exquisite golden ornaments and trinkets, many of which are pronounced to be the most perfect specimens of the high condition of art in Greece in those early times. These excavations are conducted during two or three months every year by a member of the Archæological Commission of St. Petersburg, whose labours, however, are sometimes attended with the most unsatisfactory results, when he discovers, after extensive and toilsome cuttings, that the tombs have been rifled, though outwardly restored, at some early period, perhaps by Venetian colonists in the fifteenth century, who, as is known, directed their attention to the opening of tumuli in search of treasure. Large as is the number of tumuli around Kertch, they appear fourfold on the opposite shore—the lasting necropolis of Phanagoria, a name that vies in its antiquity with Panticapæum, of which we now take leave, and bid farewell to the Crimea.

The protection afforded by the Emperor Alexander I. to the King of Georgia, upon the supplication of that monarch that he might be defended against his enemies, confirmed the annexation of his dominions to Russia in 1799. To possess Georgia, however, ceded as it had been against the nation's will, was not to keep it, unless the 'seventy nations' spoken of by Strabo as holding the fastnesses in the great mountain chain were either conciliated or subdued. Conciliation, it was soon discovered, was out of the question, and so the process of subjection was shortly commenced, the brave mountaineers offering, year after year, the same stubborn resistance, rendering abortive many a campaign, disputing each acre of ground with so much tenacity, that not until the year 1863 did the commander-in-chief feel that he was able to announce to the Emperor 'the complete subjugation of the Caucasus.' But the country was not pacified—far from it, and oppression was resorted to chiefly in the more accessible and densely-populated territory, to wit, Circassia; oppression which drove no less than 250,000 of four tribes of Circassians to seek expatriation to Turkey. The result is perceptible in the denuded condition of Circassia, the country into which we are first about to pass after crossing the Straits of Kertch, where tracts of once cultivated lands, with happy homes, now present the distressing sight of tangled growths of vegetation and human habitations in various stages of decay.

Interspersed here and there with the natives that remain, are some German

settlements, and a few Molokané, or Dukhobortsy, sectarians originally deported
hither by Alexander I., who style themselves the 'Real Spiritual Christians,' as
distinguished from all others, whom they indiscriminately call 'Worldly.' From
the Molokané (milk drinkers) sprang the Dukhobortsy, 'Wrestlers with the Spirit'
as the name implies, who refuse to recognise any kind of temporal authority,
on the principle that all men are equal and a monarchy unnecessary, our
Lord having said that 'He and His are not of this world;' and they
dissent from the Orthodox Church, because the true Church consists of an
assemblage of such as are chosen by God to walk in the Light and Life
without the use of any distinguishing signs or symbols, by which they mean
images, since God's command to Moses was in these words: 'Thou shalt
not make to thyself images,' etc.

The late Alexander II. removed from them the ban of exile, and they
are now free to go whithersoever they will; but how are these poor people
to give up their homes, their land, their cattle now? They are steady and
trustworthy, good agriculturists, and specially remarkable for their kind
treatment of animals.

The chief town of the Kouban district is Ekaterinodar, a name
which signifies, literally, 'Catherine's gift,' from having been founded by the
sovereign of that name and bestowed, in 1792, together with the adjacent
territory, on the Zaporogian, subsequently known as the Black Sea Cossacks.
Catherine mistrusted their power and influence, and tempted them to the
Kuban with grants of land and other privileges. The first service of some
20,000 of these new warrior settlers consisted in barring all egress from
the mountains, by means of a 'first fortified line' of stations that extended
to Vladikavkaz, where they united with the descendants of the Grebenski
Cossacks, with whom they are not to be confounded. The predominant
type amongst the Zaporogians is still that of the Little Russians, the
Grebenski continuing to preserve their identity with the natives of Great
Russia, whence their origin; and although the whole of this imposing force,
maintained at half a million, has long since adopted the dress of the
Caucasian mountaineers, the Cossacks remain true to the orthodox faith
and to the customs of their forefathers, whose vernacular tongue has never
been forgotten by them. The dress so universally worn by the male sex,
even from boyhood, in all parts of the Caucasus, consists of a single-breasted
garment, like a frock-coat, but reaching almost to the ankles, tightened
in closely at the waist, with a belt from which are suspended dagger,
sword, and frequently a pistol, and having on either breast a row of ten
or twelve sockets, each of a size to hold a cartridge. A rifle, which every
man possesses, is slung across the back; and a tall sheep-skin hat finished
off at its summit with a piece of coloured cloth completes the costume.

The number of Cossacks in Transcaucasia being very limited, for a few
only are stationed in each principal town, chiefly as an escort to the

FEATS OF HORSEMANSHIP BY COSSACKS OF THE CAUCASUS.

governor of the province, their duties are performed by *Chapars*, an irregular force, equally dashing horsemen, and trained in like manner from early youth in those singular exercises and break-neck evolutions for which the Cossacks of the Caucasus have become so famous. Setting their horses at full gallop, they will stand on the saddle and fire all round at an imaginary enemy; or throw the body completely over to the right, with the left heel resting on their steed's hind quarter, and fire as if at an enemy in pursuit, or turn clean round, and sitting astride facing the horse's tail, keep up a rapid fire. A favourite feat, amongst many others, is to throw their hat and rifle to the ground, wheel, and pick them up whilst going at the horse's fullest speed.

Should the traveller elect to proceed eastwards, but north of the great range, he will meet with the Kabardines, the first amongst the Circassians to enter into friendly relations with Russia; they are the ' blood ' of the Caucasus, a noble race, thoroughly domesticated, hospitable to strangers, and useful breeders of cattle. To the south of the Circassians, and occupying about one hundred miles of the coast in the Black Sea, are the Abkhases, who have enjoyed the reputation, from time immemorial, of being an indolent and lawless race, anciently given to piracy, now addicted to thieving when the opportunity is afforded them, for they are determinedly inimical to strangers. Their mountains abound in forests of magnificent walnut and box, where the enthusiastic sportsman will find the bear, hyæna, and wolf, and plenty of smaller game, with seldom a roof to cover him other than the vault of heaven; but the ordinary traveller is likely to encounter difficulties and delays that he would prefer to avoid. Christianity was here introduced by Justinian, who constructed many churches that would have been notable specimens of Byzantine architecture, had the Abkhases not destroyed them in their struggles against the Russians, every such edifice being occupied and converted by the latter into a military post. One church, at Pitzunda on the coast, remarkable as being the place to which John Chrysostom was banished at the instance of the Empress Eudoxia—although the exile never reached his destination—having escaped the general destruction, has been thoroughly restored of late years, and is a striking object to passing vessels. Being the mother church in the Caucasus, Pitzunda, then Pityus, continued to be the seat of the Catholicos of Abkhasia until the twelfth century. Practically, the Abkhases are at present heathens.

Farther south, and extending some way inland from the sea, is the principality of Mingrelia, where we again tread classic ground, inasmuch as our wanderings have brought us to the .Ea of Circe and the Argonauts. In a Mingrelian landscape we are struck at the aspect afforded by the numerous whitewashed cottages as they dot the well-wooded hills. The Mingrelians, too, like their neighbours whom we have just quitted, are incurably given to indolence, except in the making of wine from their abundant vineyards; otherwise they are content to live on the produce of their orchards, prolific through the interposition of a beneficent Providence rather than to any agricultural diligence on their part. They may certainly be included amongst the handsomest people in Transcaucasia, with their well-defined features and usually raven black hair. The Dadian, or prince, is the wealthiest of the dispossessed rulers; the foresight of his predecessor and his own European training having taught him the danger of disposing of land and squandering the proceeds, rather than preserving the property and contenting himself with a smaller income.

Between Mingrelia and Abkhasia courses the Ingur, and if we ascended to near its water-shed—a journey easily accomplished on horseback, say from Sougdidi, the well-known military station—we should find ourselves amongst

a very wild and singular people, the Svanni, whose complete subjugation dates back no farther it may be said than 1876, although they made a formal submission in 1833. They occupy some forty or fifty miles of the upper valley of the Ingur, at no part exceeding ten miles in width, and are cut off from all outside communication between the beginning of September and the end of May, in consequence of the passes being blocked with snow. 'The scenery in this valley,' writes a recent traveller, 'is of great beauty and wildness, and grand beyond description; amid the most profuse vegetation, every imaginable flower is seen in its wild state, and bank, meadow, hill-side and grass plot are literally covered with all that is most lovely; in every forest and grove, and all undergrowth even, indeed wherever the pure air of heaven and its divine

A MINGRELIAN PEASANT.

light is not obstructed, the earth is thus gorgeously arrayed.'

Since the ordination of a priesthood in 1859, the Svanni have been required to keep to the observances of the Russian Church, but in most communities their own priests, if they may be so designated, continue to officiate after ancient custom. For instance, when a couple is about to be married, their garments are attached to each other at the hips by the minister, who utters a sentence or two, and they thenceforth become man and wife; or at funerals and burials, after the disposal of the body with strange rites, the mourners abandon themselves to feasting over the grave, the day ending in drunkenness and brawls. Christianity was first upheld in Svanneti by the sovereigns of Georgia as early as the tenth century, and at several villages in the valley are churches of comparatively recent date—

but they remain empty, the services being conducted mechanically by Russian or Georgian priests in a tongue quite unknown to the people, whose language is a very distinct dialect of the Georgian. The Svanni fast on Wednesdays and Saturdays, and keep Lent without knowing why they do so: they fix the skulls of animals about the fences and walls of their habitations for the purpose of warding off evil influences, filling the churches with the horns as offerings, and yet they will erect a tall staff surmounted by a cross as a caution to trespassers. They do not commit depredations upon each other, but are ever ready to steal from strangers. Murder is rife, the

A VILLAGE IN SVANNETI.

crime being met by the one inviolable law, that the price of blood shall be paid or the life of the murderer forfeited. The price of a life is estimated at six hundred roubles, equal to £70 to £80, but there being no money in circulation, the amount has to be made up in cattle or land. A very notable feature in their villages are the towers of defence, fully sixty feet in height, with which each cottage is provided, used as a place of refuge in days of feud by a member or even an entire family. The Russians have been careless and doubtlessly prudent in rarely undertaking to attack the Svanni in their isolated strongholds, preferring rather to leave this strange

population to its own gradual extinction, a contingency that is certain as
the result of frequent deaths through personal animosities, and the destruction of female infant life, the birth of a female child being usually deemed
a reproach to its parents.

The upper valley of the Ingur has been brought to notice of late
years by reason of its having become the starting-point from which
the members of our Alpine Club have effected the ascent of Elbruz,
Koshtan-tau, and other of the highest peaks in the great range. Contrary
to earlier experience, recent travellers speak in more favourable terms of the
Svanni, of their feelings towards strangers, and of their hospitality ; but as
regards their consideration for the property of others there is much yet to
be desired.

BATOUM.

Returning to Mingrelia, we find it bounded on the south by the River
Rion, the ancient Phasis, which flows through the country whence was
introduced into Europe the Phasian bird—our pheasant. The Rion divides
Mingrelia from Guria, another principality, where is situated Batoum, a
somewhat pestiferous but important military station and commercial port,
that has tended in no small degree, since its annexation to Russia in 1878,
towards the development of the resources of this beautiful country, intersected
with good roads through valleys highly cultivated with maize, corn, and
barley, the hills and their declivities being overspread with the oak and box,
exported in large quantities, and yielding handsome returns. Ozurgheti,

the chief town, attractively situated, was the residence of the rulers who lie interred at the ancient monastery and episcopal church, Chemokmedy, about six miles distant.

Passengers from Odessa and the Crimea landing at Batoum find the train in readiness to convey them to Tiflis, the capital of the whole of Transcaucasia, reached in about fifteen hours, the train travelling slowly enough, but through a land of much interest, historically and pictorially. On the right, in the distance, are the highlands of the old kingdom of Armenia, to the left is Imeritia, a glory, like Mingrelia and Guria, of the past. If so inclined, the traveller may exchange, at Rion station, the main for a branch line, which will take him to Kutais, the chief town of the old kingdom of Imeritia, where he may tarry for a while to great advantage. It is the ancient Khytæa, the residence of Ætes; at any rate a city of great antiquity, beautifully situated on the banks of the Rion.

AN IMERITIAN NOBLE, WEARING THE PAPANAKY.

The natives pride themselves not a little on the distinctness of their nationality, not forgetful that at one period or other their dominion extended over neighbouring territories. Although many of the well-to-do women, here noted for their beauty, affect European fashions in assuming the bonnet or hat, the men, less frivolous, do not disdain to wear the *papanaky*, a small lozenge-shaped piece of leather, silk, or velvet, which lies over the front part of the head, and is fastened with strings under the chin. The head-dress generally in use amongst females of the upper classes, chiefly in Georgia, Imeritia, and Kakhety, may be described as consisting of a narrow black velvet band, stiffened, and worn round

AN IMERITIAN LADY.

the brow like a coronet; it is embroidered with gold or silk thread, and is sometimes ornamented with gems, a thin white veil, cleverly arranged, falling from it in loose folds.

Archæologists would delight in an inspection of what remains of the cathedral, an edifice of the eleventh century, and the first ever constructed in the style now accepted as Georgian, but which is a mixture of the Armenian and Byzantine. The Turks destroyed it in 1691, carrying away with them every movable decoration of value. An old and equally-interesting edifice is the Episcopal Church of Genath at Ghelaty, six miles away, a restoration of the eleventh century, after which date it became the sepulchre of the sovereigns of Imeritia, and is believed to have been the burial-place of the great Queen Thamara.

Between Kutais and Tiflis is the Pass of Suram, at an altitude of three thousand and twenty-seven feet, over which are laid the lines of rail by gradients of one in twenty-two feet over a distance of about eight miles : a triumph of engineering skill due, as is the entire railway, to British capital and enterprise. Beyond this pass the train stops at Gori, situated at the limits of a glorious plain, watered by the Kur and its tributaries. Since fairly good accommodation is obtainable, it were well to halt at this station for the purpose of visiting the unique rock-cut town, Uplytz-tzykhé, some eight miles off. Here is a town—there can be no other designation for it—consisting of public edifices—if such a term may be employed—of large habitations, presumably for the great, smaller dwellings for others, each being conveniently divided, and having doorways, openings for light, and partitions, while many are ornamented with cornices, mouldings, beams and pillars. The groups are separated by streets and lanes, and grooves have been cut, unquestionably for water-courses, and yet the whole has been entirely hewn and shaped out of the solid rock.[1] Tradition is replete with incidents in the history of these remarkable excavations, but faithful historiographers have hitherto refrained from endorsing any of the tales that have been handed down by the romancers of Georgia.

Tiflis, the chief seat of Government and residence of the Governor-General, having a population of about one hundred thousand souls, is unpleasantly situated between ranges of perfectly barren hills, and but for the River Kur, on the banks of which it is built, would be almost uninhabitable. Having driven through the suburbs on his way from the railway terminus, the traveller crosses the Kur over the Woronzoff Bridge, which at once brings him to the principal street, where he passes in succession the public gardens, gymnasium, law-courts, palace of the Governor-General, the main guard-house, public library, museum, etc. ; by which time he will have reached Palace Street and Erivan Square, where are situated the best hotels and restaurants, and the National Theatre. From the square three main thoroughfares lead to as many separate quarters, viz. : the European, where the wealthy live in well-built houses of elegant construction ; the native bazaars, and the market-place and Russian bazaar. An extensive view of the city and an interesting sight is obtained from the eminence

[1] *The Crimea and Transcaucasia.* By Captain Telfer, R.N.

crowned by the old fortress which immediately overlooks the Asiatic quarter and bazaars, whence rise the confused sounds of human cries and the din from the iron, brass, and copper-workers. As is the custom elsewhere in the East, those of one trade congregate together, apart from other trades, and so are passed a succession of silversmiths in their stalls, of furriers, armourers, or eating and wine-shops, the wine of the country being kept in buffalo, goat, or sheep-skins laid on their back, and presenting the disagreeable appearance of carcases swollen after lengthened immersion in water. The Georgians are merry folk, rarely allowing themselves to be depressed

TIFLIS.

by the troubles of life. They love wine and music, and ever seek to drive away dull care by indulging in their favourite Kakhety two bottles being the usual allowance to a man's dinner, an allowance, however, greatly exceeded when, of an evening, friends meet together to join in the national dance, called the Lezghinka.

The Cathedral of Zion was formerly the church of the Patriarch of Georgia. It dates from the fifth century, and encloses that most precious relic with which the nation was converted to Christianity in the fourth century nothing less than a cross of vine stems bound with the hair of

St. Nina, the patron saint, who first preached the truth! The patriarchate has long been suppressed, and is replaced by a Russian Exarch, so that the Georgian Church may be considered in all respects identical with that of Russia. The palace of the kings has entirely disappeared, for not a vestige remains. George XIII. signed his renunciation of the crown in favour of the Emperor Paul in 1800, and died shortly afterwards amid the execrations of his late subjects, for having ignominiously betrayed them. Many of his descendants are in the service of Russia, and are the representatives of one of the most ancient monarchies of the world — for the Bagrations first rose to power in 587; and if allowance be made for interregnums it will be found that their reign extended over 1092 years, during the twelve centuries that elapsed from their earliest election.

GEORGIAN LADIES.

Some day a railway will convey passengers and goods the entire distance from Georgia into Armenia, but for the present the line is constructed as far as Akstafa only, whence travellers on their way south have to content themselves with the post-road which goes over the Delijan Pass, 7124 feet above the sea, descending by the southern slopes into the plains of Armenia. An order for post-horses may be obtained at any post-town, but special orders granted to officials or others on duty always take precedence, and frequently cause immeasurable inconvenience to the ordinary traveller.

As Georgia is the land of wine and song, so is Armenia essentially the land of legend and tradition, for which must be held in great part responsible the magnificent mountain that exhibits itself suddenly at a dip in the road long before the plains are in sight. Well may the Armenians glory in 'their' Ararat, peerless among the mighty works of the Creator, almost symmetrical in its outlines, and rising to an altitude of 16,916 feet above the sea, Lesser Ararat, 12,840 feet, looking almost dwarfed by the side of its mighty neighbour.

At Erivan, the largest city in Russian Armenia, the traveller will find fairly good accommodation, but the place is dull enough, whether in the Persian quarter, where crooked lanes are lined with high walls, that mask the dwellings within like the defences of a fortress, or in the broad streets and unpaved quarter laid out by the Russians since their occupation of the province in 1829, even though enlivened by a boulevard and gardens fair to look upon. The population is Armenian and Persian, for Persia ruled here during a considerable period until vanquished by Russia; but at the bazaars one meets with other nationalities, such as Tartars from the steppes, Kurds, Greeks, and Turkish dealers in search of good horses, upon which they will fly across the frontier, defying Cossacks and custom officers alike.

Within a short distance of Erivan, and the post-station nearest to the Persian frontier, is Nahitchevan, the first abode of Noah after he came forth from the ark, and probably also his last, since his tomb is reverently shown by the inhabitants, who eagerly escort strangers to see it. Other still more important towns in Armenia, available by carriage-road, are Alexandropol and Kars, the former being the largest and most powerful fortress and the principal arsenal in Transcaucasia; the latter, long a Turkish fortress town, was gallantly defended in 1855 by Sir Fenwick Williams and a few British officers, until the garrison was starved into surrender by General Mouravieff. Kars was finally ceded to Russia by the Treaty of Berlin in 1878.

As in most Russian towns, excellent carriages are obtainable at Erivan, whence a two hours' drive over a good road brings the visitor to the Monastery of Etchmiadzin, the cradle of the Gregorian Church, and so called because 'the only-begotten Son of God here descended and appeared to Gregory,' the founder, surnamed 'the Enlightener.' The convent, a beautiful edifice standing within high battlemented walls presenting the appearance of a fortress, encloses in its treasury one of the most extraordinary of sacred relics—the identical spear-head with which our Lord's side was pierced, brought hither by the Apostle Thaddeus in the year 34! Another priceless relic is the hand of St. Gregory, in a silver-gilt case, which is carried about for the purpose of healing the sick and performing other miracles, and it is also employed in the consecration of the patriarchs. The library contains some early MSS., being Gospels and devotional works, and from the printing-press issue all religious books for the use of Gregorian congregations in various parts of the globe.

A Tartar city brought into prominence of late years through the introduction of railways is Elizavetpol, on the line between Tiflis and the Caspian, where we must now pick ourselves up after having retraced our steps from the plains, to journey by rail to dismal-looking Bakù—a town of recent creation, approached through a desert of sand and stones, where neither vegetable nor animal life can possibly find an existence. Viewed from

NAPHTHA WELLS AT BAKÙ.

the sea, Bakù presents a distinctly picturesque appearance, with its sombre citadel, numerous minarets, and the palace of the princes of bygone days towering above the old town, where the houses look as if they were piled the one above the other—the new or Russian quarter being at the base, and lining the shore of the pretty little bay. Modern Bakù contains some handsome residences and well-paved streets, the principal being the busy quay, constructed of massive blocks of greystone masonry, where the naphtha, the wealth of Bakù, is embarked for transport to the interior of Russia by the Volga, or for conveyance across the Caspian to Central Asia. Numerous refineries, worth inspecting, at the west end of Bakù compose the Black Town, so called from its begrimed condition, and from being ever enveloped in clouds of the densest smoke. Since a remote period has this neighbourhood been considered holy by fire-worshippers, because of the many naphtha springs that were constantly burning, some even perpetually; indeed, the fires at Surakan, a suburb of Bakù, continued to be guarded by fire-worshippers from Yezd in Persia, and even from India, until, with the connivance of the Government, they were hustled away some ten years ago by the increasing number of speculators engaged in a trade which has now completely driven out of the market all American produce.

Georgians are rarely met with outside the confines of their country proper, the foremost and most enterprising trader encountered everywhere being the Armenian, who is no favourite among the different populations, because of his prosperity, which he owes entirely to his own industry and thrift; and from being strictly a trader, the Armenian is careless about agriculture, which, in Georgia, is the work of its own people. Stretching from the province of Bakù, and even from the shores of the Caspian, as far as the slopes of the great range, the vine is successfully cultivated in the Georgian district of Kakhety, the richest vineyards being in the Valley of Alazan, watered by the river of that name. It is with the wine of Kakhety, red and white, grateful even in the days of Strabo, that the Georgian makes merry, giving it the preference over the wine of Mingrelia, which is thin and acid. The two principal towns in this wine country are Telav in Upper, and Sygnak in Lower, Kakhety, where still stands the wall constructed by King Heraclius as a defence against the frequent attacks of the mountaineers of Daghestan, who invaded the plain from time to time, and carried off females and the young of both sexes. The Lesghians, as these marauders are called, occupy the mountainous region known as Interior and Eastern Daghestan; they call themselves Taül mountaineers, in distinction to the Tartars who occupy the declivities and plains, are second to none in bravery, are good tacticians, and cool under fire. Nominally, the Lesghians are Mahometans, whilst in truth their religion consists of a love of independence and an unconquerable aversion to Russia.

In Daghestan is Gunib, the last stronghold of the brave Shamyl, whom the strength of Russia was unequal to subdue during the space of thirty years. 'Do the Russians say that they are numerous as the grains of sand? Then are we the waves that will carry away that sand,' said the great Tartar chief when addressing the numerous tribes who placed themselves under his leadership to repel the invader. The mountaineers posted themselves on the heights, and, hidden by trees, shot down their enemies in scores as they advanced in column up the narrow defiles.

The Chentchen are a wild, ungovernable tribe, who never fail in their hostility towards others, more especially the Lesghians, when the opportunity is afforded them, for they cannot forget that they were employed by Shamyl to assist him in subduing them. After a predatory fight, three

years ago only, with their hated neighbours, the Chentchen resorted to an
ancient and cruel custom that of amputating the hands of their wounded
enemies, and nailing them to the doors of their dwellings. Other tribes
scattered to the west of the Chentchen are the Ingush and Kysty,
agriculturists and breeders of cattle, whose religion, like that of the
Chentchen, is a singular mixture of Christianity and Paganism, tinged with
not a little Mahometanism, the talismans they wear about their persons
being inscribed with passages from the Koran in Arabic or Persian. Adjoining the Ingush and Kysty, and near the Kabardines, whose acquaintance
we made in Circassia, are the Ossets, a numerous tribe to the west of the
River Terek and in the valley of the Ardon, whose origin and history, long
a subject of debate amongst ethnologists, has finally resulted in an almost
general admission that the Ossets or Osses are descended from and inhabit
the same parts as were anciently peopled by the Alains or Alans, mentioned
for the first time by Josephus.

The Ossets occupy the right as well as the left bank of the Terek, in
the hilly parts where they adjoin the Hefsurs, Ph'tchavy, and Tushines,
all rude tribes of puzzling religious tendencies, and exceedingly superstitious.
The Hefsurs are a proud and supercilious race, inimical to Russia, as are
the Ph'tchavy and Tushines, so that they rarely quit their impregnable
homes in the most inaccessible sites on the mountains, and live much the
same life they led a hundred years ago.

The great thoroughfare between Transcaucasia and Russia is from
Tiflis to Vladikavkaz, the terminus of the Moscow-Rostof railway, by way
of the Dariel road, a stupendous engineering success completed in the reign
of Nicholas. This road winds over a pass 7977 feet above the sea, and is
kept in repair and clear for traffic in winter by the Ossets, whose country it
traverses, in return for which service they are exempt from all taxes. The
post stations are the best in the Caucasus, and the distance, 126 miles, is
usually accomplished in something less than twenty-four hours. The first
station at which horses are changed after leaving Tiflis is Mz'hett, the site
of the most ancient city in Georgia, its first capital, and residence of its
first king, Pharnawaz, 302-237 B.C. The cathedral, restored in the seventeenth century, in which many monarchs and patriarchs are interred, is worth
inspecting as a perfect example of Georgian architecture. For ages was here
preserved ' the seamless garment of our Lord, the handiwork of the blessed
Virgin ;' but unhappily when the Persians overran Georgia, the precious relic
was sent for safe custody to Moscow, where it has remained ever since.

From another station on this road is obtained a near and beautiful view
of Kazbek, ascended, twenty years ago, to its very summit, 16,546 feet, by
several members of our Alpine Club, notwithstanding local traditions which
assert that the peak of Kazbek, being a holy place, is inhabited by a spirit,
and that the man who attempts to reach it is seized by an unseen power

or arrested by a storm, and compelled to retrace his steps. Beyond the Kazbek station the road, keeping the right bank of the Terek, leads through the celebrated Dariel Pass, of which Mr. Douglas D. Freshfield,[1] a practical mountaineer, says : 'The bold and broken forms of the gigantic cliffs must arrest the attention of even the most indifferent observer of Nature. The mere fact of the existence of a carriage road is some detraction from the impressiveness of a mountain gorge ; . . . . yet we agreed unanimously that it had nothing to fear from a comparison with the finest defiles of the Alps.'

When the traveller will have completed the journey from Tiflis to Vladikavkaz, he will have arrived at the depôt and point of transit for all goods brought by rail from Russia, and there transferred, for conveyance to the Transcaucasian provinces, to clumsy, unwieldy carts or vans drawn by horses or oxen ; those in charge of the caravans never being in a hurry, completely indifferent as to when they start, or when they arrive at their destination, and rejoicing in a lengthened stay at Mlety station, after having accomplished the most toilsome part of the distance—the ascent and descent of the pass. Vladikavkaz was founded in 1785 on the site of an Osset village, and became the headquarters and chief military depôt of the Russians during their lengthened struggle for supremacy with the stout-hearted hillmen ; it is now the chief town and seat of government for the province of Kuban, and still an important military station. The population is made up of Circassians, Armenians, and Russians, and a few Ossets at the bazaars, for the natives made off long ago. The chief industries are the manufacture of silver and gold lace, arms, *burkas*, the Caucasian's all-weathers cloak, silver ornaments, etc. The hotels are fairly good, but there being nothing at Vladikavkaz itself sufficiently inviting to encourage a longer stay than is absolutely necessary, the following choice of routes lays before the stranger. He may post through Eastern Caucasus and embark at Petrovsk for Astrakhan and the tedious voyage up the Volga ; or take the railway to Rostof *en route* to Moscow ; or travel by rail to Novorossisk on the Black Sea, and there embark ; or, following that line as far as Ekaterinodar, post thence to Taman and cross the straits to Kertch.

[1] *Travels in the Central Caucasus and Bashan.*

AN ILLUMINATION OF THE FIFTEENTH CENTURY IN THE LIBRARY OF THE MONASTERY
OF SAINT SERGIUS, MOSCOW.

CHAPTER IX.

SIBERIA.

WE have, within the compass of a very few pages, to sketch the leading features of Asiatic Siberia, which, having an area of nearly five million English square miles, is almost three million square miles larger than the whole of European Russia, including Poland and Finland. It comprises, in fact, one thirteenth part of the globe. On the other hand, the population, sparsely scattered over eight provinces, is scarcely that of London, for it amounts to little more than four millions, giving less than one inhabitant per square mile, against forty-one in European Russia. For thousands of miles Siberia has a northern seaboard on the Arctic Ocean, and an eastern coast line on the Pacific and the Sea of Okhotsk that embraces nearly twenty-five degrees of latitude. On the west, the Ural Mountains separate it from Europe, and on the south its limits come into contact with the empire of China and with the dominions of Russia in Central Asia.

A gloomy desert of frozen *tundras*, or mossy boglands, on the north, the rest of this vast country is in some parts green and fertile as the prairies and pampas of America, in others mountainous, with alpine lakes, glaciers, and snow-clad peaks. The principal rivers are the Ob, the Enisei, and the Lena, which, after being fed by numerous tributaries, discharge their mighty waters into the Arctic Ocean, on points of the seaboard practically inaccessible

KIAKHTA.

to shipping for the steady and reliable prosecution of trade. Railways will soon be constructed to bring the rich produce of the great Siberian rivers to a westerly harbour on the Polar Ocean, more free from ice than the fjords, or bays, in the Kara Sea. On the south, Siberia has a convenient waterway into the Gulf of Tartary, namely, the great Amùr river, with its tributary, the Usuri, which was diplomatically acquired from China in 1859 and 1860.

So far, Asiatic Siberia is tapped by only one railway, that from Perm, on the European side of the Ural Mountains, to Ekaterinburg and Tiumen, but it will not be long before the Ural chain is pierced at a more southerly point by the Great Siberian Trunk Line, which was opened in 1888 as far as Ufa, the point of departure for Omsk, Tomsk, Krasnoyarsk, and Irkutsk. Pekin and the Russian coast on the Pacific are the objective points of the railways in construction or under contemplation.

Known to the generality of our readers only as a land of penal or political exile, from early impressions conveyed by

OSTIAKS SPINNING AND NURSING.

Elizabeth, or the Exiles of Siberia, and more recently from the reports of travellers who have devoted their attention to the Russian convict system, Siberia, except in the extreme north, may be said to be a land 'flowing with milk and honey,' requiring only the energy of man and the resources of civilization to raise it to a condition of great affluence. The sparseness of its population is an obstacle which greater facilities of communication are rapidly removing. A strong tide of immigration has set in from Central and Southern Russia, even towards the distant basins of the Amúr and the Usuri, where the Russian peasant finds himself in contact, not with bears, but with tigers.

The natives whom the Russians have displaced as masters of Siberia are no longer to be dreaded, and their numbers are dwindling rather than increasing. Ethnographically, the aboriginal races are grouped as the *Arctic*, roaming on the frozen lands of the Arctic Circle, from the mouth of the Lena

TUNGUZ GIRLS.

to Behring's Straits, and extending from thence to the Kamchatka peninsula, with settlements also at the mouth of the Amúr and on the island of Sakhalin; the *Ural-Altaic*, composed of Samoyedes and of Ostiaks, and other Finnish tribes, who reign supreme in the north-western part of Siberia, principally between the Ural Mountains and the Enisei, from the shores of the Polar Sea down to the sources of the Enisei, from which, however, they are cut off by strong Slav settlements in the districts of Eniseisk and Krasnoyarsk; the *Turkish*, which supplies fishing and hunting Yakuts to a large tract of country intersected by the Lena, and nomadic Khirghizes, Nogais and Bashkirs, to the steppes west of the Irtysh; and the *Mongol*, represented by Buriäts and Kalmucks, who, starting as a narrow ethnological wedge from the Arctic shore east of the Enisei, extend southwards until they meet the Tunguz and Lamut tribes of the *Manchu* race, dominant from the head of the Sea of Okhotsk to the Russian outpost at Vladivostok, on the Gulf of Tartary.

The origin of Russian dominion in this part of Asia is worth tracing. In the most remote times, the Slavs, and mainly the Novgorodians, had commercial intercourse with the tribes settled on the Asiatic slopes of the Ural Mountains, and traders from Novgorod the Great are known to have descended the tributary streams of the Ob river in search of furs, of which the principal mart was at Isker, on the Irtysh, a little above the site of the present city of Tobolsk. Isker was the capital of a Tartar kingdom, and was known to ancient Arab merchants and missionaries. Early in the sixteenth century the Muscovite Tsars, having annexed the wide dominions of Novgorod, began to style themselves 'Lords of the territories of the Ob and the Kanda,' that is to say, of the lands within the basin of the Ob, which had long been 'exploited' by agents of the Stroganoff family, which derived great riches from its Siberian trade. A Cossack robber band under Ermak followed in the footsteps of the traders and trappers, and on a second expedition, in 1581, succeeded in capturing Isker, but with the loss of over half of the Cossacks who had crossed the Ural. Ermak was soon after drowned in the Irtysh, and the Cossacks, demoralized also by the danger of their position in the face of inimical

A SIBERIAN MERCHANT IN WINTER TRAVELLING DRESS.

native tribes, were forced to abandon a conquest which was virtually effected later by Muscovite troops. The Tsars thus became masters of the Trans-Ural territory, or Siberia, and established their power at Sibir (the name which the Russians gave to Isker), Tobolsk, and Tiumen.

The Buriäts on the Angara, the Koriaks, and other aborigines, long resisted; but the construction of fortified Cossack posts at the confluence of rivers, at portages, and in mountain passes, eventually reduced them to entire submission. Isker, or Sibir, having been swept away by a flood, Tobolsk became the central seat of government, from which Russian dominion was consolidated and extended.

In 1689, under the Treaty of Nerchinsk, the Tsar was compelled to order the evacuation of the settlements formed by Cossacks on the Amûr, on Chinese territory, a century and a half previously. But a desire to possess an outlet in the Pacific for the huge continent of Siberia led the Russian Government, in spite of that treaty, to establish, in 1851, 'trading factories' at the mouth of the Amûr, and at the two extremities of the portage connecting that river with De Castries Bay, in the Gulf of Tartary. During the Crimean War the left bank of the Amûr was militarily occupied, and nine points in the law having thus been gained, the remainder was dealt with, as we have already said, by skilful diplomacy; and the Chinese Government made a formal cession, in 1860, of the territory through which the Celestial empire is now dangerously vulnerable.

The plains of Mongolia, from which had issued, in the thirteenth century, the hordes that devastated Russia, arrested her in a development common to the rest of Europe, and ultimately, by successive invasions, established a semi-Asiatic form of government at Moscow, are now in the hands of those on whom the Mongols and Tartars inflicted such well-nigh ineffaceable injury and suffering. Russians and Poles, representing the Slav race, preponderate numerically in Siberia. The Russian trappers, traders, and Cossacks, of whom we have spoken, were succeeded, from the seventeenth century, by exiles, first only political, but later both criminal and political. Strange to say, the first sufferer in this respect was the tocsin bell of the town of Uglitch, on the Volga, which was formally banished in 1591 to Pelym, near Tobolsk, and condemned, like a human criminal, to lose its tongue and ears, for the offence of ringing out an alarm while the emissaries of the usurper, Boris Godunof, were doing to death the young Prince Dimitri, son of Ivan the Terrible. Among the earliest State criminals exiled to Siberia were the citizens of the town in which that tragedy took place. Towards the end of the seventeenth century, contumacious Little Russians of the Ukraine, just annexed to Muscovy, were exiled in batches to Siberia, of which the population was later increased by Dissenters from the Russo-Greek Church, and by the small remnant of the Streltsi whom Peter the Great had spared, and sent to guard, in isolated forts, the most distant confines of his empire. Some of their descendants are settled in villages along the banks of the Lena.'

The sovereigns who more immediately succeeded Peter I. began to supply Siberia with a new class of exiles—noblemen and ex-favourites, victims of Court intrigue, or perpetrators of fraud and crime against the State. Many of them, branded or maimed in tongue, nose, or ears, perished

---

' Russian revised Edition of *Keller*, to which we are indebted for much information in a concise form.

miserably in the forests and *tundras* of Siberia, where no friendly hand could help them, and where, even if pardoned, the messenger of glad tidings was generally unable to find them. Catherine II. deported to the same wilds large bodies of Poles. In the reign of Alexander I. about 600 Poles, who had served under the banners of Napoleon, were sent to join their countrymen in Siberia, and the last considerable contingent of Polish exiles performed the same dreary journey after the suppression of the insurrection of 1863. Of these, 972 were sent as convicts, and about 1500 as settlers within certain circumscribed districts.

Like the ordinary criminals of every grade who have been poured into Siberia for the last century and a half, the political exiles had, until recent days, to make journeys of four or five thousand miles on foot, tied, or chained in gangs to long iron poles. It took them two years to reach places of banishment in the Trans Baikal province, where, as well as in other parts of Siberia, it was, in days happily gone by, the custom to guard against the escape of convicts by tearing out their nostrils. Until 1864 they were branded with a hot iron on the forehead and on both cheeks; but at present runaways are simply placed beyond the pale of the law, and left to the tender mercies of the Tunguzes and Buriäts, who are reported to prefer the chase of an escaped convict to that of 'a wild goat, which has only one skin, while the leanest fugitive has three—his shirt, his

SIBERIAN CONVICT.

kaftan,[1] and some kind of sheepskin coat.' Nevertheless many still escape entirely, in obedience to the call of 'General Kokushka,' that is, the cuckoo when it proclaims the advent of spring.[2] The Howard Association has recently drawn attention to the dreadful sufferings still endured by exiles in Siberia, more especially to 'the crowding of political offenders and criminals, with the

---

[1] The long coat worn by peasants.—Russian edition of *Reclus*, p. 685.
[2] See Dr. Kennan's articles in *The Century*, vols. xxxvi and xxxvii.

innocent wives and children of the former, in filthy prisons,' in one of the largest of which 'more than twenty-five per cent. of the inmates are constantly ill . . . and more than ten per cent. die.'

No honest critic can accuse the present government or the superior officials of Russia of intentional cruelty or negligence in the matter of deportation ; but, although a very great deal has already been done to mitigate the sufferings of condemned felons and banished revolutionists, a Russian Howard would undoubtedly still find a large field of activity in watching over and improving the system in its details, at centres remote from the eyes of philanthropic governors. In some respects, even, the present punishment by exile might be made more impressive and more effectively deterrent of crime. Siberia is a pleasant land to convicted plunderers of banks and other public institutions, and to numerous other felons, who lead a free, happy, and perhaps luxurious life at Tomsk or Tobolsk, thanks to the habitual lenity of Russian juries, and to their proneness, when unable to acquit a prisoner clearly culpable, to give him the benefit of 'extenuating circumstances,' which save him from the full rigour of the law. A great amount of crime thus escapes punishment in Russia, and it has become a serious question to Russian statesmen whether trial by jury, suddenly introduced in 1865, has not done more harm than good to the moral condition of the people. Corporal punishment having been abolished in 1863, the penalty of death is now inflicted only in cases of political and other crimes 'requiring special measures of repression,' and the punishment for the most atrocious murder or series of murders does not exceed twenty years' hard labour. In this respect it appears necessary that a doom of labour in the mines of Nerchinsk should have a considerable amount of salutary terror to prospective criminals. We may, however, here observe that the worst criminals are now deported to the island of Sakhalien, on the Gulf of Tartary, in ocean steamers which embark their miserable and dangerous freight at Odessa.

As regards the generality of political exiles, it cannot in truth be said that their lot in Siberia, except in its polar region, is now a very hard one, after they have once reached the places of their banishment. They are cordially received by the local inhabitants, themselves to a great extent the descendants of exiles, and are able to find occupation and recreation of one kind or another. The intellectual level of the Siberians is markedly higher than that of the population of European Russia, owing to the continuous influx of educated exiles, Polish and Russian ; and the university recently established at Tomsk will, no doubt, do much both to sustain and to raise that level.

Without pretending to bring forward a typical case of comparative felicity in exile, we may interest our readers by mentioning that a Polish gentleman banished in 1863 met, among the Bashkirs, to whose steppes he was relegated, and with whom he followed the sport of hawking, an Irish deserter from the British army in the Crimea, who taught him the English language. Recalled after a couple of years, the liberated exile settled at St. Petersburg, resuming work in his original profession of an advocate ; and the knowledge he had acquired from his Irish friend enabled him to undertake English business, and to retire after a very few years with a considerable fortune.

We must now visit some of the principal Siberian towns. Until the railway to Ufa is carried across the Ural, we have to reach the great country we have been sketching *vià* Perm, on the River Kama, a voyage of four days from Nijni Novgorod by steamer. Although within the confines of Europe, the aspect of a Siberian city is given to Perm by

A SIBERIAN GOLD MINE.

its low wooden houses, irregularly disposed. It is an important centre of metallurgic industry, started by a Stroganoff in the sixteenth century. Here we take rail to Ekaterinburg, and at Aziatskaya station begins our descent into Asia, down the eastern side of the Ural Mountains. At their foot lies Nijni Taghil, in proximity with the famous Demidoff copper mines, from which much malachite is raised. Not far from the principal works, of which there are eleven, we find a museum well stocked with specimens of the many minerals found in Siberia. The great iron works of Neviansk are some thirty

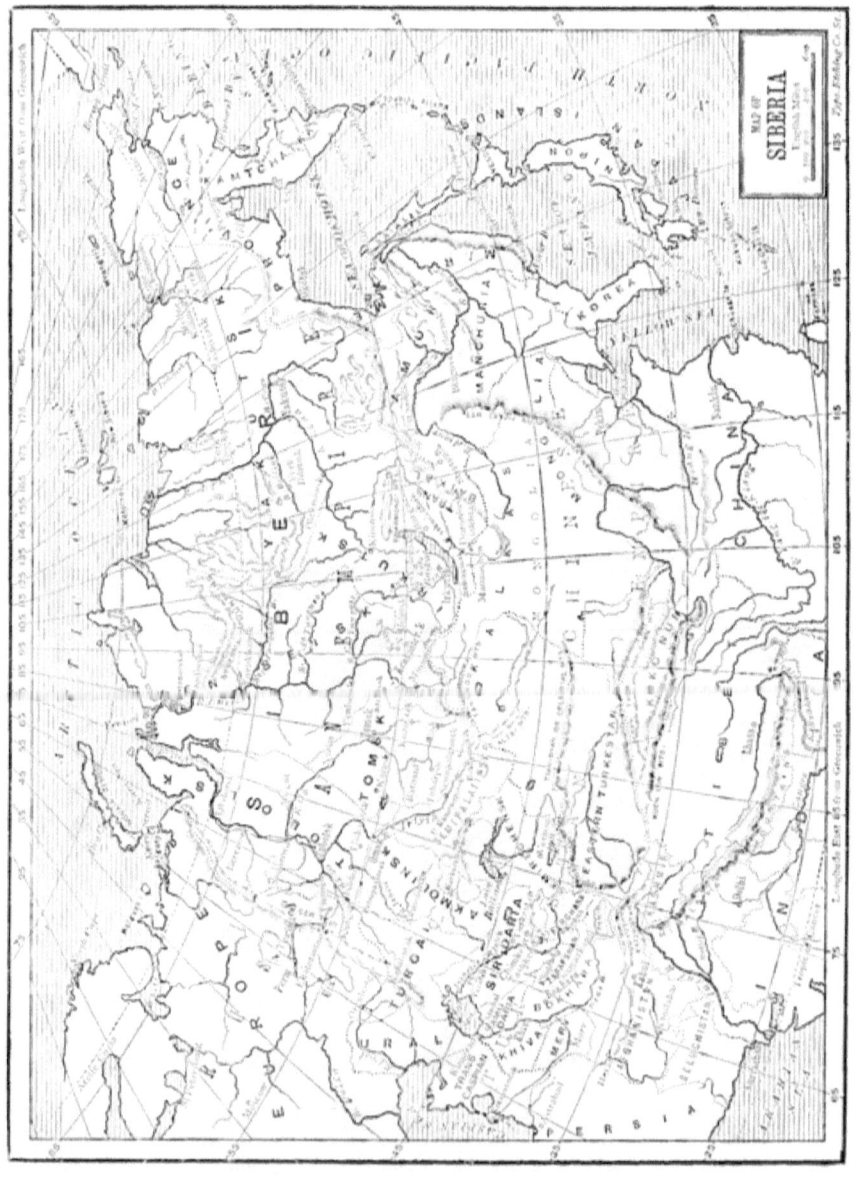

MAP 67
SIBERIA
English Miles

miles beyond, and in their immediate neighbourhood are the first gold washings to which we come in Siberia. In 1884, thirty-two tons of gold (£4,600,000), or more than a quarter of the total gold production in the world (estimated at about 144 tons), was yielded by Siberia.

Ekaterinburg, named by Peter the Great after Catherine I., was founded in 1723, and is a handsome city, of great importance as the centre of rich and extensive mining districts, and the seat of the State 'administration of the mines.' The Crown possesses in it a factory in which are cut and polished local gems and stones, such as garnets, jacinths, opals, beryl, topaz, aqua marine, lapis lazuli, jasper, alexandrite (crimson by day and green by night), and a number of other stones more or less rare and precious. There is also a laboratory in which the gold raised in Siberia is smelted into ingots. In addition to iron and copper works, and to several gold washings in the neighbourhood of the city, there is a mine of gold quartz at Berezof which most travellers are induced to inspect. We are told of the emerald mines that belong to the State, but as they are more than a hundred miles away, it must suffice to take note of the fact of their existence, as we also do of the presence, in large numbers, of elk, wolves, and bears in the forests that have not yet disappeared under the great demand for wood fuel used in smelting ore.

Our railway journey ends, like that of many an exile, at Tiumen, on the Tura River, a town founded in 1586 on the site of an ancient Tartar city. This is the most important commercial centre in Western Siberia, for while it has water communication with the Ob, through its great affluent the Irtysh, it is also the goal of caravans from China and other parts of the distant East. Exiles are distributed from this point over Eastern Siberia, and the British and Foreign Bible Society have consequently selected it as the most suitable place for a thorough and systematic dissemination of the Word of God among the political prisoners.

Steamers run from Tiumen in a day and a half to Tobolsk, the capital of a province of the same name, the oldest and most populated in Siberia, and seven times as large as Great Britain and Ireland. The upper town and the fortress of Tobolsk occupy a commanding position on a hill with a precipitous front, and from which we gain an extensive view of the Irtysh, joined not far from the city by the Tobol, and at our feet spreads out the lower town, bristling with domes and spires. Of the twenty churches that stand out from among the modest wooden houses of Tobolsk, the Cathedral of St. Sophia is the most handsome. Close to it is a belfry in which hangs the exiled bell of Uglitch, already referred to.

In eight days more, by descending first the Irtysh, and then ascending the Ob in a steamer, we find ourselves at Tomsk, after a somewhat monotonous voyage between low and flat banks inhabited by Ostiaks and other aborigines. Although the Ostiaks in these regions still live in tents,

they are more or less Russianized, and have not, like their congeners on the
Enisei, retained their ancient dress.   Built in 1604. Tomsk remained a centre
of subjugation and annexation until the towns of Eniseisk and Krasnoyarsk
were founded for the same purpose on the Enisei River.   Its prosperity and
importance will revive now that it has become the seat of a university for

TOBOLSK.

Siberia, and it can also look forward to the benefits of the great railway
which is destined sooner or later to pass through it in the direction, *viâ*
Irkutsk, both of China and the Pacific coast.   At present it takes a fortnight
to reach Irkutsk with post horses, along roads (in the neighbouring Enisei
province) as well made and kept as any in England.

LAKE BAIKAL IN WINTER.

Irkutsk, the seat of the administration of Eastern Siberia, lies on the picturesque Angara River, which rises not far off in Lake Baikal. It has a population of 36,000, and before a great fire in 1879 was the finest town in Siberia. Rapid recovery is, however, being made under the impetus of industry and trade. Its leather, soap, and candle works are being continued on a large scale, and the transit trade in tea, &c., from Kiakhta which it enjoys is likely to attain a considerable development after the establishment of railway communication.

Travellers bound to Kiakhta can reach it from Irkutsk in four days by post and steamer. The road winds along the wooded part of the Angara valley, and presents magnificent views of hills crowned and covered to the foot of their slopes with pines, cedars, and other trees. After passing a

THE BURNING OF IRKUTSK IN 1879.

more rugged part of the valley, the Angara will be found rolling down a steep decline and forming rapids nearly four miles in length. A great mass of rock, held sacred by the followers of Shamanism, and never passed by them without an act of devotion, rises picturesquely in the middle of the rushing waters. A beautiful view is soon obtained of Lake Baikal, also called the Holy Sea. This sheet of water, 400 miles long by 20 to 50 in breadth, and occupying an area of 14,000 English square miles, is one of the largest fresh water lakes in the world. It is 1364 feet above the ocean, and is surrounded by mountains which occasionally attain a height of 7000 feet. At the station from which it is crossed by a steamer the depth close in shore is a thousand fathoms. Fine fish in great variety abound in its waters, which are also tenanted by the ocean seal.

At Verkhnéudinsk, on the opposite side, is the junction of the roads that lead severally to Pekin and to Vladivostok on the Pacific; and at Selenginsk, a small and modern town, 110 miles beyond, we reach the scene of the labours of the English missionaries who, between 1817 and 1840, devoted themselves to the conversion of the Mongolian Buriäts. On the

GILYAKS IN WINTER COSTUME ON THE LOWER AMUR.

left bank of the Selenga are still extant some of the outbuildings of the house in which they lived, and in an enclosed cemetery we find the graves of Mrs. Yule, Mrs. Stallybrass, and three of their children. Sixty miles further on, at the end of a heavy and sandy road that runs along a parched and undulating tract of land covered here and there with a little grass, is

Troitskosavsk, where we have to alight in a dirty inn infested with vermin. In its so-called square—a corn and hay market—we stop to gaze at the Mongolian carts drawn by oxen, and mounted on wooden discs instead of wheels.

A walk along a macadamized road brings us to the Russian frontier town of Kiakhta, where, under existing arrangements with China, even Russian officials are not allowed to sleep. It was founded as a fort about 1728, and is still a miserable-looking place, notwithstanding that its cathedral is so richly endowed with gold and jewelled church properties. A Buriat Lamasery is among the principal sights of this place. Neutral ground, 220 yards wide, separates the Russian and Chinese empires. The latter is entered through a gate in the palisade of Maimachen, a town inhabited by three thousand male Celestials, women being rigidly excluded (from beyond the great wall of Kalgan), in order to prevent the subjects of His Chinese Majesty from 'becoming rooted to the soil.' Notwithstanding the competition of sea-borne tea, imported *via* Odessa and St. Petersburg, and which forms the bulk of the tea consumed in European Russia, a great trade still exists in that article. The theory that tea carried overland is superior to that which travels by sea, and thereby becomes deteriorated in strength or aroma, has long been exploded. As a matter of fact, the leaf brought to Kiakhta is exclusively the growth of the northern provinces of China, where a better quality is produced than in the south, which enjoys, on the other hand, the advantage of cheaper carriage by sea.

From want of space we cannot return to Verkhneudinsk, and follow the long road to the Pacific by way of the grand country of the Amùr—a vast kingdom in itself, and one also of high importance to Russia from a strategical point of view. Our readers must be content with the sketch we have already made of Siberia, which can no longer be considered as the land of the icy north, for the gravitation of its development is towards the genial south, nor as exclusively the land of the exile, since its free population, mingling with the honest banished, is making rapid strides in numbers and in prosperity, bidding fair to render 'Sibir' one of the most valuable jewels in the richly-studded Crown of All the Russias. The Russian is already seen to greater advantage in it than on his native dreary plains, for there has been a great mingling of blood in this new country, and an incessant interchange of thought of a high intellectual order, resulting in a spirit of freedom and a broadness of view, in strong contrast with the comparatively low level of general culture in the European parts of Russia Proper.

CHAPTER X.

CENTRAL ASIA.

SINCE the days of the Crimean War and the Indian Mutiny the question of Central Asia, a *terra* then almost *incognita*, has been more and more prominently brought to the notice of the British public in connection with Russian advances in the direction of India; and the country is now so well within focus in its physical and political aspects that none of our readers will expect or require to derive any additional light from our sketchy pages. The time has arrived when we should set aside the vague geographical designation of Central Asia, indicating the territories beyond the Caspian, bounded on the south by the dominions of Persia and Afghanistan, abutting on the east on the empire of China, and merging on the north into the steppes of Siberia. To our immediate forefathers the greater part of the country thus bounded was known as Independent Tartary, but the final consolidation of Russian dominion in Central Asia has converted this large, and historically and politically important, portion of the earth's surface into three distinctive provinces: the Transcaspian region, stretching from the south-eastern shores of the Caspian to Merv and the Afghan frontier; the Khirghiz steppe country, beginning at the southern limits of Siberia, including the Aral Sea, and bounded on the south by the governor-generalship of the third great division: Turkestan, within which are comprised the lands between the Oxus and the Jaxartes, terminating on the east at the Tianshan

A KHIRGHIZ BRIDE.

Mountains and the Pamir, at the foot of the great tablelands of Thibet and Chinese Tartary. On the south, the limits of Turkestan are marked by the Hindu Kush, which gradually merges into the Kopet Dagh range of mountains, separating Northern Persia from the Turcoman deserts and oases. The combined area of these three satrapies is over a million and a half English square miles, while their total population is little more than five millions.

Our first glimpse into the interior of this region is afforded by the famous expedition of Alexander the Great, when in the year 329 B.C. he passed the Hindu Kush, hunted the fugitive Persians across the Oxus, crossed then, as the natives do even now, on inflated skins or trusses of hay; laid

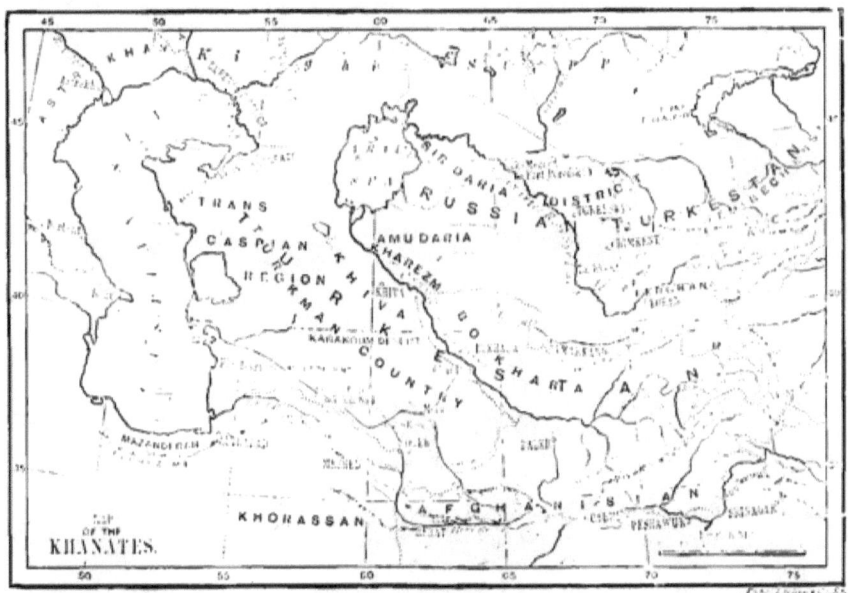

MAP OF THE KHANATES.

waste Maracanda (Samarkand), advanced to the Jaxartes, and founded the Bactrian kingdom, which survived for several centuries. On their way to the Indus, the Scythians overwhelmed the Bactrian empire, ruled afterwards in turn by the Persians, Parthians, and Chinese. They were succeeded by the Arabs of the Khalifate, who, early in the eighth century, proselytized with fire and sword, and planted the roots of Mahometanism so deeply that to this day the most orthodox champions of Islam are to be found in the mosques of Khiva, Samarkand, and Bokhara.[1]

[1] For this digest, and for much other information tersely conveyed, we are to a great extent indebted to Mr. J. Geddie's excellent work on *The Russian Empire*.

The countries traversed by the Oxus and the Jaxartes, peopled principally by races of Iranian origin, had no title to the name of Turkestan, until the Seljuk Turks burst in from the north-east, and selected as the seat of their power Khorassan, behind the mountain screen of Persia, from which they entered upon a deadly struggle with the nomads who held the steppes or deserts. The Shahs who ruled over Kharesm (Khiva) established themselves at Samarkand as the ruling power in the country, which thus became known as Turkestan; but the Mongol hordes of Chinghiz Khan, in 1219, took and laid waste Bokhara and Samarkand, massacred the subjects of the Shah, whom they defeated and slew, and chased the remnants of his army through the Afghan passes and across the Indus. Long and cruel wars, waged between the direct descendants of Chinghiz and their neighbours and kinsmen—the chiefs of the Golden Horde—were brought to an

KOKAN.

issue by Tamerlane (Timûr-Leng, or the lame), the terror of the world, in the latter half of the fourteenth century, who made Samarkand his capital.

Another flood of invasion from the northern steppes overthrew the rule of the successors of Timûr in Bokhara and in Kokan, then, and now again, called the province of Ferghana. Twice the famous Baber, the ruler of Ferghana, established himself at Samarkand, but he was unable to withstand the onset of the Uzbegs, and fleeing ultimately through Afghanistan to India, conquered Delhi (1525), and founded the 'Empire of the Great Mogul.' The subsequent national history of Turkestan is largely made up of struggles for ascendency between the Khanates of Bokhara, Khiva, and Kokan, but the last of the great 'scourges of humanity' reared in the Turcoman deserts was Nadir Shah, who overthrew the Persian and Mogul empires, and was assassinated in 1747, in the height of his fame.

The gravitation of Muscovy towards the countries of the Far East (the Russian *Drang Nach Osten*) began after 1480, when the Tartar yoke was thrown off, and all further fear of a barbaric invasion of the rest of Europe was removed. Ivan III., the powerful and ambitious prince who then began to lay the foundations of the Russian empire, entered into relations with the neighbouring states of Western Europe and with the Sultan of Turkey. In the reign of Ivan IV., the Terrible, the 'Chinese Wall,' by which Muscovy had long been surrounded, was finally broken down, and foreigners began to visit it. So early as 1520, we find Paul Centurione, a Genoese, inquiring at Moscow into the possibility of trading to India by way of the Caspian and the Oxus. A similar object brought Marco Foscarini, a Venetian, in 1537, to the court of Ivan IV., who had annexed the Tartar kingdoms of Kazan, Astrakhan, and Siberia. The geographical position acquired by those conquests brought Muscovy into commercial communication with the Khanates of Central Asia.

Meanwhile, the English, the Dutch, and the Italians were occupied with the idea of reaching India and China by an overland route, the sea approaches to those countries being then jealously guarded by the Spaniards and Portuguese; and several unsuccessful attempts were made. In 1558 Anthony Jenkinson equipped a small war vessel on the Caspian, which he crossed flying the flag of St. George. He reached Bokhara with his merchandise, after defeating the Turcomans who opposed his passage.

Between 1669 and 1672, two adventurous Russians from Astrakhan reached Balkh and Cabul, and brought back the first direct intelligence of the wealth of India. During the reign of Alexis, Muscovy sent her first embassy to Pekin, and two missions to Bokhara, whose silks had come into great request. The mission of 1675 was instructed to report on the Oxus, on the roads to India, and to establish commercial relations with the Central Asiatics. In 1695, a large caravan, also with the character of a mission, was despatched to Persia, Khiva, Bokhara, Balkh, and India. When in Holland, Peter the Great had heard much of India, the land of gold, from which the Dutch, Portuguese, and the other maritime nations brought home treasure in abundance; and he, therefore, gave the first strong impulse to Russian trade and travel in Central Asia. It was his master-mind that first pointed out to his countrymen, as the most convenient route to Bokhara, the road now traversed by a military railway. In 1694, Peter I. established a military line of frontier to the west of Tsaritsyn, on the Volga. With an army of forty thousand men, he appeared suddenly, in 1722, at the mouth of the Terek, attacked Persia, and took Bakû and Derbent, with the provinces in which those towns were situated. This enabled him to advance his frontier to the Terek, on which he planted a thousand families of Don Cossacks. The prosecution of his plans required the conquest of the Caucasus, a scheme which though begun in his day was not completed until 1864.

Parallel with these operations in the Caucasus was an advance made eastwards from Siberia. The Kirghiz Kaisaks obtained the 'protection' of Russia against their enemies the Kalmucks, in 1718, and in 1732 the 'middle' Kirghiz horde recognised the sovereignty of Russia. Small war vessels were next built on the Sea of Aral, and forts established at the confluence of the Or and the Ural and at Orenburg. By the year 1827, when the 'Great Horde' submitted, all the Kirghiz tribes who held the country between Siberia and the present possessions of Russia in Central Asia were brought within the sphere of Russian administration.

A solid basis was now acquired for further progress in Asia:[1] in the north, by the possession of Siberia; in the south, by dominion over the Caucasus; in the centre, by fortified places in the province of Orenburg; and in the Ural Mountains. Although thus confronted by an irresistible force, the Khanates long and ignorantly disdained the power of Russia; but in 1700 and 1703 the Khivans, sorely pressed by the Bokharians, had, after the interchange of some missions since 1629, submitted to Peter the Great, and had also, in 1714, supplicated his aid against the robber Turcomans. A military expedition sent by Peter for the purpose of establishing the ascendency of Russia terminated in a disaster that encouraged the Central Asiatics to believe in their impregnability. Prince Bekovitch Cherkaski and his army were massacred, or perished miserably in the desert between the Aral and the Caspian. Peter the Great left a legacy of vengeance to his successors, and these found it necessary to carry out his behests slowly and deliberately, by careful study of the Khanates and the approaches to them. Not a year passed, from 1718 to 1850, without agents and expeditions, scientific, diplomatic, or military, being despatched by Russia. A large force was sent in 1839, under General Perofski, against Khiva; but it was unable to overcome the hardships of crossing the steppes in winter, and returned to Orenburg with the loss of one third of the troops from disease and exhaustion. Frightened at last by the evident intention of the Russians to renew their attempt to reach Khiva, the Khivans entered into negotiations for peace, liberated a great number of Russians whom they had kidnapped and held in bondage as slaves, and agreed to admit Russian traders to Khiva.

From Siberia, the original base of operations against Central Asia, the Russians began to descend systematically in the year 1845, when the fort of Uralsk (Irghiz) was established in the Kirghiz steppe.

Three years later another fort was planted on the Irghiz River, and by the year 1853 Ak-mechcd (Fort Perofski), the first Kokandian stronghold on the Jaxartes, was taken after a severe combat. A flotilla also was established on the Sea of Aral, which is in reality only a lagoon two

[1] *Transkaspien und seine Eisenbahn nach Acten des Erbauers, Gen. Lieut. M. Annenkof.* By Dr. O. Heyfelder. Hanover, 1888.

hundred and sixty-five miles in length by forty-five miles in breadth. In 1858 all the Kirghizes between Orenburg and the Jaxartes submitted to Russia, and operations in the directions of Khiva, Bokhara, and Kokan became comparatively easy. The Kokandians lost their fortress of Chemkend in 1864, and Tashkent became, a year later, the capital of a Russian 'Turkestan province.' General Cherniayeff consolidated the conquests made in 1864 and 1865 by beating the Bokharians at Idjar. Samarkand was taken in 1868, and Shahrisiabs in 1870.

At about the same time the eastern coast of the Caspian to the Persian frontier at the Atrek became Russian, and the sea itself a Russian lake. Even Persian trading companies have no right to sail merchant vessels on it. It now bears on its frequently boisterous waters (ninety-eight feet below

TURCOMAN WOMEN.

the level of the Euxine) a multitude of Russian steamers and sailing craft. But their dimensions are necessarily small; the bays and inlets on the eastern side being mostly shallow, and fringed with barren sand dunes and salt marshes. Except where at long intervals a Russian fort has been built, these dismal shores are visited only by wandering bands of Kirghizes and Turcomans. On the west coast the white walls of a few old cities, such as Derbent and Bakû (the emporium of petroleum), overhang the blue waters. Its southern shores belong to Persia, which still holds the port of Resht, and eastward of it the city of Astrabad, near which disembogues the river Gurghen, anciently defended by a wall against the inroads of nomads, whom Arabian writers in the Middle Ages called the 'Gog and Magog,' now

O 2

represented in effigy at the Guildhall, London. At the back of the rich slopes of Ghilan and Mazanderan are the lofty ranges of the Elbruz, with their sides clothed with forests, and their highest summits crowned with eternal snow.

From the year 1868, when Krasnovodsk was taken and fortified, the eastern coast of the Caspian began to be utilized as a basis of operations against the marauding Tekkes and the Khivans. Some reverses and the necessity of avenging them impelled General Scobelef to recommend the construction of a railway from his fortified position at Mihailofsk, at the head of Krasnovodsk Bay. This 'Transcaspian Railway' is one of the greatest feats of modern engineering, and reflects imperishable credit on its constructor, General Annenkof. Built in 1880-81, its extension from the original terminus at Kizyl Arvat was commenced in 1885, and completed in 1888 at Samarkand. We have no space for a description of the enormous difficulties that were surmounted by the active and zealous general, such as shifting sands, want of water, almost tropical heat, unpopulated wastes, and the absence of wood or other fuel. These necessitated the planting of shrubs on embankments, the boring of artesian wells and the establishment of other waterworks, the importation of labourers from Smolensk and Kief in aid of two 'Transcaspian Railway Battalions,' and the introduction of petroleum refuse from Bakù for purposes of fuel and light.

All the materials, from sleepers to rails and rolling-stock, were Russian.' Shy at first, Tekke Turkomans and Persians flocked to the earth-works until close upon eighteen thousand of them obtained employment.

The old caravan route from Orenburg to Tashkent, Samarkand, and Bokhara, over 1500 miles long, has now been almost entirely abandoned, for the route established by rail from Uzun-Ada, the present starting-point on the eastern shore of the Caspian, to the ancient capital of Tamerlane (about nine hundred miles) can be reached in nine and a half days from St. Petersburg, including a passage of three days across the Caspian from Astrakhan. As soon as Bakù obtains direct railway communication with St. Petersburg, the journey will be easily performed within a week.

Travelling at the rate of twenty-five to thirty-five miles an hour, the train brings us across the Ust-urt Desert to Kizyl Arvat, the first of the Tekke forts seized by the Russians in 1877, but permanently occupied only in 1880, when it became one of the bases of operations which resulted in the total discomfiture of the Turcomans, and the extension of Russian dominion to Sarakhs and Merv. At Geok-Tèpé, where those who have obtained permission to travel on this military line stop for refreshment at a European buffet, we are in proximity to the fortress which Scobelef captured from the Tekkes in 1881 with great slaughter. Askhabad, the next station but one, was occupied in the same year. The *Times* correspondent in 1888 says that it is decidedly the best built

---

¹ The greater part of the rails were manufactured and supplied by English mills near the Sea of Azof.

place on all the railway. There are some very good streets, full of shops, a fine public garden, and a profusion of wild grapes. A monument perpetuates the memory of Scobelef, whose ancestor in Russia was Mr. Scobie, a Scotch schoolmaster. The frontier of Khorassan has for some time been on our right, and we soon reach a point which is scarcely more than eighty miles distant from Meshed, the sacred city of the Shiite Persians—the burial-place of their saint Mahmud Riza.

Before reaching the station of Tedjen, the line crosses the river of that name which flows past Sarakhs, a future station on the way to Herat. Eighty miles beyond we are at Merv, 'The Queen and Pearl of the World,' once a vast and glorious city, supposed to have been built by Alexander

A TEKKE VILLAGE.

the Great. The oasis of Merv, rendered fertile by irrigation, has an area of 2,400 square miles, intersected by the Murghab River. While only crumbling ruins remain of the old city, the new town, built by the Russians on the left bank of the Murghab, and surrounded by a brick wall, consists of several parallel streets and neat-looking houses of brick. According to the most recent statistics, the energetic and warlike Tekkes of the Merv oasis number about 105,000 souls. Taken together with other tribes, such as the Saryks, Salors, etc., the total Turcoman population is at least 700,000.

The semi-nomadic and once predatory Turcomans are, as their name implies, of Turkish race, but differ in their characteristics from their neighbours the Persians, Afghans and Kurds, as well as from the Bokharians and the

Mongols, although there has been a considerable intermingling of blood amongst them all. From early youth the Turcoman is accustomed to long journeys on horseback over the desert, and to endure fatigue, hunger, and thirst. Considering also the excellence of their horses, they are capable of supplying the best irregular cavalry in the world. Devoting themselves to the chase and to robber raids, they have so far left agriculture to their slaves and women. The latter are clever in spinning, knitting, and weaving, and produce carpets of such high quality in taste and texture that they are largely exported to Russia, Persia, and France. The men wear high sheep-skin hats to preserve their heads from the sun in summer and the cold in winter, and a wadded *khalat* or robe, from which hangs a sword, generally of the

TEKKES.

finest metal. They are also provided with other weapons, from the matchlock fired from a stand to the modern breech-loading rifle. Their women are attired in Turkey-red trousers and a shirt, and not unfrequently in a jacket beautifully embroidered. In cold weather a *khalat* is worn. Gold and silver ornaments are in common use; horses alone sharing with the women the distinction of being thus adorned.

Merv is only two hundred miles from Herat, and Herat about three hundred and fifty miles from our outpost at Candahar. The great Karakoum desert is left on the borders of Bokhara at Chardjui. Here we reach the Amu-Daria, the Oxus of the Greeks and the Jihun of the Arabs, which, like the Jaxartes, falls into the Sea of Aral after a course of fifteen hundred miles. A Russian town, with a church, steam mill, and theatre, adjoins the railway station, which is one of great commercial importance, from the quantity of native products floated down the river for land carriage at this point. Like the Khanate of Khiva, Bokhara is nominally independent, but practically neither can have any other will than that of Russia.

The town of Bokhara is sixty miles further to the north-east. Surrounded by a wall of sun-baked mud, and pierced by eleven gates, it still contains some interesting buildings. The Khan's palace, more than a thousand years old, is planted on a conical elevation within the Ark, or citadel. Nearly four hundred mosques and over one hundred *medressèh*, or colleges, stand out from among low-lying, mud-built dwelling-houses ensconced in gardens. The principal mosque, built by Tamerlane, is in the Reghistan, or square, in front of the palace. Its dome is one hundred feet in height, and attached to it is a minaret two hundred feet high, faced with glazed white and blue tiles, arranged in curious designs. Sentences of death were formerly carried out by hurling the condemned from its summit. Close by is the mosque of Mir Arab, with fine columns; and another ancient mosque, also built by Tamerlane, is that of Baliand.

At one side of the artificial hill that supports the citadel, and approached by tortuous alleys and dirty thoroughfares, stands the prison in which Stoddart and Conolly, two Englishmen, were executed in 1842. It is a low building with a mud dome on one side like the top of a Turkish bath at Constantinople. Writing in 1888, the *Times* correspondent described the room, in which he saw twenty-five half-naked, dirty prisoners, as not more than twenty feet long by ten feet broad, with a ceiling that nearly touched the heads of the visitors. In a well, approached by a small door in the right-hand wall of this chamber, he saw twenty more men huddled together with hardly room to move. Below this well, again, was a still deeper one — the hole into which our countrymen were let down, to be devoured by insects and vermin. Happily, under Russian pressure, the lower dungeons have been filled up and closed for ever; and it is to be hoped that ere long the Khan will be compelled to raze these barbarous dungeons to the ground. Whatever may be the political and commercial aspects of the question, humanity has undeniably gained much from the establishment of Russian authority in the Khanates; but it is to be hoped that the Tsar's mission of civilization will be carried out no less fully and rigorously than the establishment of his military power. The unsanitary condition of Bokhara is well worthy of the attention of Russian administrators.

At Sary-Bulak, one hundred and eighty-five miles from Bokhara, we are again on territory not ostensibly but *de facto* annexed by Russia, namely, in the new province of Turkestan; and four stations beyond this we arrive at Samarkand, 'the head of Islam,' as Mecca is its 'heart.' Its history is associated with two great names: Alexander of Macedon, who conquered it B.C. 325, and

Tamerlane the Great, who lavishly expended the pillage of the rich countries
to the south and west in rearing and beautifying its palaces, mosques, and
colleges. It was under his care that Samarkand became the centre of the
learning and power of the Eastern world.

The city preserves some remains of its ancient magnificence. Its chief
architectural glory is the immense mosque of Shah-Zindeh, now outside its
attenuated precincts. This is in fact a collection of mosques surrounding the
resting-place of a martyred prophet, the belief in whose re-appearance at a

SAMARKAND.

date—1868—which has passed is signified by the title of 'Living King.'
The buildings are much out of repair; but the lofty portals and domes, faced
with blue and white porcelain tiles, forming mosaic patterns and tints, the
marble and tiled staircases, the interior walls overlaid with arabesques, the
arches and ceilings covered with pendent alabaster work, and the finely
carved wooden pillars that support them, make it worthy of being a type of
the palmy era of Samarkand. The most interesting ruin is that of Gur
Amir, or Tomb of Timur, but it has suffered sadly from the destroyer's

hand, and even the great block of greenish-black stone which marks the cenotaph of the conqueror has been broken in twain. On a hill in the centre of the bazaar we see the ruins of the Ulug Beg Observatory—the first erected in Asia. Within its walls are the crumbling remains, still surmounted by a high minaret, of the college or home of the astronomers attached by that ruler to his capital.

The well laid-out Russian town, with a boulevard and an excellent pavement, stretches out on the north side of the citadel. Here the visitor can hire a real Muscovite *drojki*, get a cup of fragrant tea, and otherwise avail himself of the benefits of European civilization. He will be interested in the native population, which, numbering about 30,000, consists of Iranian Tajiks (Sarts), who occupied Sogdiania before it became the land of the 'Turks,' and of Uzbegs of the Turanian tribes that were wont to descend upon the lands watered by the Jaxartes and the Oxus since the days of Chinghiz Khan. The bazaars are also full of Persians, Hindoos, Jews, and gipsies.

A prolongation of the line to Tashkent, the administrative centre of the Province of Turkestan, about two hundred miles distant from Samarkand, is only a question of time. The city, captured by Cherniayef in 1865, and occupying an area as wide as that of Paris, is prettily situated on a branch of the Chirchik River, and its quaint and bizarre native quarter is separated by a ravine from the new Russian town, in which the finest building is the residence of the Governor-General. There are two large squares bright with turf and flowers, and with an orthodox church in the centre of each. Nor have the Russians omitted to satisfy the religious requirements of their new Mahometan subjects. Among the numerous mosques of Tashkend, almost the only one of any antiquity is that of Khoja Akhrar, over four hundred years old. This was restored by the Russian Government in 1888, and opened with great ceremony in the presence of the Governor-General, the officiating Imam on that occasion making an address descriptive of the benefits conferred by the Russian Government, and stating that never had the native population of Turkestan enjoyed so tranquil and prosperous an existence as now. Surrounded by gardens, and in great part composed of them, the pride of the city is its park of a thousand apricot trees, now somewhat rivalled by the prettily laid-out garden that adjoins the residence. With all these attractions, however, Tashkent has long been considered a place of exile or temporary retirement by the Russians who repaired to it. We remember a young officer of the Imperial Guards being asked: 'Are you also going to Tashkent?' To which the significant reply was, 'Why should I? I have no debts.'

Chimkent, the Green Town, lies eighty miles to the north of the capital of Turkestan, and is equally buried in verdure and intersected by streams and irrigation works. It was taken in 1864, when the population suffered severely at the hands of the Cossacks. A large citadel now half ruined,

towers above it, and testifies to the ancient strategical importance of the
place.

At Turkestan, one hundred and five miles to the north-east, we approach
the Syr Daria, or Jaxartes, which rises in several streams in the Celestial
Mountains, and falls, like the Oxus, into the Sea of Aral. So much of its
upper waters are deflected for irrigation that its middle and lower courses
are sluggish and shallow, and but little available for navigation. It is,

THE GRAND MINARET, KHIVA.

therefore, along a post road that we travel hence to Orenburg—the old
starting-point for Central Asia.

All we have space to say of the ancient town of Turkestan is that, as
Hazret-i-Turkestan, it gave its name to a province which was called Jassy
in the days of Tamerlane, who in 1397 began the construction of a huge
mosque in honour of Hazret-Yusufi, a Mahometan saint held to this day in
high veneration. It is an interesting and curious group of buildings,

evidently unfinished by its Persian architect. The glazed bricks and incised inscriptions of its outer walls have suffered from the Russian cannonade directed in 1864 against the citadel in which it stands, and earthquakes have in many places fissured this 'seventh wonder of the world.'

Khiva is not legitimately within the scope of our sketches of the Russian empire, but requires a passing notice as the capital of a large, semi-independent Khanate, occupying an oasis bordered by the left bank of the lower course of the Oxus, and within easy striking distance from the Russian military station on the opposite side of the river. Its fame is chiefly that of a slave mart—the chief slave market in Asia—at which Persians, Afghans, and Russians, kidnapped by the Turcomans on the shores of the Caspian, or on the tablelands of Persia and Afghanistan, found a ready sale. A Russian military expedition in 1873 put an end for ever to that traffic, and gave liberty to 37,000 slaves; but only a relatively small

THE MOSQUE OF HAZRET-I-TURKESTAN.

number reached their original homes. They were attacked by disease or massacred by the Turcomans on their march in small detachments across the desert. Under the influence of Russia, the torturing of prisoners has quite recently been forbidden by the Khan, who, like his brother of Bokhara, is now constrained to be on his best behaviour.

The city is little more than a collection of hovels of baked mud, surrounded by a low earthen wall, flanked here and there by pools of foul, stagnant water; and travellers (Kostenko and MacGahan) have described it as containing more cemeteries than gardens. Its mosques and *medressch* are in the citadel, within which dwell the Khan and his principal officers. These are almost the only buildings of brick at Khiva, and the only mosque with any pretensions to architectural beauty is that which holds the tomb of Polvan, the patron saint of the Khivites. Our illustration shows the minaret in front of that mosque.

ILLUMINATION FROM A MS. OF THE FIFTEENTH CENTURY, IN THE LIBRARY OF THE TROITSA MONASTERY, MOSCOW.

CHAPTER XI.

POLAND.

THE Czar still bears the title of King of Poland, but the constitutional kingdom created at the great settlement of political accounts in 1815 has been officially styled 'The Cis-Vistula Provinces,' ever since the absolute incorporation with the Russian empire in 1868. The provinces in question, ten in number, have an aggregate area of 49,157 English square miles, and a population of eight millions, composed to the extent of sixty-five per cent. of Poles, the remainder being Jews (in the proportion of thirteen per cent., and settled chiefly in towns), Lithuanians, Russians, Germans, and other aliens.

The Poles (the Polacks of Shakespeare) are a branch of the Slav race, their language differing but little from that of the Russians, Czechs (Bohemians), Servians, Bulgarians, and other odd kindred remnants. Contact and co-operation with Western civilization, and escape from Tartar subjugation, permitted the Poles to work out their own development on lines so widely apart from those pursued by their Russian brethren, that the complete amalgamation of these two great Slav branches has long been a matter of practical impossibility.

Polish history begins, like that of Russia, with Scandinavian invasion; Szainocha, a reliable authority of the present century, asserting that the Northmen descended on the Polish coast of the Baltic, and became, as in

Russia, ancestors of noble houses. On the other hand, it is on record that the first Grand Duke of Poland (about A.D. 842) was Piastus, a peasant, who founded a dynasty that was superseded only in 1385 by the Lithuanian Jagellons. Christianity was introduced by the fourth of the Piasts, A.D. 964, and it was a sovereign of the same House, Boleslas I., the Brave, who gave a solid foundation to the Polish State. He conquered Dantzig and Pomerania, Silesia, Moravia, and White Russia, as far as the Dnieper. After being partitioned, in accordance with the principle that long obtained in the neighbouring Russian principalities, the component territories of Poland were reunited by Vladislaf (Ladislas) the Short, who established his capital, in 1320, at Cracow, where the Polish kings were ever after crowned. Casimir the Great, the Polish Justinian (1334–1370), gained for himself the title of *Rex Rusticorum*, by the bestowal of benefits on the peasantry, who were *adscripti glebæ*, and by the limitation of the power of the nobles, or free-holders. On his death, Louis, King of Hungary, his sister's son, was called to the throne : but in order to ensure its continued possession he was compelled to re-instate the nobles in all their privileges, under a *Pacta Conventa*, which, subject to alterations made at Diets, was retained as part of the Coronation Oath so long as there were Polish kings to be consecrated. He was the last sovereign of the Piast period. After compelling his daughter to marry, not William of Austria, whom she loved, but Jagellon, Duke of Lithuania, who offered to unite his extensive and adjacent dominions with those of Poland, and to convert his own pagan subjects to Christianity, the nobles, in virtue of their Magna Charta, elected Jagellon (baptised under the name of Ladislas) to the throne of Poland, which thus became dynastically united (1386) with that of Lithuania.

On the death, in 1572, of Sigismund II., Augustus, the last of the Jagellons, the power of the king, already limited by that of two chambers, was still further diminished, and the crown became elective. While occupied in besieging the Huguenots at Rochelle, and at a time when Poland enjoyed more religious liberty than any other country in Europe, Henry of Valois was elected to the throne, in succession to Sigismund II. ; but he quickly absconded from Cracow in order to become Henry III. of France. The Jesuits, introduced in the next reign, that of Stephen Bathori, brought strong intolerance with them, and one of the reasons that led the Cossacks of the Polish Ukraine to solicit Russian protection was the inferior position to which their Greek religion had been reduced in relation to Roman Catholicism. The Russians and Poles had been at war with each other for two centuries. Moscow had been occupied in 1610 by the Poles in the name of Ladislas, son of Sigismund III., of the Swedish Wasa family, elected to the Muscovite throne by the Russian boyars, but soon expelled by the patriots, under Minin and Pojarski. Sobieski, who had saved Vienna for the Austrians, could not keep Kief and Little Russia for the Poles.

Such was the outcome of disorders and revolutions in the State, and of wars with Muscovy, Turkey, and Sweden, as well as with Tartars and Cossacks. Frederick Augustus II., Elector of Saxony, succeeded Sobieski, and reigned until 1733, with an interval of five years, during which he was superseded by Stanislas I.

Dissension and anarchy became still more general in the reign of the next sovereign, Augustus III. Civil war, in which the question of the rights of Lutherans, Calvinists, and other 'dissidents' obnoxious to the Roman Catholic Church played a great part, resulted in the intervention of Prussia and Russia, and in 1772 the first partition of Poland was consummated.

KAMENETS IN PODOLIA.

The second followed in 1793, under an arrangement between the same countries, which had taken alarm at a liberal constitution voted by the Polish Diet in 1791, especially as it had provided for the emancipation of the *adscripti glebæ*. The struggle made by Thaddeus Kosciuszko ended in the entry of Suvoroff into Warsaw over the ashes of the Prague suburb, and in the third dismemberment (1795) of ancient Poland, under which even Warsaw was absorbed by Russia.

Previous to these several partitions, Poland occupied a territory much more extensive than that of France. In addition to the kingdom proper, it included the province of Posen and part of West Prussia, Cracow, and

Galicia, Lithuania, the provinces of Volhynia and Podolia, and part of the present province of Kief. In 1772 Dantzig was a seaport of Poland, Kaminets, in Podolia, its border stronghold against Turkey; while to the west and north its frontier extended almost to the walls of Riga, and to within a short distance from Moscow. In still earlier times, Bessarabia, Moldavia, Silesia, and Livonia were embraced within the Polish possessions.

These successive partitions gave the most extensive portion of Polish territory to Russia, the most populous to Austria, and the most commercial to Prussia. Napoleon I. revived a Polish state out of the provinces that had been seized by Prussia and Austria. This was first constituted into a Grand Duchy under the King of Saxony, and in 1815, when Galicia (with Cracow) was restored to Austria, and Posen to Prussia, Warsaw became again a kingdom under a constitution granted by Alexander I. The old Polish provinces that had fallen to the share of Catherine II. at the partitions remained incorporated with the Russian empire, but were not fully subjected to a Russian administration until after the great Polish insurrection of 1830, when also the constitution of 1815 was withdrawn, the national army abolished, and the Polish language proscribed in the public offices.

Notwithstanding the wide measures of Home Rule introduced by Alexander II. into the administration of the kingdom, and which, in combination with many liberal and pregnant reforms in Russia Proper, appeared to offer to the Poles the prospect of no inconsiderable influence over the destinies of the Russian empire, the old spirit of national independence began to manifest itself, and in 1862, not without encouragement from Napoleon III., an insurrection broke out at Warsaw, with the result we have indicated at the head of this chapter.

Outside Warsaw and its immediate vicinity there is little in Russian Poland to interest the tourist. The country is generally level and monotonous, with wide expanses of sand, heath, and forest, and it is only towards the north and east that the ground may be said to be heavily timbered. Dense forests stretch down from the Russian, anciently Polish, province of Grodno, and now form the last retreat in Europe of the *Bison Europaeus*, the survivor of the Aurochs (*Bos primigenius*), which is supposed to have been the original stock of our horned cattle. Although much worried by the wolf, the bear, and the lynx, the bison are strictly preserved from the hunter, and are therefore not likely to disappear like the *Bos Americanus*, or buffalo, which has so long been ruthlessly slaughtered in the United States.

Interspersed among these barren or wooded tracts are areas containing some of the finest corn-bearing soil in Europe, supplying from time immemorial vast quantities of superior grain for shipment from ports in the Baltic. It is produced on the larger estates of two hundred to fifteen hundred acres, belonging to more than eight thousand proprietors. The

peasantry, who hold more than 240,000 farms—seldom exceeding forty acres—
contribute next to nothing towards exportation, their mode of agriculture
being almost as rude as that of the Russian peasantry, and their habits of
life but little superior, especially in the matter of drink. Towns, large and
small, occur more frequently than in Russia, and while some are rich and
industrial, others—we may say the great majority—are poor and squalid,

THE CHURCH OF THE HOLY CROSS, WARSAW, WITH UNIVERSITY IN THE BACKGROUND.

affording no accommodation that would render possible the visit of even the
least fastidious traveller.

Consequently we confine ourselves to Warsaw, which we take on our
way by rail to or from St. Petersburg or Moscow. Founded in the twelfth
century, and, during the Piast period, the seat of the appanaged Dukes of
Masovia, Warszawa, replaced Cracow as the residence of the Polish kings

and therefore as the capital of Poland, on the election of Sigismund III. (1586). It has now a population of about 445,000, not including the Russian garrison of 31,500 officers and men. The left bank of the Vistula, on which Warsaw is chiefly built, is high, and the pretty, gay, and animated city, with its stately lines of streets, wide squares, and spacious gardens, is picturesquely disposed along the brow of the cliff and on the plains above. Across the broad sandy bed of the stream, here 'shallow, ever-changing, and divided as Poland itself,' and which is on its way from the Carpathians to the Baltic, is the Prague suburb, which, formerly fortified, has never recovered from the assault by Suvoroff in 1794, when its sixteen thousand inhabitants were indiscriminately put to the sword. A vast panorama spreads out in every direction from this melancholy and dirty point of vantage. Opposite is the Zamek, or castle, built by the Dukes of Masovia, and enlarged and restored by several of the Polish kings, from Sigismund III. to Stanislas Augustus Poniatovski. Its pictures and objects of art are now at St. Petersburg and Moscow, and the old royal apartments are occupied by the Governor-General. The square in front of the castle was the scene of the last Polish 'demonstrations,' in 1861, when it was twice stained with blood.

In the Stare Miasto, or Old Town, strongly old German in aspect, stands the cathedral, built in the thirteenth century, and restored on the last occasion by King John Sobieski. A still more ancient sacred edifice is the Church of Our Lady in the Nove Miasto, or New Town ; but it certainly retains no traces of deep antiquity. Beyond the great Sapieha and Sierakovski Barracks towers the Alexander Citadel, with its outlying fortifications, built in 1832–35, at the expense of the city, as a penalty for the insurrection in 1830. In the same direction, but a considerable distance from the town, is Mariemont, the country seat of the consort of John Sobieski ; also Kaskada, a place of entertainment much frequented by the inhabitants of Warsaw, and Bielany, a pretty spot on the Vistula commanding a fine view. The churches and chapels, mostly Roman Catholic, are numerous (eighty-five), and so are the monasteries and convents (twenty-two).

Near Novi Sviat (New World) Street, we find the Avenues, or *Champs Elysées*, bordered by fine lime-trees in front of elegant private residences. Crossing a large square, in which the troops are exercised, and the military hospital at Ujazdov, formerly a castle of the Kings of Poland, we reach the fine park of Lazienki, a country seat of much elegance built by King Stanislas Augustus, and now the residence of the Emperor when he visits Warsaw. The ceilings of this chateau were painted by Bacciarelli, and its walls are hung with portraits of numerous beautiful women. On page 205 we give an illustration of the prettiest portion of the grounds.

Contiguous to the Lazienki Park are the extensive gardens of the Belvedere Palace, in which the Poles attempted in 1830 to get rid of their viceroy, the Grand Duke Constantine. We drive hence in less than an

hour to one of the most interesting places near Warsaw. This is the Castle
of Villanov, built by John Sobieski, who died in it. To this retreat he
brought back the trophies of his mighty deeds in arms, and here sought
repose after driving the Turks from the walls of Vienna. The château, now
the property of Countess Potoçka, is full of historical portraits, objects of
art, and other curiosities, of which the most interesting is the magnificent
suit of armour presented by the Pope to Sobieski in memory of his great

POLISH PEASANTS.

victory. The apartments of his beautiful consort are of great elegance. In
the gallery of pictures we notice an admirable Rubens—the Death of
Seneca; although we are more strongly attracted by an original portrait of
Bacon, which is but little known in England.

For want of space, again we must plead guilty of omitting to describe
many palatial residences, and several noticeable monuments, among which is
one to Copernicus, the Polish founder of modern astronomy. On the same

ground we pass over handsome public buildings, theatres, gardens, and cemeteries, in one of which, the Evangelical Cemetery, is buried John Cockerell, to whom Belgium owes so much of her industrial prosperity.

THE IRON GATE MARKET (AT THE BACK OF THE SAXONY GARDEN).

CHAPTER XII.

FINLAND.

THE 'Land of a Thousand Lakes,' as Finland is poetically called by her loving sons, possesses physical charms which, in the North of Europe, are second only to those of Norway. It has a superficial area of 144,255 English square miles, and a population slightly in excess of two millions, or about sixteen inhabitants to the square mile. In both these respects it resembles Norway very closely. The long coast-line on the Gulf of Bothnia, from the Swedish frontier on the Torneå River, and a good part of its sea-margin on the Gulf of Finland, present a succession of fiords and rocky headlands similar to those of Norway, but not equally wide, deep, or grand. The hilly interior is intersected by a vast number of lakes and streams, a peculiarity from which has been derived the poetical designation of the country. Fertile plains, formed by the recession of the sea, occur occasionally, but inland, the poor stony patches of soil afford but a scanty sustenance to the peasantry, who form about eighty-five per cent. of the population, and who are almost as much driven to emigration as the Norwegians. Along the coasts, the people are more thriving, for the sea gives them lucrative occupation.

In 1809 Sweden ceded to Russia her rights over Finland, and after a separate negotiation between the Finnish Diet and Alexander I., the Estates swore allegiance to the Emperor as the Grand Duke of Finland,

HELSINGFORS.

The maintenance of the Lutheran religion and the integrity of their constitution, together with all previous rights and privileges, were assured to the Finlanders in a solemn manifesto, which continues to this day to be their jealously guarded Charter of Rights. In virtue of it, they have a Diet composed of four Estates (nobles, clergy, burgesses, and peasantry), as in Sweden until 1866, when a Parliament of two Chambers was established in the mother country. Extensive powers are reserved to the sovereign, including the right of veto. He is represented at Helsingfors by a Governor-General, who is also Commander-in-Chief of the national army, established in recent years under a system of general military conscription, and placed under the Russian War Department.

A committee composed of a Secretary of State and four other members acts at St. Petersburg as a kind of delegation of the Senate at Helsingfors, which, nominated by the Crown, administers the affairs of the Grand Duchy, excepting only its foreign relations. The latter are dealt with by the Imperial Foreign Office. Among the most important privileges thus enjoyed by the Finlanders are: a separate budget, bearing no imperial charge or contribution; a distinct coinage, which renders the Finnish mare, or franc, independent of the fluctuations of the Russian rouble; and an independent tariff much more liberal than that of Russia, and therefore best calculated to sustain a sound system of finance and to promote trade and navigation.

These are already highly developed. Timber, tar, and dairy produce are the principal exports, and they are carried chiefly by the national merchant navy, which gives employment to more than twelve thousand men. In regard to religion and education, the Finlanders have reason to be proud of the results of the legacy bequeathed to them by their old Scandinavian masters. There is scarcely a man or woman in that well-ordered country that cannot read the Bible. An excellent system of education is zealously carried out under the superintendence of the Lutheran clergy, who do not admit to the Communion any person who is unable to read or write.

The Finnish language, so different from all other European tongues, is a great stumbling-block to the exploration of the less frequented parts of the Finnish interior. But the enterprising and intelligent traveller armed with a handbook or a dictionary can easily make his way, and enjoy not only scenery and life which comparatively few tourists have witnessed, but also excellent sport, in the shape of salmon, trout, char, and grayling fishing. In winter he can shoot as many wolves as he chooses to pursue on a sledge, with a sucking-pig as a lure. The pig is kept in a bag, and made to squeak by twisting his tail, upon which the wolf darts out from the dark forest and attempts to seize his prey, deceitfully represented by the wisp of straw smeared with lard that is attached to a long rope at the back of the sledge.

The accommodation outside of the towns is of a somewhat rougher

description than in Norway, but with a well-assorted stock of absolute
necessaries (including insect powder and mosquito netting), and the willing-
ness to brave slight discomforts, personal acquaintance can soon be made,
via Gothenburg and Stockholm, with this fascinating country. In fifteen
hours we cross over from the Swedish capital to Abo, in smooth and
sheltered water except for about two and a half hours, while the steamer
passes through the moderate waves of the open part of the Gulf of Bothnia.
As we steam up the small and shallow Aura *joki*, or river, to the quay
where our passports and luggage are examined, we have a pretty view of
the city.

It is disappointing, on landing, after the charming landscape we have

ABO CATHEDRAL.

enjoyed, to find an air of desolation reigning over the place. This is
imparted by the wide, roughly-paved streets, by the prevalence of low wooden
houses, and by the deserted appearance of the thoroughfares. A fire which
raged for two days in 1827, and destroyed two-thirds of the city, including
the university (established in 1640), a valuable library, and such of its
public buildings as had been spared from many previous conflagrations,
taught the citizens the necessity of rebuilding their public edifices and private
houses at considerable distances from each other. Although the Cathedral
of St. Henry was completely gutted on that occasion, yet its rude and heavy
Gothic exterior has been preserved, its interior renovated without detriment

to previous architectural features. The first episcopal chair of Finland was instituted within its walls after their consecration by Bishop Magnus in A.D. 1300, when the city itself was removed to its present site from its pagan foundations a short distance up the river. The consort of Eric XIV., a peasant girl before she wore the Swedish diadem, lies in one of the chapels, which is embellished by a stained window allegorical of her misfortunes and of her love for Sweden and Finland.

The stained windows, designed by V. Svertschkoff, a native of Abo, but whose name betrays a Russian origin, and the frescoes in the chancel by Ekman, a Finlander, add to the interest of the cathedral. The secular buildings of the city are unimportant, excepting the Residence, a large block opposite the cathedral, built by Gustavus IV. (Adolphus) for the University (transferred after 1827 to Helsingfors), and now occupied by government officers.

A large number of charming excursions can be made from Abo, foremost among which is the trip to the pretty island of Runsala, an old royal domain now dotted with villas.

The sun may be seen at midnight from Mount Aavasaksa, and salmon fishing abounds in most of the rivers that fall into the Gulf of Bothnia. A trip by water to Torneå affords the opportunity of inspecting several snug little ports, such as Björneborg, founded in 1558, at the mouth of the Kumo River, the border of ancient Osterbothnia; and not far from which is a wooden house, surrounded since 1857 by a stone wall, in which Bishop Henry, an Englishman, first preached Christianity in Finland; Kristinestad, in the two neighbouring parishes of which the Finnish national costume is still though exceptionally worn; Nikolaistad, or Vasa, one of the most progressive towns in Finland, with a Russo-Greek church commanding a splendid view of the gulf and the islands on it; Gamla Karleby, an active-looking town of tarred roofs, and black-haired Finlanders (all others being very light); Brahestad, the creation of Count Per Brahe in 1649, and possessing a considerable amount of shipping; and lastly Uleaborg, the present terminus of the railway from St. Petersburg.

Uleaborg lies at the mouth of a great and rapid river which flows out of Lake Ulea, some sixty miles distant, and is one of the principal ports in Finland, with a good deal of shipbuilding and a considerable amount of trade, chiefly with Great Britain, in tar and deals. The tar is brought down from the interior in peculiar boats made of thin planks, which bend as if they were made of pasteboard, when shooting the numerous rapids of the Ulea. Those who are in search of excitement cannot do better than drive to a place called Vaala, near the Myllyranta Ironworks on Lake Ulea, and descend the river in a hired boat, or in one of the tar-ladened craft that have so fragile an appearance. The scenery, especially at the largest and midway rapids of Pyhäkoski, is very fine, and there is in reality no danger of death by drowning on such an excursion.

Tornea, the most northerly town in Finland, is separated from the Swedish town of Haparanda by a dried-up branch of the Tornea River, and was once distinguished by the appellation of 'Little Stockholm,' from its brisk trade, until 1809, with the Swedish capital. In winter, when daylight lasts only three hours, it is visited by Laplanders, with their swift reindeer and sledges, to sell the tongues, hams, and skins of the animals from which they derive their whole support; while in summer, on the night of the 23rd–24th of June (St. John's Eve and Day) swarms of travellers arrive to see the midnight sun, leaving only the most energetic to post fifty miles to Mount Aavasaksa, from which the sun is visible at midnight for fourteen days, although it does not remain entirely above the horizon for more than seventy-two hours. The extension of the railway from Uleåborg to Tornea

FINLANDERS.

will no doubt deflect from the present yachting route to the North Cape the many would-be travellers who dread the sea, however calm and sheltered, or cabin accommodation ever so roomy and convenient, and who yet would like to gaze at a phenomenon which not only fascinates the eye by its strange grandeur and by the weird effect of light it produces, but also impresses the mind most deeply and with more awe than any other cosmic marvel among the great and glorious works of the Omnipotent Creator.

As a contrast to this coast trip the railway may be taken to Tammerfors, the Manchester of Finland, at the junction of two lakes which supply an immense water power to cotton, flax, and paper mills, and many other industrial establishments, in which a goodly number of Englishmen are employed as foremen. As almost everywhere else in this country of wood, water, and rock, the views obtained on this journey are lovely, and particularly the view from the bridge that spans the Tammerfors Rapids.

Helsingfors has been the capital of the Grand Duchy since 1819, and the seat of a university since 1827, and owes much of its prosperity to the political connection of Finland with Russia. The most prominent object in the city, and a far-seen landmark from seaward, is the Church of St. Nicholas, raised (1830-52) in Senate Square, on a mass of granite fifty-nine feet high. Its style is that of the Renaissance, and the Russian form of a Greek cross distinguishes it from the usual architecture of Lutheran churches. The two porticoes of Corinthian columns, reached by flights of steps, are very handsome; and no finer view of Helsingfors and its pretty environs can be obtained than from the top of the splendid dome. Facing this church, which can easily accommodate three thousand worshippers, is the Senate House, with a central hall, used on great occasions, and in which stands the throne of the Grand Duke, whose life-sized portrait hangs in each of the rooms occupied by the several administrative divisions of the Senate. On the south side of the same square we find the Alexander University, constructed in 1832, and attended by nearly a thousand students. The University Library contains about 150,000 volumes, over and above the 50,000 books in Russian and Polish, which form a separate collection.

Resuming our railway journey, we soon come to the picturesque old town of Tavastehus. Just before reaching it, our attention is called to a modern castellated villa lying in a pretty park to the left of the line. There is but little to see in this town beyond a church in which the altar is placed in the centre of the edifice, with the pews radiating from it. The clergyman preaches from the altar, with his back towards the congregation; but, owing to the curious acoustic properties of the edifice, an echo repeats the discourse.

At Lahtis Station the railway brings us to the southern extremity of Päijänne Lake, one of the largest in Finland, being eighty miles long by about eighteen at its widest part. Steamers run hence to a pretty place called Heinola, and to Jyväskilä, a charming little town, with a large seminary for teachers, and from which Kuopio, the seat of a bishopric and a district renowned for the trotting capacities of its horses, can be reached by road in a two-wheeled cart, but little inferior to the Norwegian carriole. But, not as in Norway, the driving in Finland may be called furious. Sharp pitches in the road are descended at full gallop, and a good part of the next hill ascended at a round trot. The small horses are as quiet, hardy, and intelligent as the Norwegian animal, although perhaps not as well taken care of by the small boys who drive them. The speed at which Finlanders travel is curiously out of keeping with the general dilatoriness of their character, exemplified as it is in one of their favourite proverbs, 'Hurry only when catching fleas.' Norwegians are also taught the same maxim.

In summer the Imatra hotel, situated in the midst of enchanting scenery, is crowded with tourists, not only from St. Petersburg, but from all parts of Europe and America, who come to see the Imatra Falls, or rapids, formed by the Vuoksi rushing through a narrow chasm between two steep granite rocks. The fall is not perpendicular, but with a gradual slope over about half a mile, giving a difference of sixty-one feet between the top and the end of the rapids. The rush and roar of the waters are very grand and imposing. It grinds into small fragments the

FINNISH PEASANT-CHILDREN.

empty barrels that are thrown into it for the edification of visitors, who watch for hours the seething water, taking at last no heed of the deafening noise it produces. Sunrise is the best time to see the Imatra-Koski, when, the mist having risen, this awe-inspiring work of Nature is seen through a golden light.

Viborg can be reached either by returning to the railway at Villmanstrand, or by taking the pretty canal route from Lauritsala. Viborg, where stands an old castle, built in 1293, is now a town of seventeen thousand inhabitants, with a considerable trade in timber, shipped from its port in Trangsund Bay. Its show place is the domain of Baron Nicolai, *Mon Répos*, where the scenery of Finland is artificially represented in miniature, the home park being full of fine statuary and monuments. Here we may appropriately terminate the labour of attempting to describe, by pen and pencil, within a narrow compass, the principal features of the great Russian empire, both in Europe and in Asia.

VIBORG CASTLE.

INDEX.

LONDON: WILLIAM CLOWES AND SONS, LIMITED, STAMFORD STREET AND CHARING CROSS.

ILLUSTRATED BOOKS OF TRAVEL.

Australian Pictures:

DRAWN WITH PEN & PENCIL.

By HOWARD WILLOUGHBY,

of "The Melbourne Argus,"

With a large Map and 107 Illustrations
from Photographs and Sketches,

Engraved by E. Whymper and others.

*Imperial 8vo, cloth boards, gilt edges
or 7/6 in morocco elegant.*

COACHING SCENES.

NORWEGIAN PICTURES.

Drawn with Pen and Pencil.

With a glance at Sweden and the Gotha Canal.

By RICHARD LOVETT, M.A.

With a Map and One Hundred and Twenty-seven Illustrations, engraved by E. WHYMPER, R. TAYLOR, and others.

Imperial 8vo. 8s. cloth boards, gilt edges.

THE SVÆRHOLTKLUBBEN, OR BIRD ROCK.

OTTAWA.

CANADIAN PICTURES,

Drawn with Pen and Pencil.

By the MARQUIS OF LORNE, K.T.

With numerous Illustrations from Objects and Photographs in the possession of, and Sketches by, the MARQUIS OF LORNE, SIDNEY HALL, etc.

ENGRAVED BY EDWARD WHYMPER.

Imperial 8vo., elegantly bound in cloth, gilt edges, 8s.; morocco elegant, 25s.

SEA PICTURES.

Drawn with Pen and Pencil. By James Macaulay, M.A., M.D. Editor of the "Leisure Hour."

Imperial 8vo., handsomely bound, gilt edges, 81.: morocco elegant, 25s.

CLOVELLY.

UNIFORM WITH THE ABOVE IN STYLE AND PRICE.

ENGLISH PICTURES.

DRAWN WITH PEN AND PENCIL.

By the Rev. S. MANNING, LL.D.
and
Rev. S. G. GREEN, D.D.

With Coloured Frontispiece and Numerous Wood Engravings.

THE GRAMPIANS.

SCOTTISH PICTURES.

DRAWN WITH PEN AND PENCIL.

By SAMUEL G. GREEN, D.D.

Illustrated by Eminent Artists.

Imperial 8vo., handsomely bound, gilt edges, 8s; morocco elegant, 26s.

ST. OUEN, ROUEN.

LUTHER'S HOUSE, FRANKFURT.

FRENCH PICTURES,

DRAWN WITH PEN AND PENCIL.

By the Rev. Samuel G. Green, D.D. With upwards
of 150 Fine Engravings.

Imperial 8vo., elegantly bound in cloth, gilt edges, 8s.; morocco, 25s.

PICTURES FROM THE GERMAN FATHERLAND,

Drawn with Pen and Pencil. By the Rev. Samuel G.
Green, D.D. Profusely Illustrated with superior
Engravings.

Bound in handsome cloth boards, full gilt, 8s.; morocco, 25s.

RUINS OF A SYNAGOGUE AT SHILOH

THOSE HOLY FIELDS.

Palestine Illustrated by Pen and Pencil. By the Rev. Samuel Manning, LL D
With Numerous Fine Engravings.

COLUMNS OF TEMPLE AT LUXOR.

THE LAND OF THE PHARAOHS.

Egypt and Sinai Illustrated by Pen and Pencil. By the Rev. Samuel Manning, LL D.
With Numerous Fine Engravings.

Imperial 8vo, elegantly bound in cloth, gilt edges, 8s.; morocco, 25s.

SACRED TANK AND TEMPLE, MADURA.

Indian Pictures.
DRAWN WITH PEN AND PENCIL.
By the Rev. WILLIAM URWICK, M.A.
PROFUSELY ILLUSTRATED BY ENGLISH AND
FOREIGN ARTISTS.

*Imperial 8vo., handsomely bound, gilt edges, 8s.;
morocco, elegant, 25s.*

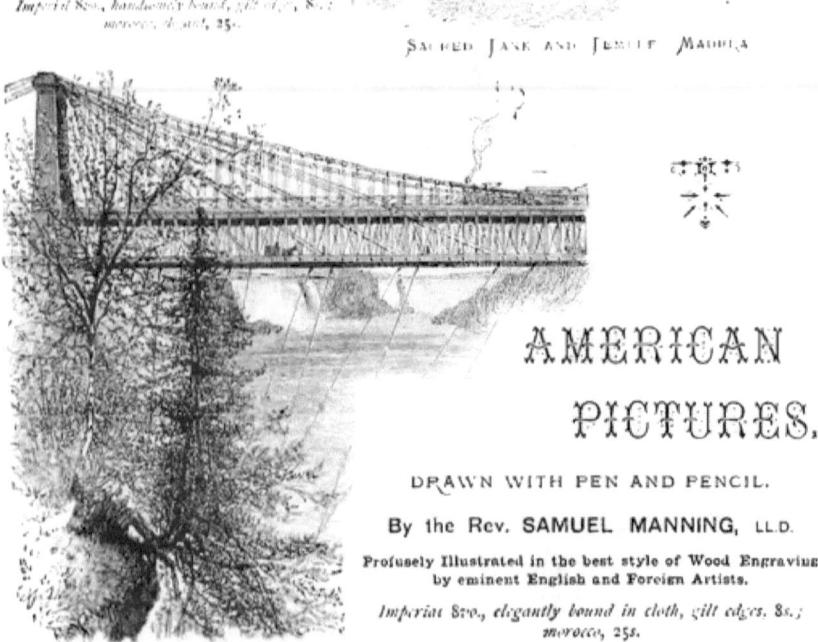

NIAGARA BRIDGE.

AMERICAN
PICTURES.

DRAWN WITH PEN AND PENCIL.

By the Rev. SAMUEL MANNING, LL.D.

Profusely Illustrated in the best style of Wood Engraving
by eminent English and Foreign Artists.

*Imperial 8vo., elegantly bound in cloth, gilt edges, 8s.;
morocco, 25s.*